Previous page: *A cyclist surveys Cape Arago State Park, south of Coos Bay, Oregon.*
Top: *Invasive jubata grass dots the California coast and sports impressive flowering tufts in late summer.*

A craggy coastal scene

Grilling oysters at Taylor Shellfish Company on Chuckanut Drive in northwest Washington.

A selfie stick comes in handy.

Opposite: *The family that bikes together camps together.*
Top: *The water-bottle salute*

Cyclists from Japan and Ireland meet on the road in southwest Washington.

Previous page: *The rugged California coast*
Top: *Engineers fire up the steam-powered locomotive at the Oregon Coast Scenic Railroad, roadside in Rockaway Beach, Oregon.*

Scarecrow of a bicycling farmer graces an orchard on Washington's San Juan Island.

Vineyards are planted in a pleasing bicycle-tire arc on terraces in central California's Santa Ynez wine country.

A cyclist seems to float through the tall beach grass, intersected by a smooth asphalt trail, on the Long Beach peninsula in southwest Washington.

Opposite: *Cycling the magnificent Founders Grove in the California redwoods*
Top: *A generous bike rack on the foredeck of the MV Coho makes it easy for cyclists to wheel on and off the boat, which travels between Victoria, BC, in Canada and Port Angeles, Washington, in the United States.*

Bottom left: *Deluxe storage boxes are installed in some Oregon hiker-biker campgrounds. This one has an electrical outlet for charging your electronics and a lock. Some even have powered USB ports.*
Bottom right: *The Banks-Vernonia State Trail, part of the Portland to Astoria side trip*

Previous page: *You will undoubtedly soak up plenty of ocean sunsets on your Pacific Coast journey.*
Top: *Renna and Sam show off their cycling mascot Martín at a shady rest break in Oregon.*

Driftwood-strewn Rialto Beach near La Push, Washington, on the Olympic Peninsula alternate route

Top: *Admiralty Head Lighthouse, at Fort Casey State Park on Whidbey Island, Washington*
Next page: *Bull Creek Flats Road meanders through giant redwoods on the Lost Coast alternate route in Northern California.*

CYCLING
THE PACIFIC COAST

CYCLING
THE PACIFIC COAST

THE COMPLETE GUIDE
from CANADA to MEXICO

BILL THORNESS

MOUNTAINEERS
BOOKS

To the trailblazers and builders of our coastal roads; to advocates of wide shoulders, bike lanes, and trails; to the dedicated saviors of the giant redwoods; to all who preserve, respect, and revel in nature

Mountaineers Books is the publishing division of The Mountaineers, an organization founded in 1906 and dedicated to the exploration, preservation, and enjoyment of outdoor and wilderness areas.

MOUNTAINEERS BOOKS

1001 SW Klickitat Way, Suite 201, Seattle, WA 98134
800.553.4453, www.mountaineersbooks.org

Printed in the United States of America
Distributed in the United Kingdom by Cordee, www.cordee.co.uk

First edition 2017

Copyeditor: Kris Fulsaas
Design and layout: Jen Grable
Cartographer: Bart Wright, Lohnes+Wright
Cover photographs: Front: *The Pacific Coast route offers plenty of opportunities for beach sunsets.* (Russ Roca, Laura Crawford/pathlesspedaled.com) Back: *Cyclists head for the Cattle Point Lighthouse on Washington's San Juan Isalnd.*
Frontispiece: *The author crosses the Golden Gate Bridge.*

Library of Congress Cataloging-in-Publication Data
Names: Thorness, Bill, 1960-
Title: Cycling the pacific coast : the complete guide from Canada to Mexico / by Bill Thorness.
Description: Seattle : Mountaineers Books, [2017] | Includes bibliographical references and index.
Identifiers: LCCN 2017012248| ISBN 9781594859861 (ppb) | ISBN 9781594859878 (ebook)
Subjects: LCSH: Bicycle touring—Pacific Coast (North America)—Guidebooks. | Pacific Coast (North America)—Guidebooks.
Classification: LCC GV1045.5.P3 T56 2017 | DDC 910.979—dc23
LC record available at https://lccn.loc.gov/2017012248

Mountaineers Books titles may be purchased for corporate, educational, or other promotional sales, and our authors are available for a wide range of events. For information on special discounts or booking an author, contact our customer service at 800-553-4453 or mbooks@mountaineersbooks.org.

♻ Printed on recycled paper

ISBN (paperback): 978-1-59485-986-1
ISBN (ebook): 978-1-59485-987-8

CONTENTS

OREGON

NORTHERN CALIFORNIA

CENTRAL CALIFORNIA

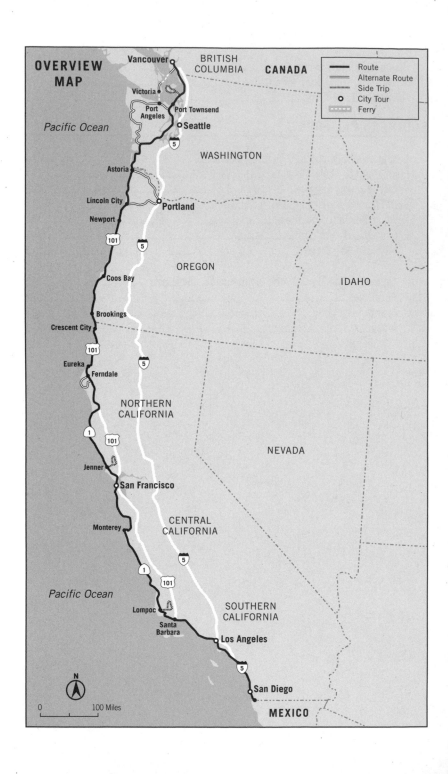

OVERVIEW
MAP

Pacific Ocean

| Route |
| Alternate Route |
| Side Trip |
| City Tour |
| Ferry |

Vancouver

BRITISH
COLUMBIA

CANADA

Victoria

Port
Angeles

Port Townsend

Seattle

5

WASHINGTON

Astoria

Lincoln City

Newport

Portland

101

5

OREGON

IDAHO

Coos Bay

Brookings

Crescent City

101

5

Eureka

Ferndale

NORTHERN
CALIFORNIA

1

101

NEVADA

Jenner

San Francisco

CENTRAL
CALIFORNIA

Monterey

5

1

101

Pacific Ocean

Lompoc

Santa
Barbara

SOUTHERN
CALIFORNIA

Los Angeles

5

N

San Diego

0   100 Miles

MEXICO

ROUTE AT A GLANCE

	DISTANCE (MILES)	ELEVATION GAIN (FEET)	HIGHLIGHTS
BRITISH COLUMBIA, CANADA			
City Tour: Vancouver, BC	24.0	1120	Stanley Park seawall trail, Granville Island Public Market
Vancouver to US Border	39.5	1680	Alex Fraser Bridge
ALTERNATE ROUTE: LOWER VANCOUVER ISLAND			Lochside Trail, Galloping Goose Trail, British-style city
Delta to Swartz Bay via Tsawwassen Ferry	17.6	250	
Swartz Bay to Victoria	21.7	560	
WASHINGTON			
US Border to Bay View	49.8	1460	Bellingham's Fairhaven district, Chuckanut Drive
Bay View to Port Townsend	44.6	2030	Deception Pass, Whidbey Island military forts
Side Trip: San Juan Islands			Orca whale watching, quiet island roads, harbor towns
San Juan Island	40.0	2520	
Lopez Island	35.9	1880	
Anacortes Connector	8.2	230	
Port Townsend to Belfair	72.5	3770	Larry Scott Trail, Hood Canal floating bridge
City Tour: Seattle	25.3	1380	Pike Place Market, Hiram Chittenden Locks, city bike trails
Belfair to Elma	54.9	2090	Quiet country roads
Elma to Bruceport	47.5	1920	Raymond steel sculptures
ALTERNATE ROUTE: OLYMPIC PENINSULA			Olympic Discovery Trail, Lake Crescent, temperate rain forest, Olympic National Park, pristine lake, Kurt Cobain Memorial Park, Willapa Bay, Raymond steel sculptures
Port Townsend to Sequim	43.8	1690	
Sequim to Fairholme	51.5	2930	
Fairholme to Kalaloch	64.9	2250	
Kalaloch to Lake Quinault	33.7	1370	
Lake Quinault to Westport	63.6	1740	
Westport to Bruceport	41.1	1180	
Bruceport to Astoria	66.2	1990	Willapa Bay, Long Beach towns, Cape Disappointment, historic Astoria

	DISTANCE (MILES)	ELEVATION GAIN (FEET)	HIGHLIGHTS
OREGON			
City Tour: Portland	21.3	1280	Pearl District, bridges, riverfront trails
ALTERNATE ROUTE: PORTLAND TO ASTORIA Portland to Stub Stewart Stub Stewart to Astoria	40.8 82.4	2110 3600	Rural rail trail, historic Astoria
ALTERNATE ROUTE: PORTLAND TO LINCOLN CITY Portland to Champoeg Champoeg to Lincoln City	34.6 70.2	1250 2240	Urban bike trails, historic park, Willamette Valley
Astoria to Manzanita	46.3	3070	Lewis and Clark National Historical Park, beach towns
Manzanita to Cape Lookout	39.3	1430	Tillamook Bay, cheese factory
Cape Lookout to Otter Rock	61.4	3770	Otter Crest Loop
Otter Rock to Washburne	42.5	2020	Lighthouses, bridges, coastal towns
Washburne to Winchester Bay	42.1	2530	Sea Lion Caves, Oregon Dunes
Winchester Bay to Bullards Beach	47.0	2140	South Slough National Estuarine Research Reserve
Bullards Beach to Humbug Mountain	37.8	1780	Bandon's reclaimed-plastic sculptures
Humbug Mountain to Brookings	51.7	3300	Prehistoric Gardens
NORTHERN CALIFORNIA			
Brookings to Elk Prairie	66.4	3600	Redwood forests
Elk Prairie to Arcata	46.3	1910	Coastal scenery
Arcata to Burlington	61.8	2610	All-American Ferndale, Avenue of the Giants redwood drive
ALTERNATE ROUTE: THE LOST COAST Ferndale to Burlington	70.1	8110	Quiet, remote roads
Burlington to Leggett	47.4	3680	Avenue of the Giants, rural towns
Leggett to Fort Bragg	41.8	3500	Epic climb, remote coastal scenery
Fort Bragg to Gualala	64.9	4670	Mendocino, ocean views

	DISTANCE (MILES)	ELEVATION GAIN (FEET)	HIGHLIGHTS
Gualala to Bodega Bay	46.3	3420	Historic Fort Ross
Side Trip: Russian River Wine Country	45.7	1620	Vineyards, Healdsburg
Bodega Bay to Lagunitas	42.1	2260	Tomales Bay oysters
Lagunitas to San Francisco	30.7	1800	Golden Gate Bridge
City Tour: San Francisco	23.2	1200	Fishermans Wharf, Golden Gate Park, museums
CENTRAL CALIFORNIA			
San Francisco to Half Moon Bay	28.8	1680	Devils Slide Trail, beach trail
Half Moon Bay to Santa Cruz	57.3	3030	Beaches, ocean views
Santa Cruz to Monterey	42.2	1680	Monterey Bay Coastal Trail
Monterey to Big Sur	44.3	2760	Cannery Row, 17 Mile Drive
Big Sur to Pacific Valley	33.3	3230	Rugged, remote scenery
Pacific Valley to San Simeon	34.8	2720	Hearst Castle
San Simeon to Pismo Beach	53.0	1990	Morro Bay
Pismo Beach to Gaviota	64.7	3360	Monarch butterflies, Orcutt
Side Trip: Santa Ynez Wine Country	44.5	2330	Danish-style town, vineyards
Gaviota to Carpinteria	46.1	1520	Santa Barbara
SOUTHERN CALIFORNIA			
Carpinteria to Point Mugu	43.2	720	Ocean-side bike paths
Point Mugu to Santa Monica	32.0	1310	Malibu beaches, Santa Monica Pier
City Tour: Los Angeles	36.4	890	Rodeo Drive, farmers market, Hollywood Boulevard, art museum
Santa Monica to Newport Beach	54.2	680	Waterfront bike trails
Newport Beach to Encinitas	61.9	2710	Ocean beaches
Encinitas to Mexico	48.8	1370	La Jolla shore roads, San Diego waterfront, Coronado trail
City Tour: San Diego	29.5	1190	Cabrillo National Monument, Old Town, Balboa Park

INTRODUCTION

It had been a long day riding solo on a predictable road, and I was living inside my head, singing favorite songs and composing haiku. When I arrived at the shared hiker-biker campsite, three small cycling groups were tending to their tents and sourcing their suppers from the depths of their panniers. I said hi and set about making camp. But the day was not complete—something was missing. So I walked out to the campground entrance, plunked down five dollars, and hefted a bundle of firewood.

It is an anthropological experiment to make a fire in a communal campground. People gather. Stories are told, advice is given and taken. Plans are shared. Food and drink get passed. Conversation goes round, like the wood smoke shifting with the wind.

Sharing experiences is the spark that ignites the mind, which is what directs the body. Meeting others, whether they are on your path or just intersecting, stokes your resolve and renews energy. However important the achievement of tackling a long-distance bicycle trip seems, it is the human interaction that stays with you, that has the power. You pass through many places, there's a familiarity that blends them together, but people are unique, interesting, inspiring.

When you cycle the Pacific Coast and you want to go deeper, build a fire.

AN EPIC RIDE

"The Pacific Coast is epic." I've heard that phrase again and again, from friends who look admiringly at my achievement of riding it and from fellow travelers trying to explain the trip. I found it true in so many ways:

Epic is a ribbon of highway clinging to bluffs high above a craggy shore.

Epic is mile after mile of glittering coastline, silver waters sparkling like sequins on the dress of a shimmying dancer.

Epic is hulking sea stacks, dark rock looming over the crashing waves.

Epic is towering trees whose shadowy canopy shields the road from a steady rain.

Epic is a redwood forest absorbing all sound.

Epic is a roadside café serving simple, warming food or refreshingly cold drinks.

Epic is hours of steady climbing along winding switchbacks.

Epic is wind whistling through your helmet as you whiz down the other side.

Opposite: *Craggy coastlines with watery horizons will be your view for much of the ride.*

13

A touring cyclist departs Port Townsend, Washington, along the hard-packed Larry Scott Trail.

Epic is fording a mighty river on a steep, too-narrow bridge.
Epic is spotting the city skyline, then putting it in the mirror.
Epic is a hill-hugging, cliff-drop road.
Epic is a dune, a boardwalk, a pier, a trail, fish tacos, and iced tea.
Epic is pairing up for a ride with a new cycling friend met on the route.
Epic is washing off the road salt in a pounding surf.
Epic is self-supported, pedal-powered travel.
Epic is Canada to Mexico on America's Pacific Coast.

"COASTING"

Holding this book and reading these words, you must be considering taking the ride—putting everyday life on hold for a while, packing the bike, and heading on down the road. Some see it as the adventure of a lifetime, a "bucket list" experience. For others, it's just going to be this year's vacation, and maybe not as lengthy or difficult as the last long-distance cycling trip they took. There are certainly many longer or more challenging rides—Transamerica, anyone? Bhutan?

With every traveler you meet, you'll discover another reason for cycling the Pacific Coast. There are contingents of carefree, unattached young adults exploring the world before settling down. There are restless wanderers whose life is one adventure after another. There are postwork drifters, meeting up with pension checks along the way that will get them to the next state. Families bonding. Girlfriends breaking boundaries. Guys sending their stuff ahead and powering into their new city, their new job.

You'll cross paths with people from many countries. "If you like to meet people and [get to] know each other, you should do it," advises Shuhei

Akayoshi from Hiroshima, Japan. "If you are stressed out or depressed, you also should do this, for your health." The reasons for taking this ride are truly as varied as the people you meet.

An honored friend, since passed away, retired from a job in the environmental world but was still involved in organizations related to his work, which was also his passion. A board meeting was coming up in San Francisco and he, a Seattle guy for whom bicycling was a treasured value, decided to pedal there. A month on the road to make a meeting—commitment and exploration rolled into one.

Riding down the coast, stopping at tourist destinations along the road, you see a lot of people also vacationing by car. You share the view with them at roadside pullouts, walk by them on the beach, or stand in line together at the ice cream shop. They pass you on the highway, sometimes honking and waving, but other times scowling and literally or figuratively shaking a fist. They're on vacation, but sometimes, tumbling out of the car, they don't quite look like they're having a great time. The phone is more interesting than the view. Caffeine is more valued than conversation. I think that cars incite lethargy. On a bike, your senses are awake every minute, for better or worse. You are engaged.

Whatever your reason for taking this trip, whether it's a big deal, on your bucket list, or just a holiday, I urge you to plan and prepare, but also to leave your mind open to engagement and your plan open to adjustment. Both will happen.

WHAT TO EXPECT

This section approaches preparation from a few angles: knowing generally what to expect regarding weather and road conditions; charting how much time and money this trip (or these trips) might take; and gathering up the necessary gear for bicycling and camping, which is the preferred overnight approach for the long-haul cyclist.

Weather

This book tackles the Pacific Coast from north to south, as do all sane travelers, including those at the Adventure Cycling Association (ACA), whose Pacific Coast map set is the polestar for the route and also serves as the basic route for the book. The reason most people head south is to keep the wind at their backs. During the cycling seasons (all but winter), the prevailing wind along the coast is north to south. Riding the route in reverse, which might be preferable from a weather standpoint, would result in much more effort, as you'd be "bucking the wind"—cycling into it—for much of the trip.

Seasonal weather conditions need to be considered along with the wind. A Pacific Coast trip does not begin in the winter. The daylight hours are short, and the cold, wet, stormy weather on much of the route will induce misery.

If you want to start early in the spring in the Pacific Northwest, temperatures will be chilly and you are likely to encounter more rain. If you wait until early summer to compensate for that, you might be biking into fog in Northern California and extreme heat along the southern coast. If you start too late in the fall, the northern coast could already be cold and rainy again before the southern climes have cooled.

Even in the warmest summer months, the Pacific Northwest coastal weather is cool, with temperatures often 10–15 degrees lower than inland locations. Fog is common in the mornings, from southern Washington to San Francisco. The least foggy months are April, May, September, and October. That "marine effect" can be a blessing in California, where staying along the coast can mean escaping a heat wave. But cyclists need to look ahead at inland conditions if they take a side trip or a detour that veers away from the ocean.

In recent years, drought caused by climate change has entered into the equation too. Wildfires are more common in California, which makes the air unhealthy and can even cause road closures along the route, as happened in the Santa Barbara area in 2015. Heavy rainfall can cause landslides of unstable or overly dry hillsides; an amazing Oregon cape route might be closed forever because of soil eroding under the road. Winter rains are plentiful in the Northwest, but water shortages to the south can cause parks departments to shut off water to campgrounds or limit water use to drinking only. California shuttered the showers at many campgrounds south of San Francisco during drought times recently and, in some places, even closed the bathrooms and installed portable toilets. At most campgrounds, open campfires are prohibited or restricted to the provided fire pit.

Road and Traffic Conditions

The Pacific Coast route uses the major coastal highways but also side roads, arterial streets through towns and cities, and some bike trails. Where there are two coastal roads, this book attempts to use the less-trafficked route, but that can also mean the chosen route is narrower, perhaps without a striped shoulder or bicycle lane.

Many federal and state roads along the coast do not have consistent shoulders of a width necessary for comfortable bicycling. When a road is repaved, sometimes shoulders are added, but the work is done only a section at a time, so the shoulder appears and then disappears. Similarly with bridges: newer bridges generally have a generous shoulder, but older bridges account for only two lanes of traffic, so a cyclist must ride in the traffic lane to avoid the danger of being passed on a too-narrow bridge.

Some of the coast roads are secondary highways and maintaining them is simply not a high priority for the state, much less upgrading them. On those sections, as on narrow bridges, a cyclist must simply "take the lane."

Many roads feature "bikes on roadway" signs.

However, if cyclists block the lane for a significant period of time, they should expect the patience of drivers to run short. Keep an eye on the traffic behind, and if there are multiple vehicles or there have been many minutes with no opportunity for them to pass you, find a safe spot to pull off the road and let the traffic flow past, then start riding again.

The level, diversity, and speed of traffic is another challenge. Delivery trucks, up to large tractor-trailers, must use these roads to serve the coastal communities. Logging trucks are common on the Northwest roads. Any road serving vacation communities, parks, and beaches will have recreational vehicles, sometimes in significant number and jumbo sizes. Roads through popular beach towns can be clogged with cars as locals flock to the coast, especially on weekends.

Mostly, it seems, commercial drivers are respectful of cyclists and watchful of their safety. It makes sense, as those drivers stake their professional careers on a good safety record. However, your maneuvering skill may be tested by RV drivers and auto tourists who perform unexpected turns, stop on blind corners, block entrances or exits to sightseeing pullouts, and in many cases have no clue that they are causing a problem or dangerous condition for you, a cyclist—possibly because, in many cases, those problematic drivers simply don't see you. It is prudent as a cyclist to act accordingly and always be aware and defensive when in traffic. If it comes to a showdown between bikes and cars, the bike will always lose.

Cities, of course, present many challenges: dense traffic, especially at rush hours; limited bicycling infrastructure like bike lanes or grade-separated trails on the most direct routes; a slow pace due to traffic signals; and sometimes unreliable signage.

It is absolutely necessary for any cyclist planning to ride this route to be comfortable riding alongside powered-vehicle traffic under all these variable conditions.

Coastal weather can adversely affect the conditions of the roads traveled on this route as well. A dry environment or pounding surf can undermine the soil under roads that hug fragile bluffs. Salty air erodes the steel that reinforces concrete bridges, and water causes erosion. So there are spots where road repairs are needed regularly. Construction projects or detours cannot be predicted too far in advance, but cyclists should use state and local resources to learn about any major events prior to their trip.

Although road conditions and traffic are a mixed bag and the whole package sounds daunting, there are bright spots:

- **"Complete streets":** In or near towns, transportation planners are increasingly mandated to develop "complete streets," which means making a new or reconditioned road work for all users, including transit riders, pedestrians, and bicyclists.
- **Warning lights for troubling tunnels or bridges:** At the bridge or tunnel entrance, cyclists will find a button to push that activates lights alerting motorists that there are cyclists on the road.
- **Paved cycling trails:** These are becoming more numerous and longer. Known chokepoints on heavily traveled highways might receive even a short trail to enhance safety and alleviate problems.
- **More aware drivers:** The number of cyclists taking the Pacific Coast route means that most drivers will encounter us along the route, and with increasing visibility comes more tolerance and acceptance.

Bicycle touring is becoming increasingly recognized as a valuable part of tourism, too, so communities, parks, and transportation departments are taking more actions to make cycling safe and comfortable. Oregon is a great example. In recent years, repaving has added shoulders to more and more of the coast highway, reducing trouble spots. The bike route is well signed, and suggested routes to alternate roads have been developed in areas where the state department of transportation urges cyclists not to use the main highway. An Oregon Coast Bike Route Map has been created (see Resources), and campground amenities are being upgraded.

How Long and How Much?

For many people considering a bicycle adventure like the Pacific Coast, the big questions are whether they have enough time and enough money to do it. Each individual will answer these questions differently, depending on their fitness, biking speed, and standards of comfort. But some generalities can be made.

Riding the entire trip from Vancouver, British Columbia, to the Mexican border, with no days off and no side trips or city tours, takes 37 days. If you mostly camp at hiker-biker sites but take one inexpensive motel night a week, mostly cook your own food, don't have any bike repairs, and don't spend money on attractions, you might be able to do it for $2000 (not counting travel to the starting point and home).

But virtually nobody would want to ride it that way. You need days off the bike, to recuperate as you get in shape or to recover from an injury or illness. You want days off to relax and enjoy the trip because the old adage "it's not the destination, it's the journey" eminently applies here. You probably will need to repair your bike or buy some new gear en route.

You also will be lured by this book into the cities, onto the islands, through parks, into museums, and through the vineyards to be found along the Pacific Coast route. Why come all this way and go to all this effort and not experience many of the joys of traveling through this region? It is rich with culture, history, culinary expertise, artistry, and, perhaps above all, amazing natural wonders. Slow down and plan for enough time that you can enjoy it.

So here is a more realistic guideline: 45 days for just the coastal tour and rest days. Add two more days for each city tour or side trip chosen. There are also alternate routes that will add one to three days. Here's how it breaks down (without rest days).

British Columbia, Canada:
- basic route: 1 day
- using alternate Lower Vancouver Island route: 3 days
- Vancouver city tour: add 1 day

Washington:
- basic route: 6 days
- using alternate Olympic Peninsula route: 9 days
- San Juan Islands side trip: add 2 days
- Seattle city tour: add 1 day

Oregon:
- basic route: 8 days
- using either Portland alternate route: 10–12 days, depending on whether you bike or take transit
- Portland city tour: add 1 day

Northern California (Crescent City to San Francisco):
- basic route: 9 days
- using Lost Coast alternate route: 10 days
- Russian River wine country side trip: add 1–3 days
- San Francisco city tour: add 1 day

Central California (San Francisco to Santa Barbara):
- basic route: 8 days
- Santa Ynez wine country side trip: add 1 day

Southern California (Santa Barbara to Mexico):
- basic route: 5 days
- Los Angeles city tour: add 1 day
- San Diego city tour: add 1 day

This overview does not include any of those magical places where, when you come upon them, you declare, "I'm stopping here!" Add in a

Bixby Creek Bridge, south of Monterey, California

magical-places factor of at least one per route segment. So, you see, when visiting the Pacific Coast, you could be on your bicycle quite a while.

As for cost, that depends on your desired comfort level. I enjoy camping but like to sleep in a bed about every five days. In most places, hostels are $25 and up, and the cheapest motels are $75 a night. On most days, I enjoy having one meal prepared by someone else. Often that's a monster sandwich or a generous salad with some protein for lunch to break up the day. That $15–$20 meal can easily double your food budget for each day. Carrying oatmeal, coffee, and freeze-dried dinners and cooking in camp, I can get by with maybe $3 for breakfast and $7 for dinner. But I also want snacks along the way, and I'm a sucker for microbrews and ice cream. So my food budget is about $40 a day.

But let me insert an element of realism into this consideration of how much money you'll spend and how long your trip will take: Also consider how far. You don't have to do it all. Perhaps you have only a two-week vacation. That's OK, you can merge into and out of the bike lanes. Here are suggestions for tackling part of the coast route if you have only one or two weeks.

One week:

- Vancouver to Seattle using the Lower Vancouver Island alternate route or San Juan Islands side trip, then back to Vancouver by train
- Seattle to Astoria, then back to Seattle (or Portland) by bus and train

- Astoria to Lincoln City (using the bus from Portland to Astoria), then back to Portland by reversing the alternate route (Portland to Lincoln City) through the Willamette Valley
- San Francisco to Bodega Bay, including the Russian River wine country side trip, then reverse the route back to San Francisco
- Los Angeles to San Diego, then back to LA by train

Two weeks:

- Vancouver to Astoria, including San Juan Islands side trip and Seattle city tour and/or the Olympic Peninsula alternate route, then back to Seattle (or Portland) by bus and train
- Astoria to Brookings, starting with the Portland city tour, then bus to Astoria, bike the Oregon Coast to Brookings, and back to Portland by two buses and the train
- Brookings to San Francisco (using train and buses from Portland to Brookings), including the Russian River wine country side trip and/or Portland and San Francisco city tours
- San Francisco to San Diego, possibly including one city tour

Lodging

Camping is the primary choice for most Pacific Coast cyclists. State and national parks dot the coastline, and almost always there is less than a day's ride between them. Local parks, private campgrounds, and Warm Showers hosts fill in the gaps. The best campgrounds offer hiker-biker sites.

That term should be reversed, because you see far more bikers than hikers. But the theory behind these sites is that they are reserved for people arriving at campgrounds in nonmotorized ways. A few of the camps right on the water also add "kayaker" to the list.

Hiker-biker sites generally have a common area where you just choose an open spot and stake your tent. Most have communal picnic tables and fire pits (only build campfires within designated fire pits, where permitted). The best ones (I'm looking fondly at you, Oregon) offer personal storage lockers where you can securely store your food and even charge your electronics. If there are storage lockers or animal-proof food boxes, use them; otherwise, most campgrounds have their own rules for safe food storage. Oregon parks have been upgrading their gear boxes with electrical outlets or USB charging ports, some using solar power. A few of them are lockable, but you must bring your own lock.

Parks charge a nominal fee, $5–$15, for a hiker-biker site. The price for a regular campsite is generally $25–$30, although beachfront sites at some Southern California parks can approach $50. Some campgrounds include a free hot shower, although many charge for showers by the minute and by the quarter. A four-minute shower might cost a dollar. Cyclists get very proficient at washing quickly.

Along with its low price, a hiker-biker site is valuable for another reason: reservations are not required—nor are they accepted. Coast campgrounds are popular, so being able to just roll up without advanced planning is great peace of mind for cyclists ambling down the coast. Many park rangers have told me they have an unstated policy of never turning away a cyclist. If the hiker-biker camp is full, they'll set up an overflow camp.

But many campgrounds offer other options too: yurts or cabins. These are pricier than camping, often about the cost of an inexpensive motel. Also, they generally must be booked in advance. There are other campgrounds along the route, from KOA and RV resorts to sites run by cities and counties. Some are nice and reasonably priced, but the state and national park campgrounds are uniformly the cheapest and most comfortable options.

In urban areas, hostels can be a good alternative to motels, if you're OK with sharing a dorm room and bathrooms. Because they are also popular, you will likely want to book them in advance. The best ones also have off-street, secured bike storage, which is a question worth asking when making the reservation.

Loading the Bike

Water weighs 8.4 pounds per gallon (4 kilograms per 4 liters). It's a consideration when packing your panniers (saddlebags) for a long-haul trip. It's also a consideration when choosing panniers to use on the trip.

Everything that you load onto your bike adds weight, and you have to haul all that weight up hills, lug it on and off the bike at campgrounds, and possibly even unlatch those bags and take them with you into a store when you go shopping. So pannier weight, for most people, is an issue.

The question of water is probably most obvious. Many people fill two bike water bottles at the campground or motel, keep them always at hand, and refill them at rest stops throughout the day. Some people pack larger bottles of water in their panniers, which might be necessary in rare instances but on this route is generally not required.

The second consideration about water and panniers is more obscure. Choosing panniers that are waterproof means that you'll haul less water on your bike during those times when you are caught riding in the rain. Panniers that are not at least water-resistant will soak up moisture on a rainy day and become heavier. They will also let the gear inside get wet, and of course everything can take a long time to dry out. Any extra moisture you're carrying will weigh you down.

Those are just two basic considerations when planning what to carry on your bike and how to pack it all in.

In the appendix in the back of the book, you'll find a packing list that mentions just a few general theories and considerations, so that you might not have quite as much to box up and ship home on the eighth day into your trip. Below are some additional tips on what and how to pack.

Balance Your Bike Load

Think carefully about how you pack your heaviest gear and where to put it on your bike to keep the load balanced. I use four panniers: two smaller ones in front and two larger in back. Then I strap my tent to the top of my back rack. I use a small handlebar bag for my camera, lunch, and valuables. This approach distributes the weight, about 35 pounds in my case, as evenly as possible.

Pack Bike Clothes for Three Days

Many people carry three sets of bike shorts and shirts: one set to wear, one clean set, and one set to wash. It's common to see padded bike shorts lashed to the back rack to dry during the day's ride. I sweat a lot, so I cannot use clothes more than once without washing them. It is a good idea to carry liquid camp soap to wash things out at campgrounds. Some of the days you are in a town or some evenings you stay in a motel, you can then get everything much cleaner in a laundromat washing machine.

Take Travel-Size Toiletries

Small bottles of shampoo, liquid soap, shaving cream, toothpaste, and sunscreen are lightweight as well as compact, which are two great reasons to use them and just replenish as needed. Yes, they're more costly and entail more wasteful packaging. Plan to be a low-impact consumer at home, and on tour just accept the trade-off.

Stock Food for Today, Plus Emergencies

It's common to see cyclists "shopping for tonight's meal" toward the end of a cycling day. Most route segments in this book suggest provisioning locations near their end. If this is not mentioned, it's probably because the choices are many or obvious. But what if you miss that provisioning stop or it's been a long day and you just want to collapse in camp? You need a little something in the panniers to get you by (as well as a camp stove and fuel to cook it with).

Try freeze-dried meals in a pouch. They are lightweight, compact, and flavorful. Just boil water and stir it into the package—simple prep and minimal cleanup. Oregon company Mountain House, which started making MREs (meals ready to eat) for the US Special Forces 50 years ago, offers some excellent meals. I usually keep one or two in my panniers, along with breakfast fixings and a few protein snack bars. Unfortunately, the freeze-dried meals are mostly available from large outdoor retailers like REI, so it's difficult to replenish them along the route.

MUSINGS FROM THE ROAD

Friendly greetings:
>Waves. Salutes. Thumbs up. Yells of encouragement.
>Lights flashing and horns honking.
>A motorcyclist's subtle raised hand on the down low.
>Cheerio from a visiting British doctor also biking up the climb from Sausalito.
>One fine morning, a tip of the hat by a guy in a convertible.

A pedaling United Nations: Canadian, Danish, German, English, French, Indian, Japanese, Australian, Italian, Irish, American, cyclists all.

New friends: Ride along, meet in camp, a day off and paths diverge.

Cars come in waves.
Trucks come in gusts.
Motorcycles rumble on in a jumble.
RVs clatter forth and rattle by.
Bicycles come in clicks.

Headwind. Tailwind. Crosswind. Sandwind! Time to clean the chain.

Nailed, stapled, tacked, glassed, iced. Flat tire.

Haiku:
Two wheels, blue ocean
Pedaling a quiet stretch.
A harbor seal barks.

If you focus on the rock, you'll hit the rock. Look farther.

Relax. Have a midday meal.

Moment: stay in it. Here's the next. It's gone. Another gone. Collection of them: a story.

I've seen people packing canned food, one-pound bags of rice, bottles of wine, jars of peanut butter, loaves of bread, bags of carrots, boxes or bottles of juice, etc. Remember the issue of pannier weight. My strategy is to buy just enough of these things for tonight's meal, along with fresh fruit and vegetables, and to carry bulk foods only sparingly.

Pamper Your Bike

Many people don't do their own bike maintenance when at home; they just occasionally oil the chain and leave the rest for the annual service in the shop. When on a long tour, however, it's wise to do a little more and plan for emergencies. A bike pump, extra bike tubes, and a patch kit are the basics. If you invest in good new tires before the tour, you can skip carrying extra tires. Chain oil and rags are absolutely required, as is a regimen of cleaning and reoiling the chain every few days. It is wise to carry extra spokes, especially if you have odd-sized rims. It is also wise to bring a multitool to tighten and adjust things as needed. Taking a basic maintenance class from your favorite mechanic before hitting the road will mean you can actually use that multi-tool effectively.

If you're traveling in a group, some items can be shared. Each person might not need a bike pump, for instance; but then again, what if the guy with the pump is 10 miles ahead when you have a flat?

A comprehensive list of gear to bring for maintaining and repairing your bike while on tour, contributed to the book by Joshua Tack of the Adventure Cycling Association, can be found in the appendix at the back of the book.

Shield the Gear

On the Pacific Coast, it's nearly a given that you will get wet. Waterproof panniers are ideal, but you can take extra steps to ensure your comfort. Your tent needs to have a rain fly. A large garbage bag is useful to pack the wet tent into when breaking camp after a wet night. When riding in wet weather, put essential items like matches, money, maps, and electronics into resealable plastic bags. One enterprising cyclist found extremely large resealable bags the size of her panniers, which provided an extra layer of protection for everything.

"When we're riding, our bikes are always ready for the rain, instead of riding with some things on the outside of our packs," explains Sarah Hine, whom I met in the moist California redwoods with her brother and a friend. Cover it all for rain when leaving camp, and forget it for the day. Good advice.

Don't Gather Mother Nature's Souvenirs

Not picking up rocks, flowers, or other natural features will keep your panniers lighter, as well as help you follow accepted environmental ethics. Take only pictures, leave only memories.

Add Something Special

On a long climb in Northern California, I met a cyclist going north who yelled across the road, "Have you seen a monkey?" Smiling, I hollered back, "A real one? No!" But it wasn't a joke question. Renna had lost her mascot, a small stuffed sock monkey, and it was important to her, so she was retracing her route in order to find it. I pedaled on, scanning the roadside, and did indeed find "Martin" staring up at me, arms outstretched, equally alarmed at being parted from human companions. I scooped it up, pedaled on until I came upon Renna's riding partner, Sam, and then waited until she arrived back so I could triumphantly press the valuable talisman into her hands and celebrate Martín's return. The next day, meeting up in camp, she presented me with my own mascot, a cheeky yellow rubber duck, who's been peeking out of one of my panniers now for many miles.

A mascot will cheer you up on a rainy or difficult day, give you something fun to place in a photo or take selfies with—even become the spokesmascot on your trip blog.

Other special items I've admired or taken on trips: an e-reader loaded with books, a small massage tool for sore muscles, pop-up camp lights, a string of battery-powered twinkly lights, a flag of your nation to fly on the bike, special food from home (like unusual hard candies) to share with fellow travelers, a beanie umbrella strapped onto a helmet, a boom box to play dance music each time you complete an ACA map segment (coming from that same duo with the mascot Martín—they were fun!). You never know when you might want to start a little roadside dance party, right? I joined in, and encourage you to do likewise.

SAFE CYCLING

Considering safety is unfortunate but necessary. It is also important not to blow these concerns out of proportion. Over my years of cycling on the coast, I have heard of only a few incidents of concern. Mostly, people comment about how safe they feel on this route. My hope is that with a few prudent precautions, all cyclists on this route will have the same rewarding experience. To start with, always wear a well-fitting helmet. Statistics show you will live longer. Safety on the road is mostly about defensive cycling while keeping your eyes open to possible dangers.

Traffic

For the safest ride through congested areas, plan to avoid commuter routes during morning and evening rush hours. Riding a long, narrow bridge into a coastal town at 8:00 AM will be more nerve-wracking, if not more dangerous, than riding it at 9:30. Commuters are in a hurry and perhaps even as distracted as tourists in a rental car.

Exercise caution at highway exit ramps. If traffic is heavy, it might be safer to use the exit and then cross to the opposite on-ramp to reenter the highway, if you can clearly see that is possible.

The sound of traffic as it approaches can be an essential cue to safety, which is why I never cycle with earbuds playing music. If music is important, get a small speaker and mount it in your handlebar bag (this is only effective on quieter roads). Keeping your ears open for approaching vehicles will cue you to check whether you are safely on the shoulder. Granted, it is jarring to hear the clattering of a car crossing the center-line bumps or the roar of

A whimsical sculpture on the island of Coronado, adjacent to San Diego

an engine as the driver accelerates around you on a hill. You might decide to look in your mirror and see if the traffic has stacked up and possibly pull off for a break if it's too heavy. And hearing the approach of a big vehicle makes you ready to adjust your balance if a truck's trailing wind vortex might cause you to wobble.

Cycling in a group requires its own safety considerations. While you may be tempted to ride two abreast, this is dangerous on any trafficked road and should be avoided. Break up larger groups into twos or threes riding single file, with multiple car lengths between subgroups. That leaves space for other vehicles to go around you and safely get back into their lane if they meet oncoming traffic.

Hills

Uphill climbs hold safety problems, as your speed is reduced to a crawl. On steep sections, train yourself not to veer back and forth in an S pattern, as you might if you were switchbacking on a steep trail.

If you must stop and walk your bike, prepare with three steps: make space between yourself and other cyclists, check for a break in the traffic, and look for a wide, straight section. Never stop on a blind curve, and try not to stop on a narrow shoulder when traffic is right next to you or when you are in the lane. Those stops can easily spook drivers and cause them to swerve or brake, creating unexpected hazards for other motorists. When walking your bike, keep yourself and your bike entirely on the shoulder if at all possible.

By the way, I cast absolutely no aspersions on anyone walking their bike. First, I've done it myself and will again. Second, there are many reasons you might need to do it, including equipment breakdown. Third (and note to self), don't worry that others will judge you badly because of your fitness level; you are out there on the bike, not in a cushy leather car seat. Most people find that they get fitter as the trip goes on, which results in faster riding and easier climbing.

Once you crest that hill, be cognizant of the downhill run. Potholes, cattle grates, and road debris can send you tumbling on a fast descent. At the very least, it could cause loose gear to fly off the bike, which means you would need to climb back uphill to get it or leave it behind. Keep an eye out for hazards, because steering around them at high speeds can mean swerving into the traffic lane, where of course there could be a much larger vehicle traveling at a much higher speed.

Dogs

When you meet a barking dog, keep pedaling; it's harder for it to bite a moving ankle. It's unlikely you'll be greeted in such an unfriendly way on the coast highway, but it's certainly possible as you cycle down a rural road. You may be able to ward off a dog by waving a bike pump, or some other gear that's handy, at it. A shot of pepper spray will repel a dog, but I see that only as a last resort. If you're going to carry it, keep it accessible in a handlebar bag and know how to use it.

Rain and Fog

Some thought must be given to riding in rain and fog. In those conditions where visibility is low, use both front and rear lights, and make sure the batteries are fresh so the beams are strong. Many people use two or three rear lights. It is always a good idea to wear reflective clothing, but being highly visible is essential in adverse conditions. Wear bright jerseys or jackets with reflective tape or a safety vest over the top of darker clothes. A triangular orange-and-yellow hazard symbol, attached to the bike or the panniers, is also a good choice.

And if the weather gets extremely bad, consider pulling off the road altogether. In a heavy fog, can you see the next curve or oncoming traffic? If not, how can they see you? A downpour will pass; fog will come and go. Make the decision that keeps you safe, even if it slows you down.

Darkness

One final thought about safe cycling: ride only during daylight hours. Even if you have reflective clothing and good lights (and you certainly must, and must keep them on in adverse conditions), you are increasing your risk greatly by continuing through dusk and into the evening. Visibility is especially bad when the sun is low in the sky; motorists driving at night will not expect cyclists to be on the road and certainly won't see you until they get quite close.

SAFE CAMPING

The sections above concern safety while you're on the bike, but what about when you're off it? At rest stops and in campgrounds, take prudent steps to

TRAVEL LIKE WILLIE

He wouldn't want me to advise this, but I will: travel like Willie. My friend Willie Weir, bike traveler extraordinaire, happily shares his experiences in far-flung lands in his column for *Adventure Cycling* magazine, in talks to packed rooms and schools, and in books. And it seems for him it's more about the adventure, of meeting people and experiencing new places, than it is about the achievement of taking the trip on a bike.

"What did you learn?" he asks. "Who did you meet?"

Willie says he sometimes chooses a "focus for the day," to put his mind into observation mode. "Blue. Elderly people. All of a sudden when you think about birds, your ears will open up," he says. "Rather than thinking about 'it's raining, and I have 28 more miles to go,' your mind is somewhere else."

Besides being a great technique to get yourself out of a funk, going out with a theme or a goal enhances your understanding of the place you're visiting. "Say, 'OK, I'm going to have three conversations on this ride.' Stop and ask someone what they're doing in their garden, or tell people what you're doing." The latter is easy, because you are atop a great conversation starter: your loaded bike. "That in itself makes people want to know where you're going," he says.

Want some advice on where or when to stop? Get a feel for your "travel sponge," Willie says, and keep your radar up for "magic places." Learning how to be a good traveler, he notes, is a journey itself. Some people "are just one gigantic travel sponge" and can continually soak up the experiences, he says. "But the moment your travel sponge is full, you stop absorbing the sights or whatever, and you become that miserable person who's complaining about the weather."

Soaking up all the newness, how do you find the truly delightful moments? Recognize when you're in a magic place, "when you have the feeling of 'I've never been any place like this in my life,'" he advises. "A wise traveler knows, when you get there and don't slow down, you're crazy."

"If you ride 50 miles past this paradise, you're only going to regret it," he says. "All you have to do is stop pedaling." Learn more at www.willieweir.com.

A mix of freeze-dried packaged food and fresh produce from a farmers market combine for an excellent bike-camp dinner.

keep yourself safe around strangers and your gear safe when you need to step away from your bike.

Personal Safety

First, concerning yourself, I believe that cyclists on the Pacific Coast route are largely safe from criminal activity, although risks rise in the cities. Most at risk are solo cyclists and, unfortunately, solo women. Yet I have spoken to many women doing the trip on their own, and I find them self-assured, outgoing, and happy. Still, a cycling partner creates safety in numbers. If you ride solo or in a small group, take rest stops in populated areas and stay with your bike.

Gear Safety

Consider how you intend to protect your bike when you can't stay with it. The danger of having gear, or even the bike, stolen at a quick restroom stop might be low, but it does exist, especially in urban areas. A group traveling together can leave one person to watch the gear while others shop, but what about if you're solo? When I've traveled solo, I've taken a combination of steps:

1. **Lock the bike.** Securely lock your bike with a heavy chain lock. Cable locks are just too easy to cut.
2. **Keep valuables with you at all times.** I keep my money, credit cards, phone, passport, and camera all in my handlebar bag, which has a shoulder strap and comes with me into every restroom, grocery store, or roadside attraction. Any pannier holding irreplaceable or expensive gear also goes with me.

3. **Lock the panniers.** Panniers staying on the bike can be locked together and to the rack with slim cable locks. This is a minor deterrent, but it could thwart a grab-and-run act.

Camp Safety

In camp, treat your gear in a similar way. Take your most important valuables with you everywhere, and lock your bike to a picnic table or other immovable object. I carry an additional cable lock that can be snaked through the tires and linked to the main lock if the area seems sketchy (camp hosts have advised me to do this in areas where wheels have been stolen while cyclists slept). I try to get to know my neighbors, and many of us practice the unwritten code of looking out for each other. When I retire for the night, I take my panniers with most everything except food into my tent with me. Many people do not do this, but I sleep more securely knowing that my gear is nearby and out of strangers' sight.

Wildlife

One danger in campgrounds that ranges from annoying to serious is wildlife. Most rangers or hosts advise campers about the local wildlife, which can range from squirrels to large mammals. All will hunt for food at night using

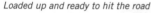
Loaded up and ready to hit the road

their noses. If campsite food-storage boxes are not available, follow campground rules for securing all food. I minimize such attraction by eating all fresh or odiferous foods every day and mostly keeping just dried or shrink-wrapped food in with my gear overnight. After dinner, clear the table, do the dishes, and properly dispose of leftover food and wrappers; don't leave them on the table for overnight visitors.

AN EPIC JOURNEY

All in all, this is an epic journey. Whether you are dipping into the route for a week or going the whole way (and farther), whether you're on a subsistence budget or exercising your credit card along with your legs, you are in for a unique experience. Preparing for the trip with proper gear, choosing a time when the weather will suit you, and using common sense measures to stay safe will ensure that you get the most out of the trip and come away with nothing but sparkling memories. And perhaps an epic suntan on your heavy-duty legs.

With your purchase of this book, you also get access to our easy-to-use, downloadable cue sheets:
- Go to our website: www.mountaineersbooks.org/PacCoastCue
- Download a complete set of mileage cues for all the segments in this book.
- When you open the document on your computer, enter the code "BIK3RID3" when prompted.

It's our way of thanking you for supporting Mountaineers Books and our mission of outdoor recreation and conservation.

HOW TO USE THIS BOOK

This book divides the 1850-mile Pacific Coast route into daily segments of mostly 40 to 60 miles, with a few longer stretches where necessary to reach the best destination for the night. Although this book largely follows the route prescribed by the Adventure Cycling Association and state and local bicycling groups (see Resources at the back of this book), I chose the safest and most scenic route, including use of bike paths where appropriate.

Each route segment begins with a summary of the distance in miles and the elevation gain in feet, followed by a description of the ride and a turn-by-turn mileage log, captured with an on-bike Garmin cyclometer and augmented by the excellent services of Ride with GPS (https://ridewithgps .com). Each route segment is also accompanied by a map and an elevation profile, compiled with these two tools as well as the ACA maps and my own two eyes.

The ride descriptions note major attractions and natural features, as well as seasonal facility limitations, road conditions or closures, and costs of pertinent services. However, because conditions change, each traveler should

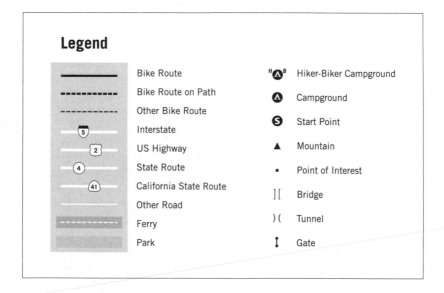

Legend

———	Bike Route	ᴴ△ᴮ	Hiker-Biker Campground
--------	Bike Route on Path	Ⓐ	Campground
--------	Other Bike Route	Ⓢ	Start Point
⑤	Interstate	▲	Mountain
②	US Highway	▪	Point of Interest
④	State Route	][	Bridge
㊶	California State Route	)(	Tunnel
	Other Road		
--------	Ferry	ⲓ	Gate
	Park		

In a hiker-biker camp corral, ground space and picnic tables are shared.

confirm critical details, such as road conditions, with local agencies prior to taking the route.

The ride descriptions also point out all campgrounds close to the route, with special focus on those with hiker-biker facilities (look for the "H-B" campground symbol on the maps). Public restrooms (please use these facilities where available) and potable water can be found at most campgrounds and public parks, but in areas where facilities are far apart, the mileage logs note the location of some public restrooms as well as camping options. Of course, commercial facilities are usually available if you buy something at a store or eat at a café.

In addition to the main Pacific Coast route, this book includes six city tours, which are mostly right along the route (one of them, Portland, requires more travel to and from the coast). There is an island-hopping side trip and two wine country side trips as well. Alternate routes of one to six days explore the southern edge of Canada's Vancouver Island, Washington's Olympic Peninsula, Oregon's Coast Range between Portland and the coast, and Northern California's Lost Coast.

Throughout the book, Connections sidebars list how to get to the major cities that provide logical starting or stopping points, with cycling-specific air and train travel information. Additional sidebars provide interesting tidbits about the route and some of its highlights.

An appendix contains a packing list, bike maintenance and repair tips, and a checklist for the touring cyclist's tool kit. Resources include books and websites, as well as information on region-specific maps and websites.

A Note About Safety

Safety is an important concern in all outdoor activities. No guidebook can alert you to every hazard or anticipate the limitations of every reader. Therefore, the descriptions of roads, trails, routes, and natural features in this book are not representations that a particular place or excursion will be safe for your party. When you follow any of the routes described in this book, you assume responsibility for your own safety. Under normal conditions, such excursions require the usual attention to traffic, road and trail conditions, weather, terrain, the capabilities of your party, and other factors. Keeping informed on current conditions and exercising common sense are the keys to a safe, enjoyable outing.

—Mountaineers Books

BRITISH COLUMBIA, CANADA

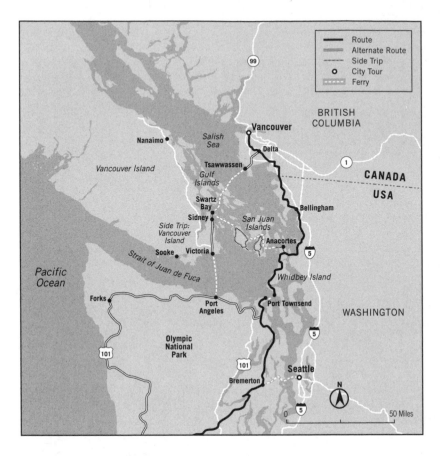

THE PACIFIC COAST ROUTE DESCRIBED in this book begins in Canada, using the Adventure Cycling Association map set as a guide and starting in Vancouver, British Columbia. If you begin this tour in Vancouver—which I hope many will do, as it is a fantastic city and welcoming to bicyclists—you can fly into that city or fly into Seattle and easily take Amtrak north to Vancouver.

But the province's premier city, just a few miles from Washington State, deserves more exploration. The centrally located train station virtually deposits you onto Vancouver's main shoreline bike path, from which city exploration begins.

From Vancouver, reaching the Canada–US border is a one-day affair, pedaling through city and suburban neighborhoods, then climbing a grand bridge into river delta and farmland. Walking your bike through customs, passport in hand, is normally a brief and comfortable border crossing.

Vancouver Island can also be briefly visited on this chapter's alternate route. It's a simple farmland ride from Vancouver to a ferry whisking you to the island's southeast corner, where you can take a leisurely ride down to the provincial capital of Victoria. From Vancouver Island, there are two ferry routes into Washington to link up with the main coastal route south.

But the rides in this chapter barely dip into British Columbia's coastal cycling possibilities. For instance, you could head north along the Strait of Georgia and visit towns along the mainland, then take a ferry across to mammoth Vancouver Island and cycle south along its protected interior shore. Additional touring can be enjoyed on the smaller Gulf Islands between the mainland and Vancouver Island. The Gulfs are part of the same archipelago as Washington's San Juan Islands, which are visited on an alternate route in the next chapter.

CITY TOUR: VANCOUVER, BC
Distance: 24 miles
Elevation gain: 1120 feet

Starting a cycling adventure down the "best coast" of North America? Not so fast. Take a break before you begin, to savor one of the West's best cities—and one that embraces cycling. Visit Vancouver.

It sounds a bit like a marketing line, but really, don't just mount the panniers and pedal south from the base of Cypress Street, away from the braced totem pole that looks after you as you leave Hadden Park. To the back of that totem, starting with the park and its Maritime Museum and stretching out to massive Stanley Park and some wonderful neighborhoods, is a network of cycling trails that allows you to safely and easily explore much of Vancouver by bike.

The city tour starts at the Telus World of Science, a glittering silver dome on the east edge of False Creek. It's only two blocks from the central train and bus station. You can immediately follow the bikes in either direction on the Seaside Greenway. In this bike-crazed city, two-wheeled transport whizzes by at a fast and regular clip, especially during the commuting hours or on a warm weekend afternoon.

Follow the trail north and then west as it curves around False Creek, then exit it at the base of Hornby Street to climb the two-way protected bike lane a few blocks and cut across the city center. You'll pass the Vancouver Art Gallery, the city's fine art museum, and end up at Coal Harbour, where the

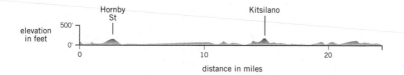

many cruise ships dock at Canada Place. Adjacent to the convention center is a visitors center outlet, where you can buy discounted tickets for theater shows.

Continue west on the Seaside Greenway and soon you'll be at the edge of Stanley Park, a 1001-acre peninsula shaped like an elephant's head. A one-way cycling path takes you counterclockwise around it, from the skyscraper view at Brockton Point (the tip of the elephant's trunk) to beneath the soaring Lions Gate Bridge (about elephant's eyebrow level) and around to English Bay. Stop at least once on the 17-mile ride: you should see the totems. Just off Brockton Point sits a meadow of totem poles, some carved as long ago as 1880, with at least one carved recently. These colorful icons of the area's First Nations heritage tell stories of their culture.

If you've planned ahead, take a picnic in the park, but if not, the cafés along English Bay beckon. Hold off if you can, because a greater culinary escapade awaits.

Depart the city center by way of the Burrard Street Bridge, which also contains a safe, generous bikeway. Drop down into the waterfront Vanier Park (where the Pacific Coast cycling route starts). Take the trail through the park and up into the funky Kitsilano neighborhood. "Kits" was the hippie

CONNECTIONS: VANCOUVER AIRPORT AND AMTRAK

If you're beginning your tour in Vancouver, perhaps you intend to arrive by airplane or train. Here are the basic connections.

Vancouver International Airport has good transit connections. The Canada Line light rail whisks you downtown in a half hour from the airport. Travel to the line's farthest station, near Canada Place, was $4 at the time of publication. If you're not staying near the rail stations, TransLink buses with bike racks also serve the airport.

To bike from the airport, about a 10-mile ride to the city center, depart east on Grant McConachie Way, then bear right onto Sea Island Way at 1.5 miles, just after the Templeton Street intersection. Caution: heavy traffic and merging lanes. Turn left on No. 3 Road at 2.4 miles, then right onto Bridgeport Road. Turn left on Great Canadian Way, then right onto a shared path at Van Horne Way to intersect with the Canada Line SkyTrain Bikeway bridge at 2.9 miles. Take the bikeway over the river and reverse the Vancouver to US Border ride into the city.

Amtrak couldn't be easier for a cycling tourist. It arrives in downtown Vancouver, just two blocks from the Seaside Greenway at Telus World of Science. Look for the science center's white geodesic dome when you exit the station to find the trail. If you are traveling from Seattle or Portland, the daily Cascades service allows bikes to be loaded (without being boxed) into the baggage car for a small additional fee.

Seaside Greenway bike trail on Vancouver's False Creek

hangout in the 1970s, and it still retains the flavor in its plentiful, colorful small shops and cafés.

Loop back to the bridge area, but turn east and take the trail to Granville Island, where you can really satiate your hunger, thirst, or sweet tooth. Here you'll find a vast, indoor public market with specialty shops serving the city's chefs. Park, purchase provisions, and eat, then cycle back on the Seaside Greenway along False Creek. Across the water, beyond the yachts and numerous small ferries, is Yaletown. Its high-rise condos provide a desirable address.

As you see the silver science dome approach, you may think the tour is done, but you've yet to see three more neighborhoods that will tell you much about the history of Vancouver and the way the city lives today.

Pass the dome and repeat a short section of the Seaside trail, but make a right onto the connecting Carrall route, which leads, via another two-way protected bike lane, through Chinatown and down to Gastown. You'll pass the edge of Chinatown, which is worth a detour to explore. One stop is a must for garden lovers: at the corner of Keefer Street is the entrance to the Dr. Sun

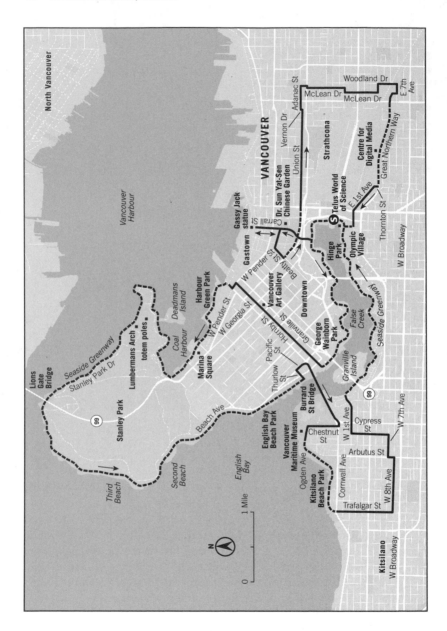

Yat-Sen Classical Chinese Garden. It is considered the finest example of its type outside China.

Next comes Gastown. This red-brick heart of old Vancouver calls up the 1800s. The trail ends at the statue of Gassy Jack, a pioneer bartender known for his voluminous . . . stories. Cycle west on Water Street for two blocks to set your watch by the famous Steam Clock, or retrace your route up Carrall to Dunsmuir. Head east on another protected lane and soon you're above Chinatown on the Dunsmuir Viaduct heading for "East Van," our last neighborhood to explore.

At the base of the viaduct you'll pick up the Adanac route, which follows Union, Adanac, and Frances streets east through most of the city and out to Simon Fraser University. This tour doesn't take you nearly that far, but it will give you a flavor of the city's residential neighborhoods and how they are made so bikeable by a set of interconnecting bike boulevards. The routes are all well marked, and the traffic is "calmed" by speed humps and periodic dead ends that allow bikes but not cars to travel through.

Turn south on the McLean route, conveniently located just beyond two welcoming microbreweries, and head back to False Creek along the Great Northern Way. This trail edges an evolving arts and technology area, which includes institutes, a digital arts gallery, and the Emily Carr University of Art and Design. With a couple of twists and turns, crossing twice under the SkyTrain elevated light rail, you return to the World of Science, having experienced nearly a dozen neighborhoods that comprise the world of Vancouver. Now, aren't you glad you took an extra day to start your trip?

MILEAGE LOG

0.0   Depart Telus World of Science, turning right (north) onto Seaside Greenway.

0.3   Pass intersection with Carrall St.

0.5   Pass Edgewater Casino.

0.7   Pass Coopers Park.

0.8   Pass under Cambie St. Bridge.

1.0   Pass Davie St.

1.4   Pass David Lam Park.

1.7   Pass George Wainborn Park.

1.8   Pass under Granville Bridge.

1.9   Forward through roundabout at Howe St. onto Seabreeze Walk (Seaside Greenway).

2.0   At roundabout, take first exit, onto Hornby St.

2.1   Forward on Hornby into protected bike lane.

2.9   Pass Vancouver Art Gallery.

3.2   Left onto W. Hastings St.

3.2   Right onto Burrard St. in two-way bike lane.

3.3   Cross W. Cordova St. into bike trail on Canada Place plaza at convention center (tourism center, discount ticket office on right).

3.4   Trail curves left around building at seaside.

3.5   Right onto trail as road becomes Thurlow St.

3.6   Left onto trail at Harbour Green Park.

4.1   Curve right to stay on trail at Cardero Park.

4.3   Left toward Coal Harbour Seawalk. In 1 block, right to stay on Seawalk at Marina Square.

4.3   Forward on trail into Devonian Harbour Park.

4.8   Forward on trail into Stanley Park. Follow Seaside Greenway along the waterfront.

5.4   Pass Deadmans Island.

6.2   Pass totem poles.

6.7   Pass Lumbermans Arch (restrooms).

7.6   Pass under Lions Gate Bridge.

8.9   Pass Third Beach.

9.6   Pass Second Beach.

10.2   Forward on trail along Beach Ave.

10.5   Pass English Bay Beach Park.

11.0   Pass Sunset Beach Park.

11.2   Left at Y at Vancouver Aquatic Center.

11.3   Left onto Beach Ave., then immediate right onto Thurlow St.

11.4   Right onto Pacific St.

11.5   Right onto Burrard St. and cross Burrard St. Bridge.

12.1   Right onto Cornwall Ave.

12.2   Right onto Chestnut St.

12.5   Left onto Ogden Ave.

12.7   Right at Maple St. onto trail, then left at Y in Hadden Park.

13.0   Pass Kitsilano Beach Park.

13.1   Bear right around Kitsilano Pool.

13.3   Forward onto trail at Kitsilano Yacht Club.

13.5   Forward onto Trafalgar St. as trail ends. Follow Valley Bikeway signs.

14.1   Left onto W. 8th Ave. (Off-Broadway Bikeway).

14.7   Left onto Arbutus St. In 1 block, right onto W. 7th Ave.

15.0   Left onto Cypress St.

15.3   Right onto W. 1st Ave.

15.6   Slight left to stay on W. 1st Ave.

15.7   Right onto Creekside Dr. (Seaside Greenway). In 1 block, left onto Island Park Walk (Seaside Greenway). In ½ block, right to stay on Island Park Walk.

15.9   Cross under Granville Bridge. (Detour left on Anderson St. under bridge to Granville Island Public Market, shops, cafés.)

16.0   Pass Sutcliffe Park.

16.2   Left at Y at Alder Bay Walk to stay on Island Park Walk.

16.3   Forward onto Ironwork Passage.

16.5   Left onto Seaside Greenway at Spruce Harbour Marina.

16.8   Slight left onto Millbank.

17.0   Bear left at Stamps Landing to return to trail.

17.3   Pass Spyglass ferry dock.

17.4   Pass under Cambie St. Bridge.

17.5   Pass Hinge Park.

17.7   Pass Olympic Village.

17.8   Bear left to stay on Seaside Greenway.

18.0   Pass Telus World of Science. Forward along Seaside Greenway, repeating original route.

18.3   Right toward Carrall St.

18.4   Left onto Carrall St.

18.6   Pass Dr. Sun Yat-Sen Chinese Garden.

18.9   Arrive at Gassy Jack statue in Gastown. Retrace route up Carrall.

19.0   Right onto W. Pender St.

19.2   Left onto Beatty St.

19.4   Left onto Dunsmuir Viaduct bike trail.

19.9   Forward across Main St. onto Adanac Bikeway (Union St.).

20.9   Left onto Vernon Dr., then immediate right onto Adanac St. to stay on Adanac Bikeway.

21.1   Right onto McLean Dr. onto Mosaic Bikeway.

21.2   Jog right then left at Venables St. to stay on Mosaic Bikeway.

21.5   Right onto Grant St.

21.6   Left onto McLean Dr.

21.9   Left onto E. 4th Ave.

22.0   Right onto Woodland Dr. to stay on Mosaic Bikeway.

22.2   Right onto E. 7th Ave.

22.3   Right onto McLean Dr., which becomes E. 6th Ave. (Central Valley Greenway).

23.0   Pass Centre for Digital Media.

23.2   Right onto Thornton St.

23.3   Left onto E. 1st Ave.

23.6   Keep left to stay on E. 1st Ave.

23.8   Right onto trail at Ontario St.

23.9   Right onto Seaside Greenway.

24.0   Arrive back at Telus World of Science.

VANCOUVER TO US BORDER
Distance: 39.5 miles
Elevation gain: 1680 feet

It's appropriate to start your 1850-mile bicycle trek in the Vancouver neighborhood of Kitsilano. About the time "adventure cycling" got started as an organized pastime, the counterculture folks of this funky neighborhood would have been way into it. Wanderlust was a feature of the 1970s hippie lifestyle, and seeing the country on the cheap (via hitchhiking or self-powered transportation) was groovy, man. You'll view a bit of that culture, updated to big vegetable gardens, Tibetan prayer flags, and Little Free Libraries, as you cycle north on the Cypress bike route.

With your back to the bay and the historic totem pole in Hadden Park, cycle up tree-lined Cypress Street. Vancouver's cycling infrastructure works so you don't have to; just follow the big green signs and enjoy a civilized feature of the city's designated bike routes: curbside, bike-height buttons to push at each major intersection to make the lights change.

Cypress begets Angus, and after making a few turns to find the bike-pedestrian bridge attached to the Canada Line SkyTrain route, you leave Vancouver and ford the north arm of the Fraser River to head into Richmond. Vancouver's largest suburb—and home to a large Asian population, which has made the area famous for its night market—is seen only briefly as you hug the river east through a warehouse district and into the countryside. Look for tidy log booms floating in the river, corralling valuable BC timber as the limbless trees wait for their turn at the sawmill.

You're riding along the north edge of Lulu Island, a flat delta edged on the south side by the Fraser's south arm. It leads, via two bridges connected on Annacis Island, to the aptly named town of Delta. The second of the two bridges is a doozy: the Alex Fraser Bridge, which was the longest cable-stay bridge in North America when it opened in 1986. Inches-thick cables arch gracefully from its two towers, sweeping down to pierce the bridge deck in an unfortunate location: on the edge of the bike-ped paths. The braided cables attach to steel girders rising from the pathway every few feet. A painted white line down the middle of the narrow decking suggests two-way travel, with each two-wheeled vehicle given about 18 inches of width. Do not open your map atop this bridge, or the strong winds could easily take it to the river.

After a fast descent from the loud, cramped, but quite safe bridge, dodge more light-industrial warehouses and head inland through Delta's sprawling subdivisions to the adjacent town of Surrey and its own suburban sprawl. Finally, the flat countryside between towns appears, and you cross two smaller rivers and skirt farmland. Side roads usher you toward the border between two major highways, so car traffic is low. At the border, you edge by big Highway 99 and drop onto 176 Street (Highway 15) to cross into the United States at Blaine.

This has been a long enough ride to convince you that you're on your way, so a well-deserved night stop on the Canadian side of the border is in order. Pedal to the Hazelmere RV Park and Campground, straight up the road

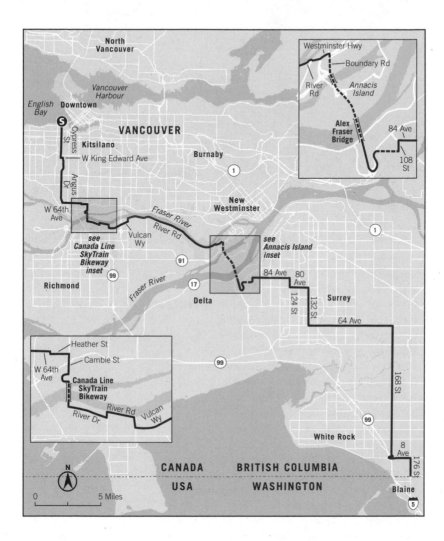

about 2 miles off the route. Tent campsites, a small store, a pool, and a hot tub will make you comfortable on your first of many nights on the road. Tomorrow, you can cross the border.

MILEAGE LOG

0.0 Depart Hadden Park heading south on Cypress St.

1.8 Left onto W. King Edward Ave.

1.9 Right on Angus Dr., which becomes East Blvd. at W. 60th Ave.

Alex Fraser Bridge

4.7   Left on W. 64th Ave.

5.7   Right onto Heather St. In 1 block, left onto W. 64th Ave.

6.1   Right onto Cambie St. Caution: traffic.

6.2   Cross SW Marine Dr. onto Canada Line SkyTrain Bikeway.

6.5   Right onto W. Kent Ave. N.

6.6   Left onto W. Ash St., which becomes W. Kent Ave. S.

6.7   Right onto ramp to elevated SkyTrain Bikeway across Fraser River.

7.2   Exit bikeway on ramps to River Dr.

7.3   Left onto River Dr.

8.0   Left onto Shell Rd.

8.1   Right onto River Rd.

8.7   Right onto No. 5 Rd.

8.8   Left onto Vulcan Wy.

9.9   Left onto No. 6 Rd., which becomes River Rd.

15.3 Left onto Westminster Hwy.

15.7 Right onto Boundary Rd.

16.2 Right onto ramps to climb to Annacis Island Bridge Bikeway.

16.8 As trail reaches ramps for Alex Fraser Bridge, cross Cliveden Ave. at crosswalk, jog left, then right immediately after off-ramp to continue on trail. Follow bike route signs across Fraser River.

18.6 Right onto trail toward Nordel Wy. when exiting bridge.

18.9 Cross under Nordel Wy., then climb to roadside path on right.

19.2 Continue on trail as it makes sharp right.

19.7 Left onto 108 St.

20.0 Right onto 84 Ave.

22.0 Right onto 124 St.

22.6 Left onto 80 Ave.

23.6 Right onto 132 St.

25.6 Left onto 64 Ave.

30.2 Right onto 168 St.

37.3 Right onto 8 Ave.: proceed west 1 block to roundabout, make complete circle, and return eastbound on 8 Ave.

38.5 Right onto Pacific Hwy. (176 St.). (Detour 2 miles east on 8 Ave. from this intersection for Hazelmere RV Park and Campground.)

39.5 Arrive at US border.

ALTERNATE ROUTE: LOWER VANCOUVER ISLAND
Distance: 39.3 miles
Elevation gain: 810 feet

If you're the type always yearning for the alternate route, why not start today, on your first leg of the long Pacific Coast route? Here's a worthy diversion that will send you island hopping.

This route takes you through the farmland and towns south of Vancouver, starting from the south bank of the Alex Fraser Bridge. Note: The distance listed here is only from the bridge south. Add 18 miles if you do the entire Vancouver-to-Sidney or -Victoria ride in one day. So total mileage from Vancouver to the campground at Swartz Bay is 38 miles, with an additional 2 miles to Sidney; total mileage from Vancouver to Victoria is about 58 miles.

It's an extra exploration of a tiny bit of Canada, and a different way to get into the United States via a ferry to Port Angeles. You'll miss a bit of the main route down Washington's north coast, but you can pick up almost all of that if you bike down to visit Victoria, then bike back up to Sidney and take the Washington State Ferries across to the San Juan Islands (see San Juans side trip in the Washington chapter). Or from Port Angeles you can take the Olympic Peninsula alternate route. No matter how you go, the coastal riding here is comfortable and scenic.

Delta to Swartz Bay via Tsawwassen Ferry
Distance: 17.6 miles
Elevation gain: 250 feet

To start this alternate route, leave Vancouver as though you were going to the US border at Blaine. Follow the main route, but after cresting the Alex Fraser Bridge at 18.6 miles, turn west toward Delta instead of east toward Surrey. You will soon be along the Fraser River heading for the big BC ferry dock at Tsawwassen. It is a flat country route through the Delta region, avoiding the main highways until the last couple of miles before the ferry dock.

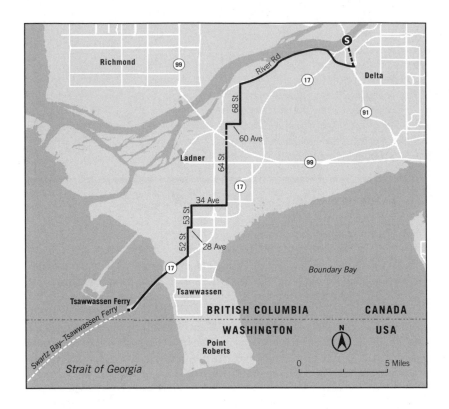

The route wends through a rural area with few services, although a convenience store can be found at Ladner Trunk Road at 9 miles. (A half mile detour west on Ladner Trunk would take you into the center of the town of Ladner in 1.5 miles. You could pick up the route to the ferry from central Ladner by heading south on Arthur Drive, which connects to 53 Street.)

Purchase ferry tickets at the Tsawwassen station, then walk your bicycle onto the big ferry as directed for the 90-minute crossing. There are many sailings daily in summer, with on-the-hour departures. Fares at the time of publication, including bicycle, were about US$20.

The ferry drops you at Swartz Bay at the north edge of the Saanich Peninsula, where a signed bike route south to Victoria can be found just beyond the ferry loading area.

MILEAGE LOG

0.0 From south end of Alex Fraser Bridge, turn right onto bike trail under bridge.
0.7 Forward onto Weigh Station Rd. as trail ends.
0.8 Left onto Nordel Wy.
0.8 Right onto Hwy. 91 Connector, which becomes 96 St.

1.7   Left onto River Rd.

5.6   Left onto 68 St.

7.2   Bear right as 68 St. becomes 60 Ave.

7.7   Left onto 64 St.

8.2   Right onto bike trail under BC 99.

8.5   Forward onto 64 St.

11.0 Right onto 34 Ave.

12.4 Left onto 53 St. (Arthur Dr.).

13.2 Right onto 28 Ave.

13.4 Left onto 52 St.

14.5 Right onto BC 17.

17.6 Arrive at ferry dock.

Swartz Bay to Victoria
Distance: 21.7 miles
Elevation gain: 560 feet

Rolling out of the ferry complex, get off the big Patricia Bay Highway in a half mile by following the bike route signs. Loop up and over the highway and continue south next to the highway on the quiet McDonald Park Road that links to Sidney, 2 miles away.

Before arriving at Sidney, pass McDonald Park Campground on the right, a worthy overnight stop if you've made the ferry ride at the end of your biking day from Vancouver. You'll find flat, wooded campsites at a cheap hiker-biker rate, and water but no showers.

Note: This alternate route visits only the tiniest corner of huge Vancouver Island. More exploration is to be had up its east coast to Nanaimo (from where you could even ferry back to Horseshoe Bay north of Vancouver and start your tour over!) or up its west side to Sooke Harbor. There's a combined trail and road route to Nanaimo, and the mellow Galloping Goose Trail, which turns from paved to gravel, up to Sooke.

But for this alternate route, head for Victoria by picking up the Lochside Trail as you enter Sidney, and very shortly you will feel like a local. Probably

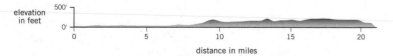

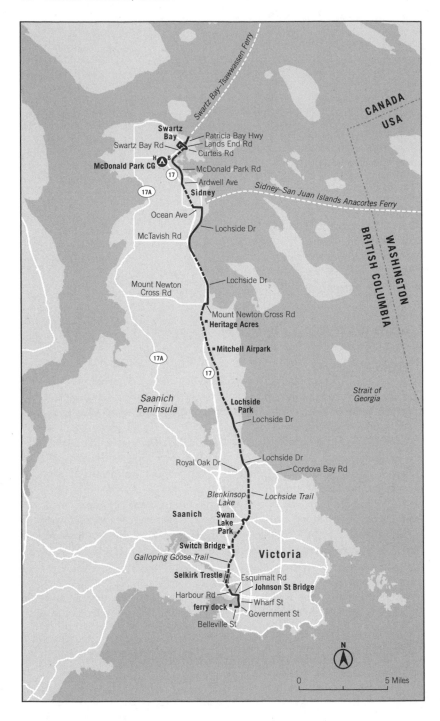

You'll meet lots of friendly locals on the rural Lochside Trail.

because, on these trails, you will mostly be riding with them. The Lochside runs north-south along the eastern edge of the peninsula, connecting Sidney with Victoria in an easy, flat 18 miles. And it links with a crossing trail, the Galloping Goose, which gets you to Victoria's harbor. The two trails provide a network that covers this little corner of Vancouver Island in style.

The Lochside began life as a railroad bed in 1917. Passengers and freight were carried up and down the route by Canadian Northern Pacific rail, initially for three cents per mile per person. It was in use as a freight rail line until 1990. With the rails replaced by asphalt and gravel, today cyclists can travel comfortably on more than 50 miles of trail from Sidney to Sooke.

Stay on the Lochside to skirt Sidney. (Or, to take a bit of a detour through town, at the big Beacon Avenue intersection, turn left and you'll be in the center of town in a half mile. Coffee shops line the street, and a bakery is a block from the harbor. Return to the route from the detour with a right turn on First Street, cycle past the Washington State Ferries dock, and pick up the route at the Fifth Street roundabout at 4.1 miles. To link this alternate route with the San Juan Islands side trip in the next chapter, you can catch a ferry here for an international crossing into the United States.)

Ride the trail south among small groups of cyclists, joggers, and moms pushing strollers. Tall, sandy-colored grasses trailside seem to grab the morning light and hold it like narrow sparks shooting skyward. You might hear a raptor overhead.

Once out of Sidney, the trail meanders through suburban neighborhoods and farming valleys. Above and between tidy waterfront homes, you get a beautiful easterly view of Mount Baker, Haro Strait, and the islands—first Sidney Island, which has a seasonal ferry from Sidney and a secluded national park preserve campground, and then Washington State's San Juan Island.

The trail turns often to Lochside Drive and back again. In some places, it is hard-packed gravel with an adjoining equestrian path. The unpaved sections traverse parks or woodlands. Mostly it's paved, and the road portions are quiet, with low-speed traffic.

Lochside Park at 12.5 miles, with its softball fields, restrooms, and cycling amenities like a repair stand and an air pump, is a welcome stop, as is the Mitchell's Farm Market, which offers sandwiches trailside at the Island View Road intersection. (For a side trip to another camping destination, go left onto Island View for 1.6 miles to a park at the water's edge.)

Nature is on verdant display at the Blenkinsop Lake Environment and Habitat, which the trail goes right through on a wooden trestle. Willows, dogwoods, birches, red alders, and Indian plums line the wetlands, which are alive with birds and waterfowl. Dainty blue chicory and climbing pink wild peas flower trailside, and thimbleberries or blackberries may be in season for snacking on your ride.

(An alternate route along the water can take you into Victoria instead of the trail. At 12.9 miles, join the Seaside Touring Route by turning south on Cordova Bay Road. The signed route, traveling scenically through residential neighborhoods, connects with Ash Road, Arbutus Road, Beach Drive, and Dallas Road to bring you to Victoria's downtown waterfront in 16 miles, adding 7 miles to this tour.)

The main tour stays on the Lochside Trail, meeting the Galloping Goose Trail at the Switch Bridge intersection, where you take the Goose into the center of Victoria. Pass by an organic bakery on Harbour Road that is popular with cyclists, and travel under a couple of concrete overpasses that are enriched with beautifully painted murals. Finally, cross the Johnson Street Bridge into downtown Victoria.

If you've taken an overnight at McDonald Park Campground or Sidney, this is a short day ride into Victoria, so plan to depart on a later ferry and set out on an exploration of this very British-style city. Enjoy high tea at the castle-like Empress Hotel or tour the manicured gardens of Government House. Visit a grove of historic totem poles in Beacon Hill Park or the home of renowned BC artist Emily Carr, and enjoy fish-and-chips at a harborside café. Be prepared for heavy tourist traffic as you explore the center of British Columbia's capital city.

Make your way to the waterfront, where you could pick up the fast, pricey Victoria Clipper and shoot straight into Seattle, then continue on the main route from there. Or head to the Black Ball Ferry dock, where the MV *Coho*, for about $25, powers across the Strait of Juan de Fuca in 90 minutes two to four times a day, taking you across the wet border into the United States at Port Angeles. From PA, you can return to the main route by cycling east on the Olympic Discovery Trail to Port Townsend, or head west on the Olympic Peninsula alternate route.

MILEAGE LOG

0.0 Depart ferry at Swartz Bay onto exit road, Patricia Bay Hwy. Keep right.

0.5 Right off road at bike lane exit sign; trail makes 180-degree turn and climbs to road above.

0.6 Right onto Lands End Rd. Follow BIKE TRAIL sign and cross over exit road; continue straight at intersection with TO TRAIL sign.

0.7 Right in 1 block onto Curteis Rd.

0.8 Forward onto Swartz Bay Rd. at intersection with Tryon Rd.

1.1 Forward onto trail at street end.

1.2 Pass first trail stop.

1.6 Exit trail left onto McDonald Park Rd. at crosswalk.

1.8 Pass McDonald Park Campground (hiker-biker campsites, water), Gulf Islands National Park Preserve of Canada.

2.6 Bear left onto Ardwell Ave. as road curves right at highway overpass. In 1 short block, right to stay on trail.

4.1 Left onto Ocean Ave.

4.2 Curve right onto 5th St. at roundabout. (Washington State Ferries dock for crossing to San Juan Islands 2 blocks ahead on Ocean; see side trip in next chapter.)

4.5 Fifth St. becomes Lochside Dr.

5.3 Left to follow Lochside Trail at highway on-ramp.

5.5 Left to stay on Lochside Dr.

8.1 Right onto Mount Newton Cross Rd. Follow Lochside Trail sign.

8.3 Left at gas station, just before intersection with BC 17, back onto trail.

9.1 Pass Heritage Acres, a Saanich Historical Artifacts Society park.

9.8 Cross Island View Rd. and Mitchell's Farm Market (café, restrooms). (Detour left here to Island View Beach Regional Park; camping.)

10.2 Pass Mitchell Airpark.

10.4 Cross Martindale Rd.

10.9 Continue straight onto unpaved trail sections, intermittent for next 2 miles.

12.5 Pass Lochside Park (restrooms).

12.7 Bear left onto trail when Cordova Bay Rd. curves to right.

12.9 Cross road to continue on trail at Sayward Hill Crescent Rd. (Detour onto the Seaside Touring Route into Victoria along Cordova Bay Rd.)

13.0   Bear right onto Lochside Dr.

14.4   Bear right to trail as Lochside Dr. curves left. In 2 blocks, return to road.

15.1   Continue straight through light at Royal Oak Dr. to continue on Lochside Dr. Intermittent trail and road sections next 2 miles.

16.5   Pass Blenkinsop Lake Environment and Habitat.

17.1   Right onto Cedar Hill Cross Rd., then left onto Borden St.; follow Lochside Trail signs.

17.3   Cross McKenzie Ave. and rejoin trail.

17.5   Cross Quadra St.

18.1   Cross Saanich Rd.

18.2   Pass Swan Lake Park.

18.6   Left onto Galloping Goose Trail at Switch Bridge intersection.

19.8   Cross Selkirk Trestle.

20.0   Bear left to stay on trail.

20.5   Left onto Harbour Rd.

20.8   Left onto Esquimalt Rd. at stoplight. Cross blue Johnson St. Bridge into downtown Victoria. Caution: traffic.

21.1   Right off bridge onto Wharf St.

21.4   Right onto Government St. at visitors information center.

21.6   Right onto Belleville St.

21.7   Arrive at Black Ball Ferry dock; use passenger entrance with bike for crossing to Port Angeles.

Opposite: *Island-hopping on a bicycle is fun and easy on a big Washington State ferry.*

WASHINGTON

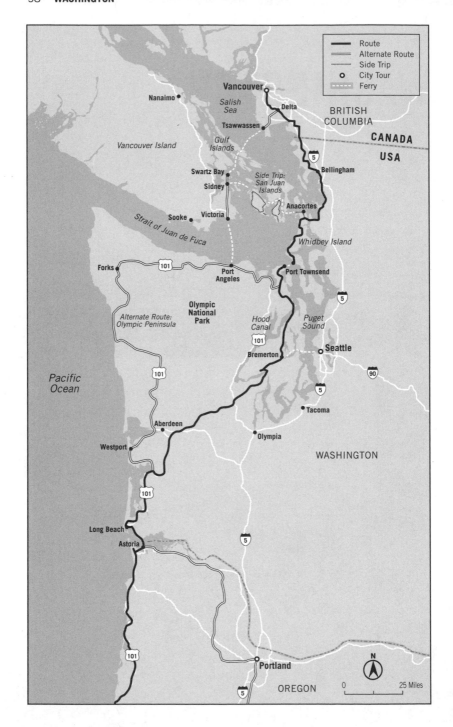

VISITING THE EVERGREEN STATE by bicycle is a coastal trip interrupted by trees. You're briefly on the northern coast, passing by or side tripping to the relaxing vacation area of the San Juan Islands, then traversing one of the nation's longest islands, Whidbey, before the route turns inland. The main route skirts Seattle and its surrounding communities on the Olympic Peninsula, but you also have another choice.

The main route heads south along Hood Canal, an extensive saltwater inlet stretching nearly to the state capital of Olympia, and along the way there is an option of detouring to a ferry that whisks you to Seattle for a city tour and air and train connections.

There is also an alternate route: instead of turning south along Hood Canal, you can turn west and pedal out around the Olympic Peninsula, skirting Olympic National Park and North America's largest temperate rain forest. This alternative keeps you as close to the Pacific Coast as possible, although much of the route consists of long stretches of road bordered on both sides by forests.

The alternate route joins the main route for the last section into southwestern Washington, where you explore verdant nature reserves before returning to the ocean for a more typical experience: sandy beaches, craggy shorelines, and windswept, whitewashed towns. A visit to the mouth of the Columbia River and the northernmost spot of Lewis and Clark's Voyage of Discovery sets the tone of exploration as you enter Oregon.

US BORDER TO BAY VIEW
Distance: 49.8 miles
Elevation gain: 1460 feet

If your papers were in order at the Blaine crossing, you are now on US soil. South of the border crossing, the route jogs east, but if you want a café, detour west here to cross over Interstate 5 and into downtown Blaine in just over a half mile (the next good stop with eateries is about halfway into today's ride, in Bellingham). Blaine is a small town with a maritime focus. A fancy retreat and golf resort, Semiahmoo, sits on the west edge of town, and a cute downtown marina park faces Boundary Bay.

You won't see much of that, though, as you continue on the main route. After some light commercial blocks, the ride continues into flat countryside.

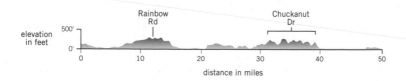

Cross I-5 and the mouth of Dakota Creek, then ride a bit on busy Blaine Road, which parallels California Creek. You truly begin to feel the rural, slower pace on Kickerville Road.

(If you're looking for a place to camp, you can detour to another coastal community, tiny Birch Bay, 2 miles west of the route, and nearby Birch Bay State Park, accessible at the Grandview Road intersection, which has hiker-biker campsites and a small store outside the park.) On the main route, Kickerville is a long, straight shot to the Lake Terrell Wildlife Area, followed by roads that skirt the Lummi Indian Reservation before leading you into Bellingham. Now here is a small city worth a bit of exploration.

Entering through the Old Town neighborhood, feel the relaxed-but-hip vibe. Old brick storefronts, some with ghostly historic murals, and water-front docks line downtown. It is a college town, home to Western Washington University, which has a renowned collection of outdoor fine art sculpture. The plentiful cafés and pubs focus on ingredients sourced from surrounding farms.

The route travels south from downtown Bellingham in the bike lane on Boulevard Street, which becomes South State Street. However, at Wharf Street you could jog right and pick up the South Bay Trail, with its scenic trestles out over the water, as you head for Fairhaven, my favorite Bellingham neighborhood.

Fairhaven was one of three towns founded in the late 1800s that voted to throw in together in 1903 to become Bellingham. This historic district is a great place to stop for coffee or lunch, with many choices and engaging window-shopping. A big ferry to Alaska, part of the Alaska Marine Highway System, departs from a dock here. A bike shop is on 11th Street just north of Mill Avenue.

After refueling, bike scenic Chuckanut Drive, a winding, rolling road well loved by area cyclists. Although traffic is not heavy, be prepared to share the road with everything from RVs to the occasional semitruck, when you will bemoan the narrow and disappearing shoulder. But there are plenty of places for cyclists to pull off and let the traffic go by. A couple are parking areas with great views of Samish Bay. Note: You may see signs for the Interurban Trail, which parallels Chuckanut for a number of miles. It is unpaved, rough and overgrown in spots, and overall more suited to a mountain biker.

Rest at Larrabee State Park, and take a quarter-mile detour down the steep side road to Taylor Shellfish Farms. It's a worthy stop. Taylor's oyster beds are visible at low tide. At the small company store—primarily a well-stocked fresh seafood case—ogle the fat foot of the giant geoduck (pronounced *GOO-ey-duck*; you're welcome) clam before maybe picking something more delec-table to try. Slurp oysters from the shell or, if you're in the mood, grill them right outside. The company provides picnic tables and Weber kettles, and you can even buy charcoal briquettes. It's a very Pacific Northwesterly scene. If you don't want to handle oysters but hanker to try some, stop at the Oyster

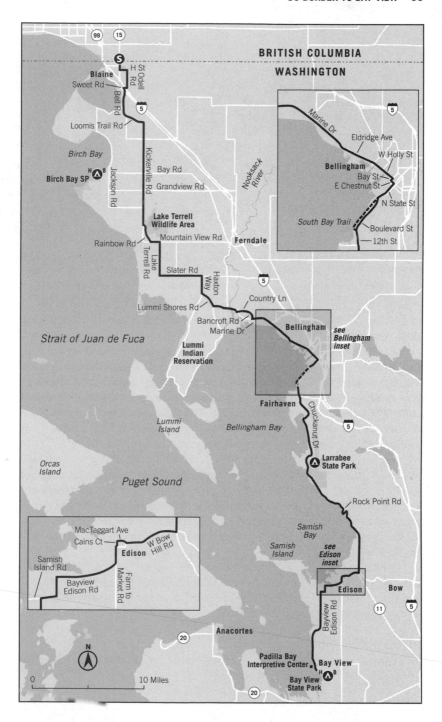

Blaine
H St
99 15
S
Sweet Rd
H Odell Rd
Bell Rd
5
Loomis Trail Rd
Birch Bay
Kickerville Rd
Bay Rd
Birch Bay SP
Jackson Rd
Grandview Rd
Lake Terrell
Wildlife Area
Rainbow Rd
Mountain View Rd
Ferndale
Lake Terrell Rd
Slater Rd
Haxton Way
5
Lummi Shores Rd
Country Ln
Bancroft Rd
Marine Dr
Bellingham
see
Bellingham
inset
Strait of Juan de Fuca
Lummi
Indian
Reservation
Lummi
Island
Fairhaven
Bellingham Bay
Chuckanut Dr
5
Orcas
Island
Larrabee
State Park
Puget Sound
Rock Point Rd
Samish
Bay
MacTaggart Ave
Cains Ct
W Bow Hill Rd
Edison
Samish
Island
see
Edison
inset
Samish
Island Rd
Farm to Market Rd
Edison
Bow
Bayview
Edison Rd
11 5
Bayview Edison Rd
Anacortes
20
N
Padilla Bay
Interpretive Center
Bay View
0   10 Miles
Bay View
State Park
20

BRITISH COLUMBIA
WASHINGTON
Marine Dr
5
Eldridge Ave
W Holly St
Bellingham
Bay St
E Chestnut St
N State St
South Bay Trail
Boulevard St
12th St

Nooksack River

Picnic tables, charcoal grills, and, most importantly, fresh shellfish are available at Taylor Shellfish Farm's waterside location on Chuckanut Drive—all the ingredients for a memorable lunch stop.

Bar Restaurant, roadside another mile down the main route. They are sure to serve Taylor's delicacies.

Chuckanut delivers you to the verdant, flat Skagit Valley and soon you're cycling past farms and into the tiny burgs of Bow and Edison. The lush farmland has attracted small-scale farmers with specialties and a holistic focus, so you could take a culinary detour and visit an artisan cheese dairy, a u-pick blueberry farm, and organic produce stands. Look for slight detours down side farm roads to delightful farm stands worth the effort. Or just find their wares at shops in the area's two artistic, resurging tiny towns.

The Rhododendron Café, at the turn onto West Bow Hill Road, is renowned for local-sourced meals. Provision for the night at the Grange-style shops of Edison, because in a few miles you'll be bedding down at Bay View State Park. An extensive day-use saltwater beach fronts the park, while the camping is wooded. The nearest grocery is 3 miles farther up the road, at a gas-station convenience store at the State Route 20 intersection that's on the next day's route.

(A final tourism note: If you're here in April, consider a detour through the Skagit Valley flower fields a few miles south of SR 20. In spring, the tulips and daffodils bloom into vast swaths of color, drawing thousands of tourists, including many cyclists, to the spectacle.)

MILEAGE LOG

0.0 Depart customs at US border, heading south in highway bike lane. Follow signs to depart highway onto brief trail.

0.5 Left onto H St. Caution: heavy traffic (detour here for Blaine).

0.9 Right onto Odell Rd.

1.9 Right onto Sweet Rd. Cross over I-5.

2.1 Left onto Bell Rd., which becomes Blaine Rd.

3.8 Bear left onto Loomis Trail Rd.

4.9 Right onto Kickerville Rd.

6.0 Cross Birch Bay Lynden Rd. Caution: fast traffic.

9.0 Cross Grandview Rd. (detour right for best access to Birch Bay State Park, camping).

11.0 Left onto Rainbow Rd.

12.1 Bear left onto Mountain View Rd.

12.6 Right onto Lake Terrell Rd.

14.7 Left onto Slater Rd.

17.1 Right onto Haxton Wy.

18.1 Left onto Lummi Shores Rd.

19.1 Bear left at Y, then left onto Marine Dr. in 100 yards.

20.2 Cross Nooksack River.

20.7 Continue straight onto Country Ln. as Marine Dr. turns sharply right.

21.5 Bear right onto Bancroft Rd. Note: Departure from ACA route.

22.1 Left onto Marine Dr., which becomes Eldridge Ave.

25.6 Bear right as Eldridge becomes W. Holly St. at stoplight.

26.3 Right onto Bay St.

26.4 Left onto E. Chestnut St.

26.7 Right onto N. State St.

27.0 Forward at roundabout onto Boulevard St. (detour right here, then left in 100 yards, to ride South Bay Trail).

27.8 Forward as Boulevard St. merges onto S. State St.

28.4 Bear left at Bayview Dr. onto 11th St.

28.7 Forward as 11th becomes Finnegan Wy., then 12th St.

29.0 Cross Harris Ave. (detour right 1 block for downtown Fairhaven).

29.3 Bear left onto Chuckanut Dr.

35.1 Pass Larrabee State Park day-use area (restrooms).

38.3 Pass Rock Point Rd. (detour right to Taylor Shellfish Farms).

42.3 Curve right onto W. Bow Hill Rd.

43.1 Curve left at Smith Rd. into village of Edison. In 1 block, curve right onto MacTaggart Ave.

43.3 Left onto Cains Ct., which becomes Farm to Market Rd.

43.7 Right onto Bayview Edison Rd.

44.7 Curve left to stay on Bayview Edison.

45.4 Left to stay on Bayview Edison at intersection with Samish Island Rd.

49.5 Pass Padilla Bay Interpretive Center.

49.8 Arrive at Bay View State Park.

BAY VIEW TO PORT TOWNSEND
Distance: 44.6 miles
Elevation gain: 2030 feet

Bridges and ferries are in your future on today's ride, which travels down the north half of one of our country's largest islands. Depart the park onto an unpaved trail that tops a dike through the Padilla Bay National Estuarine Research Reserve. The 2-mile Shore Trail helps you start the day with the tang of salt water in your nose. It's a wonderful connection to Padilla Bay.

Soon after, you reach State Route 20 and head west to climb a tall bridge over the Swinomish Channel. The bridge hosts a generous, protected bike lane, which serves cyclists going both directions. Exit the bridge onto South March Point Road next to a large casino. March Point carries you next to busy SR 20 nearly until merging onto it at March's Point. The next turn can be tricky given the traffic and speed. Merge onto SR 20 and turn left at the light to Whidbey Island, or bike in the shoulder lane to the corner and wait for the light to change to cross. (If you want to take the San Juan Islands side trip, turn right on March's Point Road and come to a trail into Anacortes in 1 mile, then the San Juan Islands ferry dock in 8 miles.)

Once you've successfully navigated cross traffic to make a left toward Whidbey, you'll find a long grade of nearly 5 miles, occasionally flattening out, before you reach the island. One of the best things about the north end of Whidbey Island is visited first: Deception Pass Bridge. Before crossing, take a moment to stop with the rest of the tourists and ogle the steel-girder bridge (well, actually two spans) and narrow waterway below. There is a more extensive visitors area on the south side of the road, if you want to cross SR 20, and even a short trail that goes under the bridge.

High above swirling waters that are treacherous to small boats (giving the pass its name), the bridge carries you from the mainland to Whidbey Island. The bridge has very narrow sidewalks, so cyclists must take over a car lane when crossing. It's good to cross this bridge in the morning, as traffic gets heavier as the day goes on.

Surrounding the bridge is Deception Pass State Park, Washington's most-visited park. Many just drive through (20,000 cars a day in summer), but there also are popular campgrounds. Hiker-biker campsites are available at the park's lower campground, at 16.4 miles. The park has wooded and shore hikes, swimming in freshwater Cranberry Lake, and saltwater beaches.

elevation in feet

distance in miles

A cyclist waits for the ferry from Whidbey Island to dock at Port Townsend, Washington.

Once on Whidbey, SR 20 sports a generous shoulder, the better to tolerate a significant traffic load. Approaching the island's largest town, Oak Harbor, the route sends you edging around Naval Air Station Whidbey Island, the US Navy's protected base. You will see and hear the overhead traffic, sometimes quite earsplitting, as you cycle Ault Field Road and head to the island's western edge. (For a detour into Oak Harbor, stay on SR 20 here and reach Oak Harbor in less than 4 miles.)

This next section of the main route has few services, plentiful rolling hills, and excellent views of Puget Sound. It aims east again at West Libbey Road, which also connects to Fort Ebey State Park, named for one of the early defensive military encampments. That park, situated on a bluff 1.5 miles off the route, also has hiker-biker campsites.

After briefly jogging onto SR 20 northbound, relax on the ribbon of road called Madrona Way. You'll spy plenty of madrona (or Pacific madrone) trees arcing precariously over the hillside on the left that drops to Penn Cove. Their peeling, rust-colored bark glows a deep red in certain light. Pass the side road to a historic log-framed hotel, the Captain Whidbey Inn. Beyond, in the water, you can see the boxy platforms and submerged piers of the commercial Penn Cove Shellfish, a revered local operation.

Enter Coupeville, a picturesque island town, and stop to visit the shops at the end of its town pier. A historical museum and two blocks of eateries and galleries beckon. From there, it's a flat 5 miles out to Fort Casey, another former defensive garrison, which sits next to the ferry dock that links to Port Townsend, the goal for tonight.

A 20-minute ferry ride (on a very regular schedule, with no reservations needed, $4–$6 at the time of publication) deposits you in downtown Port Townsend. Beyond the bluff visible when you approach town lies Fort Worden, which faces north toward Fort Casey. This is your camping spot for the night.

Ferrying from fort to fort also provides a great connection to the area's military history. Together, Forts Worden, Casey, and Ebey could triangulate on any seafaring interlopers. Today, these forts offer hiking, camping, and

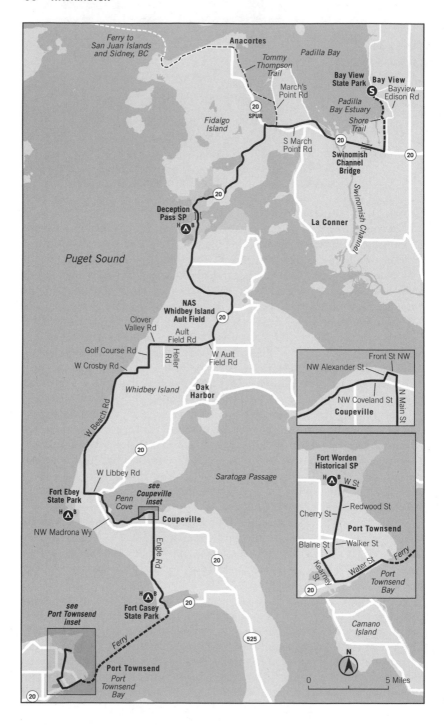

Ferry to
San Juan Islands
and Sidney, BC

Anacortes

Padilla Bay

Tommy
Thompson
Trail

March's
Point Rd

Bay View
State Park

Bay View
S

Bayview
Edison Rd

20
SPUR

Fidalgo
Island

Padilla
Bay Estuary

Shore
Trail

S March
Point Rd

20

Swinomish
Channel
Bridge

La Conner

Swinomish Channel

Deception
Pass SP
H ▲ B

Puget Sound

NAS
Whidbey Island
Ault Field

Clover
Valley Rd

20

Ault
Field Rd

Golf Course Rd

Heller Rd

W Ault
Field Rd

W Crosby Rd

Whidbey Island

Oak
Harbor

Front St NW

NW Alexander St

NW Coveland St

Coupeville

N Main St

W Beach Rd

20

W Libbey Rd

see
Coupeville
inset

Saratoga Passage

Fort Worden
Historical SP
H ▲ B   W St

Fort Ebey
State Park
H ▲ B

Penn
Cove

Coupeville

Cherry St

Redwood St

Port Townsend

NW Madrona Wy

Engle Rd

Blaine St

Walker St

20

Kearney St

Water St

Port
Townsend
Bay

see
Port Townsend
inset

Fort Casey
State Park
H ▲ B

20

20

525

Camano
Island

N

Ferry

Port Townsend
Port
Townsend
Bay

20

0   5 Miles

other activities. When you exit the ferry in downtown Port Townsend, skirt the bluff and ride a gentle grade a couple of miles up to Fort Worden's wooded hiker-biker campsites. Pitch the tent, offload the heaviest stuff, and head back into town to explore this small port city. Maybe you'll have time to visit the historic Rose movie theater after a pint or a plate in one of the many casual restaurants in town.

MILEAGE LOG

0.0 Depart Bay View State Park, turning left onto Bayview Edison Rd.

0.6 Right onto unpaved Shore Trail.

2.8 Right onto Bayview Edison Rd. as trail ends.

3.8 Right onto SR 20. Caution: fast traffic.

5.1 Merge onto sidewalk at Swinomish Channel Bridge approach.

6.2 Left onto S. March Point Rd.

7.1 Straight onto S. March Point at intersection with March's Point Rd.

8.7 Cross March's Point Rd. and continue onto SR 20 on-ramp (detour right on March's Point Rd. for San Juan Islands side trip). Caution: traffic.

9.3 Merge left into turning lane to stay on SR 20 main line to Deception Pass and Whidbey Island. Caution: fast traffic.

14.8 Continue straight across Deception Pass Bridge.

16.4 Pass Deception Pass State Park (camping, restrooms).

22.4 Right on W. Ault Field Rd. (for detour to Oak Harbor, continue straight on SR 20).

24.6 Straight onto Clover Valley Rd. at intersection with Heller Rd.

25.3 Road curves left and becomes Golf Course Rd.

26.2 Right onto W. Crosby Rd., which becomes W. Beach Rd.

33.3 Left onto W. Libbey Rd. (detour right to Fort Ebey State Park in 1.5 miles; camping, restrooms).

33.9 Left onto SR 20. Caution: fast traffic.

34.1 Right onto NW Madrona Wy.

37.2 Bear right as Madrona becomes NW Coveland St.

37.4 Left onto NW Alexander St. to reach Coupeville town center at Front St. NW.

37.5 Right onto N. Main St., which becomes Engle Rd.

41.7 Pass entrance to Fort Casey State Park (camping, restrooms).

42.1 Arrive at Coupeville ferry dock. Board ferry for Port Townsend.

42.2 Left off ferry landing in Port Townsend onto Water St., which becomes Sims Wy.

42.7 Right onto Kearney St.

43.1 Right onto Blaine St.

43.3 Left onto Walker St., which becomes Cherry St.

44.1 Bear left onto Redwood St.

44.5 Right onto W St.

44.6 Left onto Fort Worden Wy. into Fort Worden Historical State Park. Proceed to Guest Services building for campsite registration.

SIDE TRIP: SAN JUAN ISLANDS

If you took the Vancouver Island alternate route, as you approached the gargantuan island by ferry, your boat wended its way through a number of smaller islands. Covered in spiky evergreens and looking like a Bond villain's ultimate hideaway, these are the Gulf Islands, and they are certainly worthy of exploration (Salt Spring and Pender are popular by bicycle). The Gulfs are in Canadian territory, but the chain of smaller islands continues into American waters; these are the San Juan Islands.

Four of the US islands are served by the Washington State Ferries system, which docks at Sidney, BC. Cyclists have a choice of biking on one or more of these islands and continuing the mainland route or cycling them and going back to Sidney to continue via the Vancouver Island alternate route. Here are some tips if you're considering this island getaway:

- The two-hour ferry runs once a day from Sidney, BC, to Friday Harbor, Washington, on San Juan Island; it does not run January through March.
- Cost at time of publication was $15–$25 (depending on your age), bike included.
- Friday Harbor, the largest town in the San Juans, offers many overnight accommodations.
- Hiker-biker campsites are at San Juan County Park, on the opposite side of the island from Friday Harbor, about 20 miles.
- Interested in a multiday stay? Interisland ferries are free (with multiple crossings per day), so day trips to other islands (Lopez, Orcas, and Shaw) can be taken, with a return to Friday Harbor each night.
- When leaving the San Juans, take the ferry to Anacortes, Washington, on the mainland. There is no charge for the sailing from Friday Harbor to Anacortes, and there are multiple crossings per day.

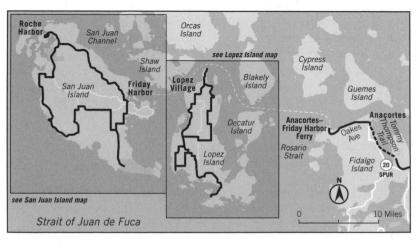

- From Anacortes, ride 8 miles southeast through the town center and on the waterfront Tommy Thompson Trail, then connect with the main route's Bay View to Port Townsend segment at the intersection with South March Point Road at 8.7 miles.

The side trip described here takes you on a two-day tour to two of the most popular islands, San Juan and Lopez. Stay the first night on San Juan and the second night on Lopez, then return to the mainland route on the third day.

San Juan Island
Distance: 40 miles
Elevation gain: 2520 feet

Ride the Washington State Ferries to Friday Harbor, the biggest town on the San Juan Islands. Plenty of cafés and shops adorn this picturesque tourist town. From the ferry dock, cycle out to the American Camp at Cattle Point, one of the two national historical parks on the island. Park signage tells the story of the Pig War between American and British settlers and soldiers. (Only one shot was fired, and it killed a pig.)

A colorful diversion awaits on Wold Road at Pelindaba Lavender Farm. Long purple rows of lavender fill the field in season (July), and refreshing lavender lemonade awaits in their shop. Although the center of the island has multiple flat farming valleys, you must climb to the perimeter road, but that elevation also comes with a great bonus: killer views. As you turn north on the perimeter road, pass Lime Kiln Point State Park, also known as Whale Watch Park, for very good reason.

"A highlight in Washington was whale watching," recalls Eamonn O'Neill, an Irish cyclist who traveled the Pacific Coast route in 2016. "They go right past the county park campsite," he says. "There were loads of them—we watched for at least a half hour." A resident pod of orcas (a.k.a. "killer whales") live in the waters off the west side of San Juan Island, so take a wildlife-viewing detour to Lime Kiln or San Juan County Park, which is 2 miles past Lime Kiln (and is the designated hiker-biker park for an overnight, should you be so inclined).

Continue up the island loop along a series of rolling hills to the English Camp, part of the island's historical park. A short (0.2-mile) gravel road takes you down through the woods to the camp, over which looms a giant Union Jack flag.

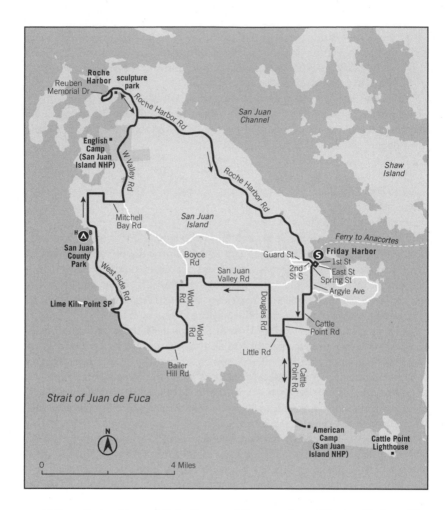

Follow that with a visit to the sparkling marina of Roche Harbor. The tiny town dates from 1886, presided over by the historic Hotel de Haro and a marina full of swanky yachts. Grab a cold drink at the Company Store on the pier in Roche Harbor and head across the parking lot to the two bocce courts for a quick game.

After Roche Harbor, stop and tour the meadows and art of the San Juan Island Sculpture Park before a mellow 7-mile return through farmland to Friday Harbor to finish the tour; then hop a ferry to another island or on to the mainland.

MILEAGE LOG

0.0   Depart ferry dock, turning right onto Front St. S.

0.1	Left onto Spring St.
0.2	Slight left onto Argyle Ave.
1.3	Left onto Cattle Point Rd.
5.8	Right into American Camp, San Juan Island National Historical Park.
6.1	Reverse route to depart park.
6.3	Left onto Cattle Point Rd.
9.0	Left onto Little Rd.
9.5	Right onto Douglas Rd.
11.0	Left onto San Juan Valley Rd.
13.6	Left onto Wold Rd.
15.5	Keep right at Hawthorne Ln. to stay on Wold Rd.
16.1	Right onto Bailer Hill Rd.
17.6	Continue onto West Side Rd.
19.2	At Y, bear left onto Lighthouse Rd. into Lime Kiln Point State Park.
19.2	Reverse route to depart park.
19.3	Left onto West Side Rd.
21.8	Pass San Juan County Park (restrooms, camping).
23.6	Continue on main road as it curves right and becomes Mitchell Bay Rd.
24.9	Left onto W. Valley Rd.
27.8	Left onto Roche Harbor Rd.
29.2	Right to stay on Roche Harbor Rd.
29.4	Right onto driveway to harbor.
29.5	Left past parking on Reuben Memorial Dr. to depart town.
29.7	Left onto Roche Harbor Rd.
30.3	Left to stay on Roche Harbor Rd. Pass sculpture park.
31.7	Bear left at intersection with W. Valley Rd. to stay on Roche Harbor Rd.
39.0	Continue onto Tucker Ave.
39.4	Left onto Guard St.
39.5	Continue onto 2nd St. S.
39.7	Left onto Spring St.
39.8	Right onto 1st St. S.
39.8	Left onto East St.
40.0	Arrive at ferry dock.

Lopez Island

Distance: 35.9 miles
Elevation gain: 1880 feet

Spend a leisurely day cycling the San Juans' rural gem, Lopez Island. There's plenty to see in this figure-eight-with-a-tail route, but you'll find plenty of reasons to stop and linger.

After the initial serious hill climb from the ferry dock, you'll find miles and miles of flat or rolling terrain, with only a couple more areas to challenge your

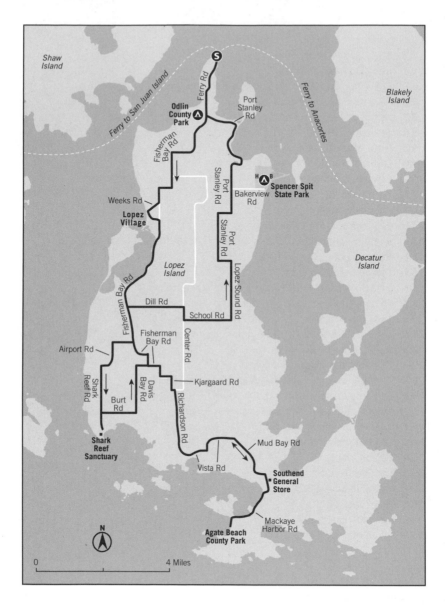

legs. Rural sights are abundant, from farms with unusual cattle breeds to old barns and nature preserves. You'll see island history at Center Church and its old cemetery. Views to the other islands and beyond are incredible. Look west to the Cattle Point Lighthouse on San Juan Island from Shark Reef Sanctuary.

This entirely paved route stays off Center Road, which handles most of the island's scant traffic, so you'll not be bothered much by cars. When you do

see one, the driver will likely give you a friendly wave. The island's residents are artistic and agrarian, and you will find their creations in small shops in town or occasionally at a roadside stand.

It's a great place to plan a picnic, but be aware that there are only two places for provisions: Lopez Village, a couple of miles from the ferry on the island's north end, and Southend General Store, near Mackaye Harbor. Lopez Village has a full-service grocery store, two great bike shops, and good eateries, including an incredible bakery and, of course, a gourmet coffee shop. Be sure to stop at the Lopez Island Vineyards tasting room in the village and try their island-grown siegerrebe or madeline angevine white wines.

Camping is very popular, but the seven hiker-biker sites at Spencer Spit State Park, about 3 miles from the ferry (at Bakerview Road, near the end of the mileage log) give you a greater chance of finding a spot. More camping is at Odlin County Park near the ferry dock or at the private Lopez Farm Cottages and Tent Camping. There also are B and Bs scattered throughout the island.

MILEAGE LOG

0.0 Depart ferry dock, heading straight up Ferry Rd.
1.2 Pass entrance to Odlin County Park (camping) on right.
2.1 Bear right onto Fisherman Bay Rd.
3.8 Right onto Weeks Rd. into Lopez Village.
4.1 Left onto Lopez Rd.
4.5 Right onto Fisherman Bay Rd.
7.3 Right onto Airport Rd.
7.8 Left onto Shark Reef Rd.

Cattle Point Lighthouse on San Juan Island

9.6   Arrive at Shark Reef Sanctuary. Retrace route to depart.

9.8   Right onto Burt Rd.

10.6   Left onto Davis Bay Rd.

11.5   Pass Center Church.

11.8   Right onto Fisherman Bay Rd.

12.1   Right onto Kjargaard Rd.

12.8   Right onto Richardson Rd.

14.2   Slight left onto Vista Rd.

14.8   Left to stay on Vista Rd.

15.5   Right onto Mud Bay Rd.

16.6   Right onto Mackaye Harbor Rd. at Southend General Store.

18.4   Arrive at Agate Beach County Park. Retrace route to return.

20.3   Left onto Mud Bay Rd.

21.4   Left onto Vista Rd.

22.2   Right to stay on Vista Rd.

22.7   Slight right onto Richardson Rd.

24.1   Left onto Kjargaard Rd.

24.9   Left onto Fisherman Bay Rd.

26.5   Right onto Dill Rd.

27.7   Right onto Center Rd.

28.0   Left onto School Rd.

29.0   Left to stay on School Rd.

29.0   Continue onto Lopez Sound Rd.

30.5   Right onto Port Stanley Rd.

32.2   Pass Bakerview Rd. (detour to Spencer Spit State Park; camping).

34.7   Right onto Ferry Rd.

35.9   Arrive at ferry dock.

Anacortes Connector

Distance: 8.2 miles
Elevation gain: 230 feet

To return to the main route traveling southbound on the mainland, take the ferry from Lopez Island to Anacortes, then bike approximately 8 miles and meet the Bay View to Port Townsend segment at its 8.7-mile point. The route through Anacortes skims the watery edge and quiet downtown, then takes a bike trail along its waterfront and a causeway called the Tommy Thompson Trail.

MILEAGE LOG

0.0 Depart ferry dock onto SR 20 spur road.

0.6 Bear left onto SR 20 at Sunset Ave.

2.9 Left onto D Ave.; in ½ block, right onto 11th St.

3.9 Cross Q Ave., then immediate right onto Tommy Thompson Trail.

4.5 Cross 22nd St., then forward to stay on trail.

6.2 Forward as trail crosses causeway over Fidalgo Bay.

7.2 Slight right onto March's Point Rd.

8.2 Meet S. March Point Rd.; continue forward on main route from Bay View to Port Townsend.

PORT TOWNSEND TO BELFAIR

Distance: 72.5 miles
Elevation gain: 3770 feet

If you take the ferry over to Port Townsend and spend the night at the excellent Fort Worden complex, you'll be rested and ready to go for today, which is one of the longest days on the Washington route, with a significant amount of climbing. On this day, you'll also experience one of the manmade wonders of Washington: one of the world's longest floating bridges.

Port Townsend is not a town to leave quickly; in fact, it would be a great place for a rest day. But on this day's 72-mile segment, fuel up at one of the downtown coffee shops and then get an early start with a ride along Port Townsend Bay. The first and last sections of today's route divert slightly from the Adventure Cycling Association map, but they are diversions focused on enjoyable roads, views, and enhanced safety around the region's burgeoning traffic areas.

Exit town on the Olympic Discovery Trail at the shipyard and enjoy an hour of shady, rural scenery before communing with gas-powered vehicles. Also called the Larry Scott Trail, this pathway's first part is an unpaved, hard-packed surface, but it is navigable by most touring tires and only a little sketchy if there have been prolonged rains. If it's very wet, turn right onto Sims Way at 1.8 miles, then right onto Mill Road at 4 miles, then left onto Discovery Road. This keeps you on pavement and cuts 2 miles off the route. But ride the trail if you can; it's a wonderful start to the day.

"That was a glorious trail," says Doug Canfield, a longtime Seattle cycling buddy who joined me on one of my trips down the coast. The uncrowded

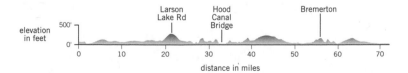

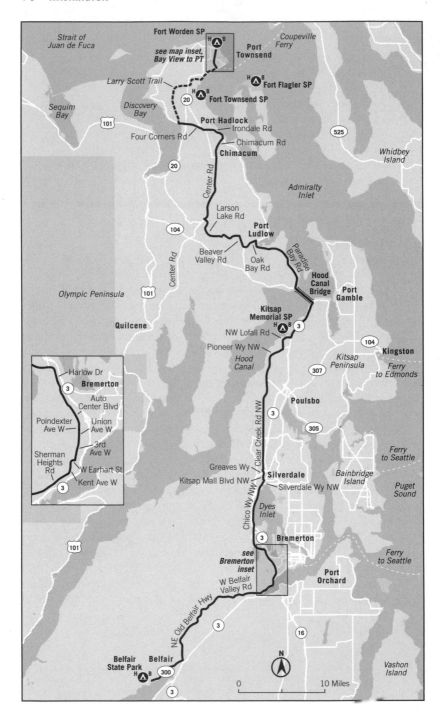

Fort Worden SP

see map inset, Bay View to PT

Port Townsend

Coupeville Ferry

Strait of Juan de Fuca

Larry Scott Trail

Fort Flagler SP

Fort Townsend SP

20

Sequim Bay

Discovery Bay

101

Port Hadlock

Irondale Rd

Four Corners Rd

Chimacum Rd

Chimacum

525

Whidbey Island

Center Rd

20

Admiralty Inlet

Larson Lake Rd

104

Port Ludlow

Beaver Valley Rd

Oak Bay Rd

Paradise Bay Rd

Hood Canal Bridge

Port Gamble

Center Rd

Olympic Peninsula

101

Kitsap Memorial SP

3

NW Lofall Rd

104

Kingston

Quilcene

Pioneer Wy NW

Hood Canal

Kitsap Peninsula

Ferry to Edmonds

307

Poulsbo

305

Ferry to Seattle

Harlow Dr

Bremerton

Auto Center Blvd

3

Poindexter Ave W

Union Ave W

3rd Ave W

Sherman Heights Rd

W Earhart St

Kent Ave W

3

Clear Creek Rd NW

Greaves Wy

Kitsap Mall Blvd NW

Silverdale

Silverdale Wy NW

Bainbridge Island

Puget Sound

Chico Wy NW

Dyes Inlet

3

Bremerton

Ferry to Seattle

see Bremerton inset

W Belfair Valley Rd

Port Orchard

101

NE Old Belfair Hwy

3

16

N

Belfair State Park

Belfair

300

Vashon Island

3

0   10 Miles

The Hood Canal Bridge, the third-longest floating bridge in the world

Larry Scott Trail "was kind of magical and mystical, among the trees and the filtered light," he recalls. Doug, who's a great outdoorsman and also the director of marketing and innovation for Mountaineers Books, thinks it could be the perfect exit from Port Townsend, "which is kind of a magical little town in itself."

The quiet trail is all too short, but follow it up by pedaling through a series of small towns that punctuate the woods and farmland. Ride through Irondale and Port Hadlock's business intersection and on to Chimacum, which is just a wide spot in the road, but a welcome one. A full-service farm stand sits prominently at the intersection with State Route 19, like a one-stop farmers market. Take a break for coffee and baked goods, and check out the farm-fresh produce, locally sourced foods, and a selection of gourmet natural eats.

Valley vistas greet you on low-traffic Center Road, which is flat and sports a nice shoulder, while wooded solitude awaits on Larson Lake Road, which has some hills and no shoulder, but few cars. Drop down to Port Ludlow and check out views of Admiralty Inlet before making a significant climb away from the water as you aim for the main highway and the Hood Canal Bridge.

Here is the aforementioned construction wonder: 1.2 miles of bridge, most of it floating on giant cement pontoons and engineered to rise and drop with the tides. The third-longest floating bridge in the world, it has a 600-foot retractable pontoon drawspan, which allows boat traffic, including US Navy nuclear submarines, to pass in and out of Hood Canal. The bridge sports a wide cycling lane for each direction of traffic, so the only challenge is dodging the fast-moving vehicles to cross SR 104 and get on it.

East of the bridge, you have moved from the Olympic Peninsula to the Kitsap Peninsula, still a ferry ride away from the Seattle metropolitan area. (A side trip to Seattle is encouraged; see the suggested route from Bremerton in City Tour: Seattle in this chapter.) As you turn south, your route roughly follows Hood Canal, but much of it is along wooded highways rather than water-view lanes.

A long stretch of side roads along Pioneer Way and Clear Creek Road keeps you off the main highway, but it is also an area with few services or diversions.

A big climb gets you onto Pioneer, after which you'll spy a few water views through the plentiful trees. Kitsap Memorial State Park, 3 miles past the big bridge, is a good option for a picnic lunch, water, and bathroom break.

From the busy town of Silverdale, skirt the west side of Dyes Inlet as you ride toward Bremerton. Chico Way delivers another big climb, but on a generous shoulder. On the main route, you just skim the edges of Bremerton, but it is worth a visit (and it is the jumping-off point for your city tour of Seattle). This is a US Navy town with a rich military history. On its downtown waterfront, an old Navy destroyer, the USS *Turner Joy*, is permanently berthed and open for tours. A free nautical museum sits next to the Washington State Ferries dock at the terminus of SR 304. The ferry has multiple daily crossings to Seattle; it's a stunning hour-long trip that delivers you to the center of the Emerald City's downtown waterfront.

At Bremerton, the last part of today's route once again diverts from the ACA route, avoiding the packed highway traffic and challenging interchange of SR 304 and SR 3. Instead, find the unsigned turn to Harlow Drive (just past the obvious Seabeck Highway turn at Northlake Way) and climb above the fray. Then you roughly parallel SR 3 until meeting the ACA route again at West Belfair Valley Road. The farm roads into Belfair are quiet, and the town sports a large grocery store at the intersection with SR 300, which allows you to provision for the evening before cycling to Belfair State Park in a scant 3 miles. A restaurant with uneven hours sits right before the park, but an espresso stand is open every morning across from its entrance, and a grocery store is a half mile beyond.

MILEAGE LOG

0.0   Depart Fort Worden, turning right onto W St.

0.1   Left onto Redwood St.

0.5   Continue straight as Redwood becomes Cherry St.

1.0   Cherry curves left and becomes Walker St.

1.3   Right onto Blaine St.

1.5   Left onto Kearney St.

1.8   Cross Sims Wy. (SR 20). Caution: traffic.

1.9   Right onto Washington St.

2.1   Jog right at Benedict St., then left to continue on Washington.

2.5   Left onto Larry Scott Trail at far edge of boatyard parking (restrooms). Caution: trail is unpaved but surface is hard-packed.

4.8   Curve right to go under SR 20, then curve right again to stay on trail (also signed Olympic Discovery Trail).

7.4   Exit trail onto gravel road; in 100 yards, rejoin trail.

8.3   Cross Discovery Rd. and continue on trail.

9.5   Left onto S. Discovery Rd. as Larry Scott Trail ends.

9.8   Continue straight across SR 20 onto Four Corners Rd. Caution: fast traffic.

11.1   Right onto Airport Cutoff Rd. (SR 19).

11.4   Left onto Irondale Rd. Caution: fast traffic as you merge to turn left.

13.5   Continue straight onto Chimacum Rd.

14.9   Continue straight onto Center Rd. at SR 19 crossroads at Chimacum farm stand.

19.8   Left onto Larson Lake Rd.

23.8   Right onto Beaver Valley Rd. (SR 19).

24.8   Left onto Oak Bay Rd. to Port Ludlow.

25.3   Arrive at Port Ludlow.

26.2   Right onto Paradise Bay Rd.

32.2   Left onto SR 104 to cross Hood Canal Bridge. Caution: fast traffic.

34.0   Curve right when exiting bridge, onto SR 3. (Detour left onto SR 104 for alternate route to Seattle via Kingston ferry to Edmonds.)

37.2   Right onto NW Lowfall Rd. (Detour straight on SR 3, then left onto SR 305 through Poulsbo, for alternate route to Seattle via Bainbridge Island ferry.)

38.6   Right onto Pioneer Wy. NW, which becomes Clear Creek Rd. NW.

48.7   Left onto Greaves Wy. when entering Silverdale.

48.9   Curve right onto Kitsap Mall Blvd. NW. Stay straight to take overpass, avoid highway exit lane.

49.7   Right onto Silverdale Wy. NW.

51.2   Left at roundabout onto Chico Wy. NW.

55.1   Chico becomes Kitsap Wy.

55.3   Right onto unsigned Harlow Dr., 1 block after Northlake Wy.

56.7   Right onto Auto Center Blvd.

57.4   Continue straight at W. Werner Rd. as street becomes Union Ave. W.

57.5   Slight left onto Poindexter Ave. W.

57.7   Right onto Union Ave., then immediately left onto 3rd Ave. W.

58.3   Right onto W. Earhart St. In 1 block, left onto Kent Ave. W.

58.6   Right onto Sherman Heights Rd.

59.1   Left to stay on Sherman Heights Rd.

59.6   Continue straight onto W. Belfair Valley Rd. as Sherman Heights ends.

66.0   Continue straight as road becomes NE Old Belfair Hwy.

69.6   Right onto SR 300 W.

72.5   Arrive at Belfair State Park.

CITY TOUR: SEATTLE
Distance: 25.3 miles
Elevation gain: 1380 feet

Now that you're four days into the long coast ride, isn't it about time to take a break? Seattle offers just the place. Although Seattle owns a well-deserved reputation for gray skies and rain, a summer day here makes you realize

Historic Pike Place Market is the most visited Seattle attraction.

why its nickname is the Emerald City. Very little rain falls between July and October, so expect blue skies and a mellow northern sun. Varied shades of green and blue await below those skies: dark evergreen trees line the hills, verdant gardens attract pollinating insects, the teal waters of Elliott Bay keep sailboats and ferries afloat, and sparkling ultramarine reflects the sky on freshwater Lake Washington and its fellows.

In between all this color, of course, are people. Many of them—working, shopping, playing, on the streets and in their cars. A latecomer to mass transit, Seattle has serious traffic problems, and as a booming high-technology metropolis, the city also has a people problem: so many newcomers that housing prices are high and density is a municipal conundrum.

Pedal through it, though, and you will see why so many cyclists call it the best place to live: a mild maritime climate with fresh breezes and low humidity, tolerant locals, and a growing infrastructure of protected trails, street lanes, and other bicycling amenities that get you away from the worst car traffic.

Of note, there are hills. Plenty of them. But with some good leg power, you can experience many of the city's best neighborhoods and attractions. This route is designed for maximum views and minimum hills, although there are two significant climbs.

Coming off the Pacific Coast route, the easiest access to Seattle is via ferry from Bremerton, although the Washington State Ferries system operates many routes from the Kitsap Peninsula to the metro Seattle area. (Alternatives are the Kingston ferry to Edmonds, 12 miles north of Seattle—access Kingston via State Route 104 from the Hood Canal Bridge—and the Bainbridge Island ferry, accessed via SR 3 a few miles south of that bridge, which goes through the town of Poulsbo and connects to SR 305 and a bridge to Bainbridge Island. The Bainbridge ferry delivers you to downtown Seattle's Colman Dock, the same terminus as the Bremerton ferry.)

Choosing Bremerton, you need to deviate only a couple of miles from the Pacific Coast route, and it shortens the long Port Townsend to Belfair segment. And after your Seattle city tour, even a late-day ferry will result in a timely arrival at Belfair State Park to continue the journey (or a bit longer ride to Lake Sylvia State Park outside Montesano on the next segment, Belfair to Elma).

During the one-hour Bremerton–Seattle ferry ride, you can enjoy the marine beauty of Puget Sound as the boat skirts Bainbridge Island, then powers into Elliott Bay around West Seattle's Alki Point. The approach into Seattle, with the delicate Space Needle and towering skyscrapers backed by the purple peaks of the Cascade Range, is not to be missed.

Once in the city, this loop tour begins through Pioneer Square, Seattle's oldest neighborhood. Hotels in this area would be a good choice, as you could drop your panniers and enjoy the city's hills with a lighter load. Ride through two tree-lined squares, then past the restored Union Station train depot and into the International District under the scarlet Chinese gate.

The neighborhood is not called Chinatown here, as it is home to people from so many Pacific Rim nations. A Japanese supermarket, Uwajimaya, sits one block to the right of the route on Sixth Avenue South. Pedal by colorful Hing Hay Park and then head east past shops and cafés to exit the neighborhood. A right turn onto 12th Avenue South takes you over the José Rizal Bridge and to your first trail—and your first view stop. The bridge provides a stunning western vista over Seattle's center city, Elliott Bay, and the mountains of the Olympic Peninsula beyond.

Turn left at the south bridge approach to join the Mountains to Sound Greenway Trail, also called the I-90 Trail. The trail runs next to Interstate 90, the Seattle-to-Boston freeway, and takes cyclists quickly to the suburbs. You're taking it only as far as the city's eastern edge, though.

The trail passes the Northwest African American Museum and two parks named for two famous Seattleites: guitarist Jimi Hendrix and city councilmember Sam Smith. Follow the trail signs through the center of these parks and then into a tunnel. This takes you to a viewpoint overlooking I-90. Here you turn around, but not before your second view stop. Drink in a view of I-90's twin floating bridges (we love our floating bridges!) that connect Seattle to its suburbs across Lake Washington.

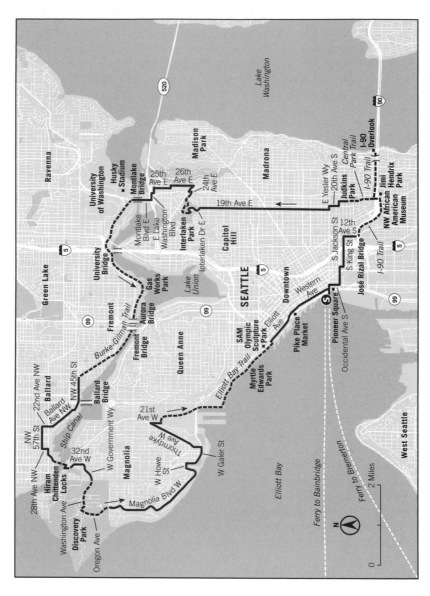

Pedal back through the tunnel, then turn north on trails through a couple of smaller parks and continue on a neighborhood greenway street, 19th Avenue East, through the Central District neighborhood. Small cafés can be found along this section.

At the north end of this street, continue forward onto Interlaken Drive East and enter a wooded ravine that contains the remaining section of

CONNECTIONS: SEA-TAC AIRPORT AND AMTRAK

If you are joining the route in Seattle, or for some reason leaving the route, you'll need travel connections.

Seattle-Tacoma International Airport (Sea-Tac): The easiest way to the airport is taking Link light rail from downtown Seattle, a cheap 45-minute ride. Two bikes can fit on each light rail car (no extra charge), and the light rail drops off and picks up at Sea-Tac's parking structure.

To bike to the airport, it's a 14-mile ride from the Colman Dock ferry terminal on Seattle's downtown waterfront. Ride south along the waterfront to the Elliott Bay Trail, which parallels East Marginal Way South to a turn toward West Seattle. Continue on the trail across Harbor Island and under the West Seattle Bridge. Turn left onto the Duwamish Trail. Follow the Duwamish Trail south along West Marginal Way SW, crossing onto the trail south of SW Idaho Street. Follow the signed trail onto the South Park neighborhood streets, Portland Street to Eighth Avenue South.

Pick up the Duwamish Trail again briefly along State Route 99, then cross over the highway to again pick up Eighth Avenue South. Go south to a left onto South 96th Street, then a right onto Des Moines Memorial Drive South. At a Y at 9.6 miles, bear left onto Military Road South, then in 0.5 mile, bear right onto 24th Avenue South.

At 12 miles, cross under SR 518 and onto Air Cargo Road, which skirts the airport. At 12.7 miles turn left onto South 160th Street, then in one block, turn right onto Host Road. In a half block, bear left onto the paved lane through Bonney-Watson Cemetery. At the cemetery's south end, turn left onto South 170th Street, then right in a half block onto Pacific Highway South (SR 99).

Turn left onto South 176th Street and immediately left to the elevator that takes you up and over Pacific Highway South into the Sea-Tac parking structure. From there, walk your bike past the Link light rail terminal 0.25 mile to Sea-Tac's main terminal.

Amtrak departs Seattle from Union Station, which is on the southern edge of downtown, at Fourth Avenue and Jackson Street. It's a half mile from the Washington State Ferries' Colman Dock and just two blocks from Link light rail, which serves Sea-Tac. The Cascades line runs between Vancouver, BC, and Eugene, Oregon, and cyclists can walk their bikes to the baggage car and load them without having to box them, for a small additional fee.

Seattle's first bicycle trail. The Lake Washington Path was opened in 1897, during a bike-crazy, pre-automobile time when there were 40,000 Seattle residents and 10,000 bicycles. End this all-too-short historic trail by rejoining the city streets and crossing the historic Montlake Bridge to arrive at the University of Washington.

Skirting the edge of U-Dub is the Burke-Gilman Trail, Seattle's oldest current bicycle path, a rail trail dating to 1978. Head west, paralleling the Montlake Cut, which connects Lake Washington with Lake Union and then a ship canal and locks operated by the US Army Corps of Engineers connecting Lake Union to Elliott Bay. Sights along this section include the rusty ruins of Gas Works Park and the funky Fremont and trendy Ballard neighborhoods.

Walk your bike across the Hiram Chittenden Locks, and stop to see if there are any salmon making their way up the 22 concrete channels of the fish ladder. This is how they return to spawn in the Cascade rivers and lakes. You cross into the Magnolia neighborhood and climb (or walk) a steep first block up from the locks to a bike-ped converted railroad trestle across Kiwanis Ravine.

Magnolia, another of Seattle's oldest neighborhoods, offers two highlights for the cycling tourist. The first is Discovery Park, which was the military encampment of Fort Lawton during the city's early days. Climb into the park and bike north to south on the paved, car-free roads. Great views to the west can be seen from this park's bluffs. Continuing south, Magnolia Boulevard West delivers more stunning city views and another angle on the center city and its bay. Drop down to the industrial-feeling Elliott Bay Trail that cuts through rail yards and you will be back on the Seattle waterfront, cycling through a series of narrow parks. The Space Needle is visible a few blocks to the left (accessible with a half-mile detour via the Thomas Street Overpass in Myrtle Edwards Park).

Continue on the waterfront, though, and soon you'll reach the Seattle Art Museum's Olympic Sculpture Park, at the corner of Alaskan Way and Broad Street. Walk your bike through this extensive, free sculpture park and then continue south in the bike lane on busy Elliott Avenue, which takes you to Western Avenue and another urban gem for visitors: Pike Place Market. Lock up your bike and walk through this historic farmers market and local-shopping oasis before continuing south on Western, which returns you to Pioneer Square to end the tour.

MILEAGE LOG

0.0   Depart Colman Dock ferry terminal heading straight onto Yesler Wy.

0.2   Right onto Occidental Ave. S.

0.3   Left onto S. Jackson St.

0.5   Pass Union Station (Amtrak).

0.6   Right onto 5th Ave. S. Pass International District Station (Link light rail). In 1 block, left onto S. King St.

1.1   Right onto 12th Ave. S. Cross over I-90 on José Rizal Bridge.

1.4   Left onto I-90 Trail (Mountains to Sound Greenway).

1.5   Keep right to continue on I-90 Trail.

2.3   Exit trail left onto sidewalk on 23rd Ave. S. In ½ block, right to cross 23rd at stoplight onto I-90 Trail.

2.5   Cross Martin Luther King Jr. Wy. S. at stoplight onto I-90 Trail in Sam Smith Park, continuing forward into tunnel.

3.0   Exit tunnel to viewpoint. Retrace route to return.

3.7   Cross 23rd Ave. S., then right onto sidewalk. In ½ block, left to join Central Park Trail.

3.8   Right to stay on Central Park Trail; in ½ block, cross S. Judkins St. into Judkins Park (restrooms).

4.1   At S. Dearborn St., continue forward on sidewalk next to 20th Pl. S.

4.2   At S. Weller St., continue forward on 20th Pl. S.

4.4   Left onto S. Jackson St.

4.4   Right onto 20th Ave. S.

4.6   Left onto E. Yesler Wy.

4.7   Right onto 19th Ave., which becomes 19th Ave. E. north of E. Denny Wy.

6.8   Continue forward onto Interlaken Dr. E.

7.3   Right onto E. Interlaken Blvd.

7.4   Forward through bollards onto Interlaken Park Trail.

7.8   Forward onto E. Interlaken Blvd. as trail ends.

7.9   Left onto 24th Ave. E.

8.0   Right onto Boyer Ave. E.

8.1   Left onto 26th Ave. E.

8.5   Left onto E. Lynn St.

8.5   Right onto 25th Ave. E.

8.8   Left onto E. University Blvd.

8.9   Right onto 24th Ave. E.

9.0   Left onto E. Lake Washington Blvd.

9.1   Right onto sidewalk at Montlake Blvd. E. Cross Montlake Bridge.

9.4   Left onto bike-ped overpass at Husky Stadium.

9.5   Keep right to continue toward Burke-Gilman Trail.

9.6   Right to cross over NE Pacific Pl.

9.6   Left onto Burke-Gilman Trail.

10.0   Cross 15th Ave. NE and, in 1 block, University Wy. NE at stoplights to continue on trail.

10.1   Cross Brooklyn Ave. NE to continue on trail.

11.3   Pass Gas Works Park (restrooms).

12.0   Pass Fremont business district.

12.2   Continue on trail under Fremont Bridge.

13.3   Slight left then right at NW 43rd St. to continue on trail.

13.6   Continue onto NW 45th St. as trail ends at 11th Ave. NW.

13.9   Left onto Shilshole Ave. NW.

14.0   Right onto 17th Ave. NW.

14.1   Left onto Ballard Ave. NW.

14.5   Slight right onto 22nd Ave. NW. Arrive at Ballard business district.

14.7   Left onto NW 57th St.

15.0   Left onto 28th Ave. NW.

15.2   Right onto NW Market St.

15.3   Slight left to stay on NW Market St.

15.4   Left into parking at Hiram Chittenden Locks (restrooms). Dismount and walk through locks.

15.8   Right onto W. Commodore Wy., and in 100 feet, left on 33rd Ave. W. As street ends, continue onto overpass trail.

16.0   Slight left onto Gilman Ave. W. as trail ends. Continue straight as Gilman becomes 32nd Ave. W.

16.1   Right onto W. Government Wy.

16.5   Continue straight onto Discovery Park Blvd. into park (restrooms). Forward onto the Discovery Park Blvd. trail at parking.

16.8   Continue onto the Washington Ave. trail in park.

16.9   Continue onto the Oregon Ave. trail in park.

17.0   Left to stay on the Oregon Ave. trail in park.

17.5   Forward through bollards to park exit.

17.6   Left onto W. Emerson St.

17.6   Right onto Magnolia Blvd. W.

19.6   Right onto W. Howe St.

19.7   Right onto Magnolia Blvd. W.

20.0   Continue straight onto W. Galer St.

20.1   Left onto Thorndyke Ave. W.

21.1   Right onto 21st Ave. W.

21.2   Left onto Elliott Bay Trail (Terminal 91 Bike Path).

22.0   Keep right to stay on Elliott Bay Trail.

23.8   Left onto Broad St. as trail ends.

23.9   Right onto Elliott Ave. in 1 block. Caution: traffic.

24.4   Bear left onto Western Ave.

24.5   Arrive at Pike Place Market.

25.2   Right onto Yesler Wy.

25.3   Arrive back at Colman Dock.

BELFAIR TO ELMA
Distance: 54.9 miles
Elevation gain: 2090 feet

The quiet environs of Belfair State Park prepare you for today's ride through the surrounding countryside, with only a couple of town visits and one stretch of significantly busy road. Terrain on the 55-mile route is mostly mellow, with only three significant climbs.

The Elma RV Park offers a comfortable lawn (and sometimes even warm cookies) to cyclists.

Retrace your route back to Belfair, where there are grocery stores and coffee shops at the 3-mile mark. Turn onto busy State Route 3 for a short ride through the Belfair business district, then veer right to SR 106, which runs alongside homes next to Hood Canal. Views of the water are significant but end abruptly with a left turn and steep climb onto East Trails Road. This soon flattens to a few rolling hills through "managed forests," which are privately owned by timber companies and can reveal a monoculture of one type of fir tree or ugly clear-cuts. In logging season, you can also experience big-truck traffic.

Skirt the northwest side of Mason Lake, visible through the trees beyond a series of summer homes along a road with a couple of small climbs. Pass Lake Limerick, which sets many an idling mind to rhyming mischief. Here's one to get you started:

There once was a lad from Lake Limerick
Who bicycled madly to catch a flick.
He pedaled it hard,
Lost all his lard,
And then he ate popcorn till he was sick.

No doubt the solitude of the quiet, tree-lined roads of Mason County will spur you to do better.

The logical lunch stop is Shelton, the largest town in this rural county. As you peruse the menus of the half-dozen downtown cafés, take a moment also to review the stunningly preserved locomotive and logging railcars permanently sided on West Railroad Avenue (where else would they be?) between

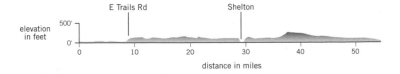

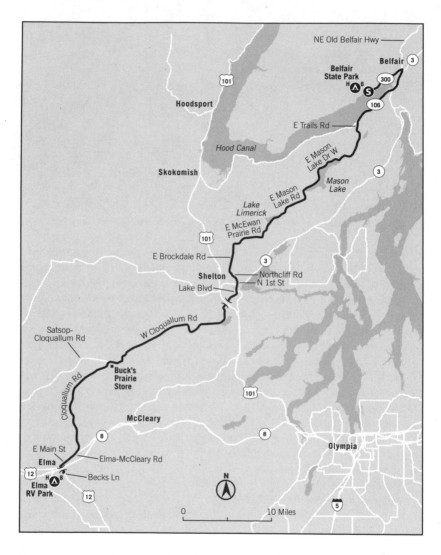

Second and Third streets. Also of note are a number of fading but entertaining murals on downtown buildings that portray a bit of area history.

Don't dine too heavily, because there's a climb right after lunch as you leave Shelton. It takes you to West Cloquallum Road, which aims toward the day's destination: the town of Elma in Grays Harbor County. Enjoy an hour paralleling Cloquallum Creek and traversing a generous river valley, in the midst of which you will find the only services on this section: Buck's Prairie Store.

The clapboard shop is certainly worth a stop for restrooms and refreshments served by the friendly proprietor. She might also serve you up a story about other cyclists, like the Kiwi man who brought his bike all the way from New Zealand and was on a trek to hit all four corners of North America, West Coast to Deep South to East Coast to Cross-Canada. Might make your legs feel a little less stressed.

SIDE TRIP: ELMA TO PORTLAND

Including Portland as a side trip on your coastal adventure requires a significant diversion. Plan on covering 100-plus additional miles and adding one or two nights. One option is to take the Adventure Cycling Association's route from Elma through southwestern Washington, then head south to Portland from the Longview-Kelso area:

Day one: Take the ACA's Washington route from Elma through Centralia to Toledo. Camp at Lewis and Clark State Park outside Toledo. It's a relatively flat 36 miles to Centralia, and another 20 miles to the park outside Toledo, with 1560 feet of elevation gain over the 56 miles. (At Centralia, you could pick up Amtrak's daily service between Seattle and Portland and take the train the rest of the way; reservations are recommended.)

Day two: At Castle Rock, 24 miles south of Toledo, turn south instead of west, and roughly parallel Interstate 5 to the sister towns of Kelso and Longview. There, cross over into Oregon on the big Lewis and Clark Bridge and head south on US Highway 30. The bridge has a wide shoulder, but it's often debris-strewn. The bridge is 1.8 miles long and steep, and the plentiful truck traffic makes it loud. This is a long stretch: the overall distance from Toledo to Portland is 90 miles, so it's unlikely to do it in one day. It also is pretty flat, with 1850 feet of elevation gain into St. Helens. There is scant camping along the route, with the best option being an RV park and campground run by the Port of St. Helens, at about 61 miles from Toledo. St. Helens is also the first town in Oregon to have motels.

Day three: If you stopped in St. Helens, you'll have a quick 29-mile, 880-foot-elevation-gain ride into Portland on US 30. From this direction, a nice approach into the city is via the St. Johns Bridge and along the Willamette River through the University Park neighborhood. After crossing the bridge, ride east along North Willamette Boulevard, past the University of Portland, east on North Ainsworth Street, then south on North Interstate Avenue to cross into central Portland on the Broadway Bridge, next to which is Union Station, home to Amtrak.

End the day in the small town of Elma, where the only camping is found at the welcoming Elma RV Park. Tents are set up on a lush lawn adjacent to the office and well-kept restrooms, for a reasonable rate. You might be given a warm cookie. A 1-mile ride to the center of town leads to a grocery store and a half-dozen dinner choices. Vance Creek Park, 1 mile west of town across SR 12 at Third Street, has a nice swimming beach.

MILEAGE LOG

0.0   Depart Belfair State Park, turning right onto SR 300.

2.9   Right onto NE Old Belfair Hwy.

3.1   Right onto SR 3.

4.6   Right onto SR 106.

8.6   Left onto E. Trails Rd. Caution: steep initial climb.

11.9   Right onto E. Mason Lake Dr. W.

18.5   Right onto unsigned E. Mason Lake Rd.

22.1   Pass Lake Limerick.

23.3   Right onto E. McEwan Prairie Rd.

25.7   Left onto unsigned E. Brockdale Rd.; follow sign for hospital.

26.7   Merge onto trail on right side of road; continue forward.

27.4   Road becomes N. 13th St.

27.9   Bear left onto Northcliff Rd.

28.7   Road becomes N. 1st St.

29.2   Arrive at downtown Shelton.

29.7   As SR 3 curves left, bear right onto Pioneer Wy. Caution: easy to miss.

30.1   Road becomes Lake Blvd.

31.1   Pass under US 101; continue forward as road becomes W. Cloquallum Rd.

40.8   Pass W. Bulb Farm Rd.

42.9   Pass Buck's Prairie Store.

43.6   Bear left at intersection with Satsop-Cloquallum Rd.

53.6   Bear right onto Elma-McCleary Rd., which becomes E. Main St.

54.5   Left onto SR 12, then forward under SR 8. Caution: busy intersection and highway ramps.

54.8   Right onto Becks Ln.

54.9   Arrive at Elma RV Park.

ELMA TO BRUCEPORT
Distance: 47.5 miles
Elevation gain: 1920 feet

Which direction will you go from here? There are a couple of options for the path to the Oregon Coast. You could follow the Adventure Cycling Association route, turning inland from Elma and then making your way to a Columbia River crossing that's 25 miles from the coast. But this book's route departs from the ACA route at Elma, turning west for a visit to Washington's southern coast, a worthy addition to the coast tour.

For this book's route, depart Elma on Main Street, which becomes the Monte Elma Road. This side road parallels busy US Highway 12, which means it really gets only the local traffic, traveling at a slower speed. A good shoulder carries you 10 miles west to the next large town, but first, along the

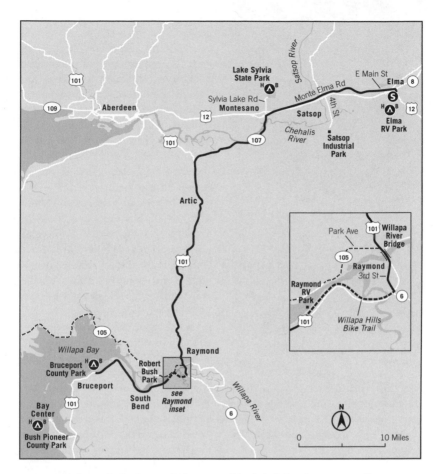

way, pass through the burg of Satsop and look left for the twin cooling towers of an unfinished nuclear power plant.

Abandoned after a financial boondoggle in 1983 when its parent agency was unable to sell the bonds needed to complete it and other planned facilities, the plant sat empty for many years. Eventually it was turned over to a regional development authority, which is transforming it into a business park. The conical concrete towers, open at the top and the base, are weathered shells into which nature is slowly seeding greenery. The site has been

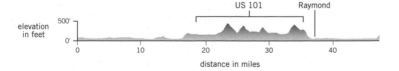

Rusty cutout sculptures are a highlight in Raymond.

a movie set in recent years, as well as a training facility for the military and for emergency tunnel-rescue operations. Its many buildings are offered as manufacturing, warehouse, or business settings. (A self-guided walking tour is possible, although the towers are fenced off. The industrial park sits 4.5 miles off the route, accessed by heading south out of Satsop from Fourth Street.)

After Satsop, you reach Montesano, which has cafés and shops in a compact town center. Two miles north is Lake Sylvia State Park, which has a secluded, wooded campground with hiker-biker sites. It's the choice for cyclists who want to get a little farther than Elma.

At Montesano, die-hard fans of the late rock star Kurt Cobain of Nirvana might want to take a detour and put in extra miles to visit his hometown of Aberdeen, where a park honors his memory with statues. (To take that detour, pedal 12 miles west on busy US 12, cross into Aberdeen's town center over the Chehalis River Bridge, and find the memorial park to the north about a dozen blocks along the Wishkah River. This area's only bike shop is in neighboring Hoquiam, 4 miles west. Rejoin the route by heading south 7 miles on US 101 to the intersection with SR 107.)

The main route turns south from Montesano, crosses the Chehalis River, and continues on SR 107 along the river and a riverine nature preserve to the intersection with US 101 at 19 miles. The section of US 101 from SR 107 to Raymond contains most of the day's climbing, including a long pull out of Artic, whose only businesses are a pub and a small RV park (with one tent site) at 21 miles. Beyond that, no services are available until Raymond at 36 miles, so you might want to pack lunch for a picnic stop en route.

Raymond (where the Olympic Peninsula alternate route joins the main route) and the nearly connected burg of South Bend are enjoyable small towns on the Willapa River. Raymond's business district consists of a couple of attractive cafés and not much else, but it does have two small museums on the river, one on area history, the other displaying historical horse-drawn carriages. A tiny farmers market is in an adjacent building seasonally on Saturdays. The town also has a multitude of delightful rusty steel sculptures depicting the locals, from Native American canoers to loggers at work, from bicyclists and runners at play to elk and eagles in repose. This is Raymond's unique feature, and the town takes advantage of it.

COMPARING THIS SEGMENT TO THE ACA ROUTE

There are advantages and drawbacks for each route for this segment.

This book's route:

- is more rural than the ACA route, with longer sections containing no services.
- takes you to the Long Beach Peninsula, a cluster of small towns on a narrow spit of sand very welcoming to visitors.
- includes Cape Disappointment State Park, the final stopping point for explorers Lewis and Clark on their historic Voyage of Discovery.
- includes an optional extra night at Cape Disappointment, followed by a relatively short ride into Astoria.
- can be done in two days if you skip Cape Disappointment, versus two and a half days for the ACA route.
- takes you into Oregon over the grand, somewhat intimidating, 4-mile-long Astoria–Megler Bridge.

The ACA route:

- includes two larger Washington towns, Centralia and Castle Rock, with services more consistently available.
- allows an easier detour to Portland, turning south at Castle Rock.
- includes a night at a quiet marina campground at tiny Cathlamet, situated on a slough, with plenty of birds and bugs.
- allows you to avoid the big Astoria–Megler Bridge, instead entering Oregon via a quaint, barge-style ferry upriver at Cathlamet.

A bike trail starting at the museums takes you along the river and out to South Bend. Parkland along the Willapa Hills Bike Trail offers benches and more river viewing and access. Plans call for this trail to continue east through the hills and farmland of two counties, connecting the Interstate 5 community of Chehalis with the coast. The Willapa Hills State Trail will run through the Willapa Valley roughly along SR 6. Sections of the rail trail, as yet unpaved, are taking shape.

South Bend has a cheery if modest waterfront centered around Robert Bush Park, which is dedicated to the area's fishing fleet and to military veterans. A well-stocked grocery and a few small cafés cluster here, along with outdoor oyster-grilling and other food available in summer. Provision here for the night, the last service stop before the campground.

Just a few miles beyond South Bend, up one final climb from the river marshland, is Bruceport County Park, a laid-back campground with hiker-biker rates that are higher than the state parks but less than the park's full camping rate. There is no hiker-biker corral; cyclists are given their own sites, some of which overlook Willapa Bay through a light tree cover. The park is open April to December. (Bruceport is also the last night's campground for the Olympic Peninsula alternate route.)

If you desire more miles, alternative campsites exist at Bush Pioneer County Park in the burg of Bay Center or the nearby Bay Center KOA. The park is primitive and remote; the KOA offers typical services and is preferred. (To reach it, continue 6 miles beyond Bruceport on US 101, then turn west on Bay Center Dike Road. The KOA is located on Bay Center Road, which has rolling climbs 3 miles back to US 101. See the map for the Bruceport to Astoria segment at the end of this chapter.)

MILEAGE LOG

0.0 Depart Elma RV Park heading straight on Becks Ln.

0.1 Left onto US 12.

0.3 Forward under SR 8. Caution: off-ramp traffic.

0.5 Left onto E. Main St.

1.2 Pass S. 3rd St. in Elma town center.

2.1 Main becomes Monte Elma Rd.

5.0 Pass Satsop town center at 4th St. (detour south to the Satsop Industrial Park walking tour).

5.7 Cross Satsop River.

6.5 Cross Middle Satsop Rd. at Brady.

9.7 Enter Montesano (detour right on 3rd St. N. to Lake Sylvia State Park; camping).

10.9 Left onto S. Main St., which becomes SR 107.

11.2 Cross under US 12. Caution: off-ramp traffic. (Detour west on US 12 to Aberdeen, home of Kurt Cobain.)

12.2 Cross Chehalis River.

19.1 Left onto US 101 (detour to Aberdeen rejoins main route here).

21.0 Pass Artic.

36.0 Enter Raymond.

36.4 Cross junction with SR 105 (Olympic Peninsula alternate route joins main route here).

36.6 Cross North Fork Willapa River.

36.8 Right onto 3rd St. into downtown Raymond.

37.2 Left onto Alder St., then immediate right onto Willapa Hills Bike Trail in park at Willapa Seaport Museum.

37.3 Bear right at Y, then keep left to continue on trail behind Northwest Carriage Museum. Bike trail curves right and parallels US 101.

37.4 Continue in protected bike lane on bridge over South Fork Willapa River.

37.6 Bear right to stay on trail at end of bridge.

37.7 Bear left onto Ocean Ave. as trail ends.

37.8 Forward on trail on south side of Willapa Pl. Wy. in front of gas station.

37.9 Cross parking area beyond businesses to continue on trail next to US 101.

38.3   Right onto Wilson Ave., then immediate left on Peters St. to continue on trail route.

38.4   Left onto Sherman Ave. as Peters ends, then slight right onto trail as Sherman ends.

39.4   Pass Raymond RV Park.

40.5   Right onto US 101 as trail ends at Monroe St. N.

41.0   Enter South Bend.

42.1   Pass Robert Bush Park on South Bend's waterfront.

47.5   Right into Bruceport County Park.

ALTERNATE ROUTE: OLYMPIC PENINSULA
Distance: 298.9 miles
Elevation gain: 11,100 feet

Let's say you are crazy for rain forests. Who wouldn't be? Looming, brooding trees, with moss draped over every branch like ragged sleeves billowing from outstretched arms. Slate-gray skies to enhance the midday darkness. Glistening raindrops on every surface, feeding glacial-blue rivers and deep, still lakes that turn your toes into a row of ice cubes.

Have I piqued your interest yet in taking the alternate route around Washington's Olympic Peninsula, home to North America's largest temperate rain forest? No? How about I throw in one last perk: Sasquatch is rumored to live there.

The unique joys of the northern Washington coast can be yours if you head west around the Olympic mountains instead of down Hood Canal on the main route's inland path to southwestern Washington's coast. You might even see the sun! You definitely will experience a landscape that Irish cycling tourist Eamonn O'Neill told me was "surprisingly more beautiful than what I expected." Having lived in Washington for more than three decades, I knew about that. However, I am still occasionally surprised by what I encounter on the lush, rainy, forested Olympic Peninsula.

This route can be approached from two directions: turn west from Port Townsend off the main route, or take the alternate route to Vancouver Island and Victoria, then take a ferry across to Port Angeles. Either way, in six days you'll travel 300 miles to Washington's southern coast, on the last day rejoining the main route from Bruceport into Astoria, Oregon. (Note: This alternate route is charted from Port Townsend. If you begin in Port Angeles, the route covers 240 miles in five days; plan for a 35-mile first-day ride from Port Angeles to the Fairholme Campground.)

On the way you'll pitch your tent in a national park, in a national forest, on tribal land, and in state and county parks. While the designated campgrounds are well spaced, other convenient camping choices are few and may be primitive. Some require a detour. Not a lot of them offer hiker-biker sites, so you'll pay a little more. Most of them are reservable and busy, so you might want to plan ahead and make reservations.

But you may be lured deeper into the mountainous terrain, too, enticed to climb a high ridge, wind your way to a hot spring, explore a driftwood-littered beach, or pedal along a river deep into the heart of the rain forest.

You also might be delighted by the warmth and welcome of locals. A pair of British cyclists who rounded the peninsula recently raved about a homespun "cycle camp" between Forks and the US Forest Service's Mora Campground. Beyond the triad of old motorcycles stacked along the highway to announce the site, they found tie-dyed camaraderie, where camping is free-form and a giant communal fireplace makes socializing easy. Farther south, they were awed first by a trio of refrigerators bordering a private garden, offering cold drinks and snacks to cyclists free of charge, with a guest book to record the raves. Called "Bicycle Haven," the oasis operated by a retired church pastor and his wife offered a bit more to these visitors: one had just broken a spoke, and the host drove him 30 miles to the nearest bike shop and back to solve the problem. Talk about hospitality!

The peninsula weather in summer and fall is not as gloomy as I've painted it, but it can be challenging. Temperatures are generally 10 degrees lower than neighboring inland climates. Storms can blow in, turning a pleasant afternoon to a rainy overnight. But they can blow out just as fast—good to remember when you are considering pitching a tent in a downpour. Wait a bit, and it might evolve into a perfect cool evening. And an afternoon exploring a small coastal town may have you reaching for the sunscreen rather than the rain slicker.

Port Townsend to Sequim
Distance: 43.8 miles
Elevation gain: 1690 feet

An 8-mile unpaved trail takes you south from the Victorian-styled small town of Port Townsend, and the south end of the Larry Scott Trail is where this alternate route departs from this book's main route (and the ACA route). Turn southwest on State Route 20 for a careful 6-mile ride along a shoulderless, winding, busy road around Discovery Bay. Head west onto the comfortingly wide shoulder of busy US Highway 101, shortly finding side roads

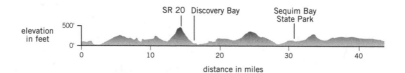

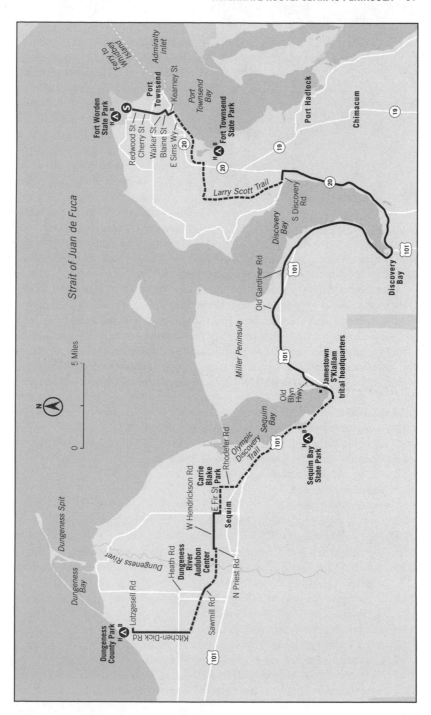

Colorful Native American totem poles mark the headquarters of the Jamestown S'Klallam tribe.

and then the welcome Olympic Discovery Trail to your destination in the hiker-biker camp at Dungeness County Park in Sequim. (It's pronounced *skwim*. You're welcome.)

Sequim is a large town in a rain shadow from the Olympic Mountains, so expect it to be slightly warmer and drier than its surroundings. There are plentiful cafés and shops; area farms focus on organic vegetables and lavender. The park has no nearby services, so before hitting camp, provision at the farm stands or the large Safeway supermarket on North Seventh Street.

Plan to spend time exploring the coast here—it's a gem. The park borders Dungeness Spit, a 5-mile-long sandbar that hooks right to form Dungeness Bay. The entire area encompasses the Dungeness National Wildlife Refuge, so take your birding binoculars on a hike once you've made camp. For dinner, may I suggest splurging on a world-famous-but-locally-caught delicacy from the sea: Dungeness crab. The rich, sweet meat, drenched in melted butter, would go perfectly with campfire-baked potatoes and an Oregon pinot noir.

MILEAGE LOG

0.0 Depart Fort Worden State Park, turning right onto W St.

0.1 Left onto Redwood St.

0.5 Continue straight as Redwood becomes Cherry St.

1.0 Cherry curves left and becomes Walker St.

1.3 Right onto Blaine St.

1.5 Left onto Kearney St.

1.8 Cross E. Sims Wy. (SR 20). Caution: traffic.

1.9 Right onto Washington St.

2.1 Jog right at Benedict St., then left to continue on Washington.

2.5 Left onto Larry Scott Trail at far edge of boatyard parking (restrooms). Caution: unpaved trail, but hard-packed surface.

4.8 Curve right to go under SR 20, then curve right again to stay on trail, also signed as Olympic Discovery Trail.

7.4 Exit trail onto gravel road; in 100 yards, rejoin trail.

8.3 Cross Discovery Rd. and continue on trail.

9.5 Left onto S. Discovery Rd. as Larry Scott Trail ends.

10.1 Right onto SR 20 onto Four Corners Rd.

16.1 Bear right onto US 101 at community of Discovery Bay.

17.8 Right onto Old Gardiner Rd.

19.7 Right onto US 101 as Old Gardiner Rd. ends.

21.2 Right onto next section of Old Gardiner Rd.

25.1 Right onto US 101.

27.5 Right onto Blyn Rd. In 100 yards, curve left to continue on Old Blyn Hwy.

28.8 Left onto Olympic Discovery Trail as Old Blyn Hwy. ends at Jamestown S'Klallam tribal headquarters.

30.4 Forward on trail at Sequim Bay State Park (hiker-biker camping, restrooms).

34.4 Cross Rhodefer Rd. at intersection with E. Washington St. to continue on trail.

34.8 Enter Carrie Blake Park.

35.5 Forward onto E. Fir St. as trail ends at park exit.

36.2 Right onto N. Sequim Ave.

36.5 Left onto W. Hendrickson Rd.

37.2 Cross N. 7th Ave. (Detour left for supermarket in 0.2 mile.)

37.9 Left onto N. Priest Rd.

38.0 Right onto Olympic Discovery Trail.

38.7 Pass Dungeness River Audubon Center (restrooms).

38.8 Cross Dungeness River.

39.3 Forward onto Sawmill Rd. as trail ends.

39.5 Jog right at Heath Rd., then left to return to trail.

41.5 Right onto Kitchen-Dick Rd.

43.6 Curve right onto Lotzgesell Rd.

43.8 Left into Dungeness County Park.

Sequim to Fairholme

Distance: 51.5 miles
Elevation gain: 2930 feet

Highlights of today's ride are the peninsula's biggest town, a trail with a unique bridge that spans a formerly dammed river, and a ride along the edges of a beautiful large lake. Today marks the first time this tour sets wheels inside one of our amazing national parks.

Port Angeles, 17 miles from camp, is reached by a fine stretch of the Olympic Discovery Trail. I can't imagine a nicer way to start the day than this quiet trail that traverses farmland, rivers, and woods, and ends with a scenic shoreline ride.

The trail passes the Black Ball Ferry terminal in downtown Port Angeles. From here, the MV *Coho* powers across the Strait of Juan de Fuca to Victoria,

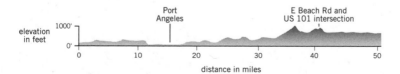

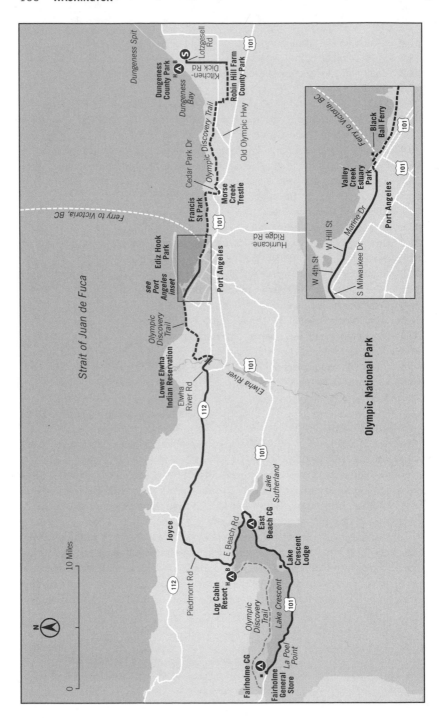

BC, in 90 minutes, two to four times daily, depending on the season. (Fares at the time of publication were $18.50 plus a whopping $6.50 for a bicycle.) If you've taken the Vancouver Island alternate route, you join the Olympic Peninsula alternate route here.

Or, if you'd like to detour to Victoria, here's your launchpad. A day trip is possible, by catching the first ferry over and an evening ferry back, but it might entail lodging in Port Angeles, which is plentiful. Or stay the night in Victoria, sampling the delights of this British-style city, and take the first boat back the next day to continue the peninsula tour.

The Port Angeles area also offers a diversion from—some people would call it an essential addition to—your peninsula route: a detour to Hurricane Ridge. It's breathtaking, in many ways. The first way is by cycling the 17-mile road to its 5242-foot high point. You will gasp as you round turn after turn in an unrelenting climb, especially to the Heart o' the Hills Campground 5 miles up. At least here you could pitch the tent (no hiker-biker sites) and offload some gear for the remaining climb.

From the top, a glistening skyline of sharp, snow-covered peaks stitches the sky to the forested slopes. Or perhaps dense, billowing clouds obscure the view, causing a sharp breath of another type. Don't be too disappointed, because often you can watch those clouds pushed eastward by nearly omnipresent winds, soon revealing but then obscuring the view again.

More breaths could be gulped in such a wind, gusting to more than 50 miles per hour, which granted the area its "hurricane" reputation. Take shelter in the ridgetop visitors center, rack the bike, and enjoy a short walk on its tree-free meadows or even glissade a little on the snow (yes, it often reaches the parking lot until midsummer, and its heavy presence explains the meadows versus the trees). Your last gasp after summiting this incredible area will be on the thrilling downhill, for which excellent brakes are a must.

This detour ride is an encouraging way to kick off the long bike journey, said Tim Joaquim of Northampton, England. "It's such a confidence boost for the trip," he told me. "If you're unsure you can do 50-, 60-mile stretches, if you get up Hurricane Ridge, you can do almost anything."

Don't let it scare you, advises Tim's partner, Chelsea Freeman. "It's definitely more mentally than physically challenging," although she admits that "every time we turned, there was more hill, with nothing to break it up." Still, "it definitely was life changing," she says. "I've never done anything like that."

Flow down that daunting climb like the rivers that stream north off the snow-covered peaks to the Strait of Juan de Fuca on Washington's north coast. Tempted by the relentless water, regional power companies dammed some of the rivers, but recently the value of diminishing power generation has been outweighed by the desire to set the rivers free and return the precious salmon runs to them. That was the story of the Elwha River, and you can witness its reconstitution along the trail west of Port Angeles.

You won't see the two dams that were demolished, but the healthy river that runs under the Elwha River Bridge is evidence. You'll know you've reached this river by its unique trail bridge, which is attached beneath the overhead vehicle bridge. The design, allowing an addition rather than a new bridge at a fraction of the cost, should be studied by other areas needing trail bridges.

Returning to the roads after crossing the Elwha, pedal up to tiny Joyce, which has a grocery and café, on gentle grades. At Joyce you could opt for a longer, more remote ride and a more distant campground (more appropriate if you have started the day in Port Angeles). Continue on winding, quiet State Route 112 for 28 miles, then turn left onto SR 113, following it for 10 miles to an intersection with US Highway 101. That stretch has no services. From here it is 12 miles to Forks on 101 and another 6 miles to Bogachiel State Park, which offers hiker-biker sites. It would result in a 73-mile day from Port Angeles, or a whopping 85-mile day from Dungeness County Park.

If you choose to visit Lake Crescent, turn left after Joyce onto a challenging climb on a mercifully quiet road. The route goes east here, past the cute, welcome respite of Log Cabin Resort (café, small store, even camping with hiker-biker sites available). You continue south, losing a little elevation, to meet US 101 at the east edge of the lake and bike its south shore.

If you're adventurous and light-footed, however, there's an alternative trail around the north side of the lake. Future plans call for this former rail line to be a continuation of the Olympic Discovery Trail, but currently it is basically a hiking trail upon which bikes are allowed. Look for the Spruce Railroad Trail signs. Expect to walk your bike over root heaves and rock-fall, maybe lift it over a downed tree, and pedal up and down a narrow trail that hugs the hillside 10–30 feet above the lakeshore. The agility of a mountain goat would be helpful. Such challenges continue for more than 4 miles, after which you are delivered to a glorious, flat, paved trail for the remaining length of the lake. It meets US 101 just above tonight's destination, Fairholme Campground.

Weigh the challenges of the rail trail against the ride along US 101, because the south shore of Lake Crescent is a narrow, winding road with no shoulder and few pullouts. Signs warn bicyclists of this problem, as the road carries all the area's traffic, including logging trucks and motor homes. Push a button, and a "bicycles on road" sign flashes for an hour, warning motorists that you are traversing the 9 miles of lakeshore to Fairholme. Pull off whenever possible to alleviate traffic pressure. Although challenged by traffic, you will be rewarded by incredible views of this deep, glacially fed lake. It glistens and reflects its deep forest backdrop.

English cyclists Tim and Chelsea didn't feel particularly threatened on their summer 2016 ride. "We didn't have any problem with vehicles," says Chelsea, to which Tim adds: "The danger at Lake Crescent was tearing your

The Olympic Discovery Trail travels along the Strait of Juan de Fuca into Port Angeles.

eyes off of the lake long enough to see what's coming. You just can't believe the color of this lake."

Fairholme Campground, open May through October, does not offer hiker-biker sites and does fill up in summer. The next campground is Klahowya, in Olympic National Forest (also no hiker-biker sites), just off the highway 9 miles farther.

MILEAGE LOG

0.0 Depart Dungeness County Park, turning right onto Lotzgesell Rd.

0.2 Left onto Kitchen-Dick Rd.

2.4 Right onto Olympic Discovery Trail.

9.2 Right onto Pristine Ln., then immediate left to return to trail.

9.8 Right onto N. Bagley Creek Rd., and in ½ block, left to return to trail.

10.9 Forward onto Deer Park Loop.

11.1 Right onto Cedar Park Dr., then immediate left at Y onto Scenic Park Dr. In 1 block, right to return to trail.

11.8 Cross Morse Creek Trestle.

12.6 Trail curves left along Port Angeles waterfront.

15.5 Bear right in Francis St. Park to continue on trail.

16.2 Forward onto E. Railroad Ave.

16.3 Pass Port Angeles Ferry Terminal (detour for Black Ball Ferry Line to Victoria or to join Olympic Peninsula alternate route from Vancouver Island). Bear right to rejoin trail.

16.4 Trail curves left to parallel N. Oak St.

16.5 Trail curves right to parallel W. Front St.
16.6 Continue on trail through Valley Creek Estuary Park.
16.7 Continue in bike lane on Marine Dr.
18.0 Left onto W. Hill St.
18.4 Bear right as W. Hill becomes W. 4th St.
18.9 Right onto S. Milwaukee Dr.
19.3 Forward onto trail as Milwaukee ends.
20.1 Right onto W. 18th St., then immediately left onto Olympic Discovery Trail.
21.1 Cross Lower Elwha Rd.
23.3 Trail curves right onto Elwha River Bridge.
23.4 Bear left after bridge; climb trail to road.
23.5 Left onto Elwha River Rd.
24.3 Right onto Strait of Juan de Fuca Hwy. (SR 112).
32.4 Arrive at Joyce.
33.0 Left onto Piedmont Rd.; follow sign for Lake Crescent and East Beach.
37.2 Pass E. Beach Rd. (detour to Spruce Railroad Trail) on right.
37.3 Pass Lady of the Lake Ln. and Log Cabin Resort on right.
38.8 Pass East Beach Campground.
40.4 Right onto trail at Bearfield Rd.
40.7 Right onto US 101.
41.1 Arrive at Lake Crescent; press button for "bicycles on road" warning.
44.4 Pass Lake Crescent Lodge.
48.6 Pass La Poel Point.
51.5 Right at Fairholme General Store into campground.

Fairholme to Kalaloch

Distance: 64.9 miles
Elevation gain: 2250 feet

Say goodbye to Lake Crescent and take to the highway for this longest day of riding around the peninsula. Today you'll see a lot of forest lining the road and little coastline until it pops into sight a few miles before tonight's camp. Trees are the main diversions on this gently graded route, and the outer peninsula's largest town, Forks, is smack-dab in the middle of the ride, making it a perfect lunch stop.

Building the Olympic Discovery Trail out here will take years, but a partial route using smaller roads has been devised to ease the highway stress in

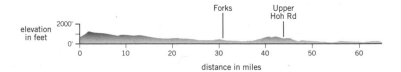

Driftwood on Rialto Beach

the meantime. From the lake, US Highway 101 offers an adequate shoulder, which disappears like a magic trick whenever you cross an old bridge, but those are mercifully few. The route is not particularly hilly either, with only a few modest climbs.

And there are four potential distractions, if you want to add a day either at the beach or deep within the rain forest:

1. At 2 miles into today's ride, turn left onto Sol Duc Hot Springs Road and head for—you guessed it—Sol Duc Hot Springs. The warm pools await 12 miles up a winding road surrounded by forest. You'll climb 1200 feet to get there, but once you do, relax in the mineral pools and swimming pool, have a drink in the lodge, and hike an old-growth trail, perhaps to Sol Duc Falls. There are tent sites (but no hiker-biker, so book in advance) as well as cabin and lodge rooms, and a small store and restaurant are onsite.

2. Head west before reaching Forks to pedal 15 miles out to the coast at La Push, on the Quileute tribal lands. A bike trail gets you off the quiet road for the last mile into the village. Camp on the beach at their oceanfront resort, or book (in advance) a small cabin or motel room. The resort has a well-stocked store and showers.

3. Near La Push is the US Forest Service's Mora Campground, a wooded site a few miles from Rialto Beach that does not offer hiker-biker sites or showers. Rialto, on Olympic National Park's wilderness beach, is worth a visit for the wall of bleached driftwood that stands between you and the beach, inviting you to clamber over it.

4. Or hold off on the beach visit and set your wheels onto winding Upper Hoh Road, which leads east with a couple of good climbs deep into the rain forest. The road ends at 17 miles with a campground and visitors

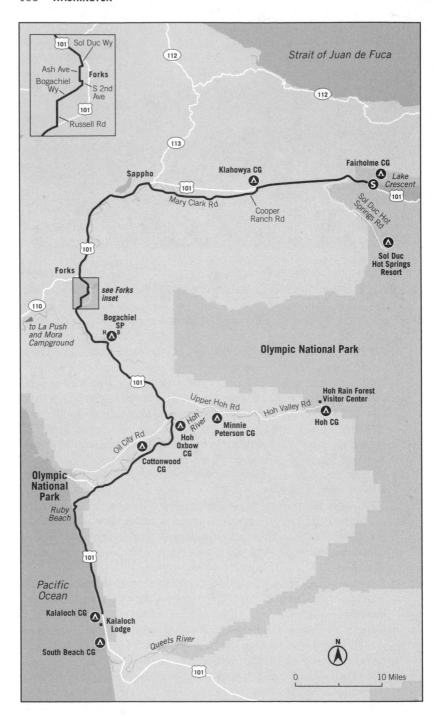

Strait of Juan de Fuca

Sol Duc Wy

Ash Ave
Forks
Bogachiel
Wy
S 2nd
Ave

Russell Rd

Fairholme CG

Klahowya CG

Sappho

Mary Clark Rd

Cooper
Ranch Rd

*Lake
Crescent*

Sol Duc Hot
Springs Rd

Sol Duc
Hot Springs
Resort

Forks

*see Forks
inset*

Bogachiel
SP
H   B

*to La Push
and Mora
Campground*

Olympic National Park

Hoh Rain Forest
Visitor Center

Upper Hoh Rd

Hoh Valley Rd

Hoh
River

Minnie
Peterson CG

Hoh CG

Oil City Rd

Hoh
Oxbow
CG

Cottonwood
CG

**Olympic
National
Park**

*Ruby
Beach*

*Pacific
Ocean*

Kalaloch CG

Kalaloch
Lodge

South Beach CG

Queets River

N

0   10 Miles

center. Here, moss covers everything but the moving water and your tent, unless you leave it long enough. A walk through moss-dripping trees along the Hoh River is enchanting.

Making any of these sites a destination would put the day's mileage from Fairholme in the 40s, followed by another 40-plus-mile ride to Kalaloch the next day. From Hoh Oxbow Campground, where the Hoh River meets US 101 (46 miles from Fairholme), you could launch all the way to Lake Quinault with a 52-mile ride and skip staying at Kalaloch (pronounced *kah-LAY-lock*; you're welcome). Hoh Oxbow, on Washington Department of Natural Resources land, offers primitive services (water but no showers) and some campsites adjacent to the river.

Other campgrounds along today's route include Bogachiel State Park, the only one out here with hiker-biker sites, at 36 miles. Off the route are Cottonwood Campground, a 3.5-mile ride southwest of 101 on Oil City Road and H 4060 (gravel), and Minnie Peterson Campground, a small primitive site 4.5 miles along rolling Upper Hoh Road.

So many choices. Whatever you decide, start by leaving Fairholme via the highway, but shortly depart US 101 at Klahowya Campground onto Cooper Ranch Road and then Mary Clark Road, which parallel the snaky Sol Duc River south of the highway to Sappho. These roads are much quieter and have much less traffic, although this is logging country, so endure the jumbled leftover look of clear-cuts and be aware of logging trucks.

The route through Forks avoids the main road, but this town needs to be visited for the cafés and grocery stores. The town's supermarket is on Forks Avenue (US 101) at Sportsman Club Road, so stay on 101 through town to access the supermarket. You're on the highway for an afternoon ride to Kalaloch, again among the trees. At 58 miles a curve south brings the coast into view at Ruby Beach, a quarter-mile walk from the highway, and the last few miles offer beach views through the forest edge. Ruby is the northernmost of Kalaloch's eight beaches, with beaches 1 through 6 numbered between Ruby and South Beach, which—naturally—is the farthest south. Beach 4, a short hike from the highway, is known for the rich sea life in its tide pools.

The historic, comfortable National Park Service lodge at Kalaloch, 7.5 miles south of Ruby Beach on US 101, offers a restaurant and a well-stocked market. The busy campground is reservable and offers no hiker-biker sites, so you may be shunted down the road another 3 miles to their overflow campground at South Beach, which has toilets but no potable water. Provision at Kalaloch before continuing there. No matter where you stay at Kalaloch, the surf will soothe you to sleep.

MILEAGE LOG

0.0   Depart Fairholme Campground, turning right onto US 101 S.

2.0   Pass Sol Duc Hot Springs Rd. on left (detour to hot springs resort; camping).

9.2	Left onto Cooper Ranch Rd. just prior to Klahowya Campground.
11.4	Right onto Mary Clark Rd.
16.4	Right to stay on Mary Clark Rd.
16.6	Left to stay on Mary Clark Rd.
19.1	Left onto US 101 S.
29.5	Pass SR 110 on right (detour to La Push, Mora, Rialto; camping).
30.3	Cross Calawah River and enter Forks.
30.5	Bear right onto Sol Duc Wy.
30.8	Right onto Klahndike Blvd.; in ½ block, left onto Ash Ave.
31.1	Left onto W. Division St., then immediate right onto S. 2nd Ave.
31.2	Right onto Bogachiel Wy.
32.0	Left onto Russell Rd.
32.6	Right onto US 101 S. (S. Forks Ave.).
36.8	Pass Bogachiel State Park (camping).
44.2	Pass Upper Hoh Rd. on left (detour to rain forest visitors center, camping).
45.3	Pass Oil City Rd. (detour for camping).
45.8	Pass Hoh Oxbow Campground.
57.9	Pass Ruby Beach.
62.1	Pass Kalaloch Beach 4.
64.9	Arrive at Kalaloch Campground.

Kalaloch to Lake Quinault

Distance: 33.7 miles
Elevation gain: 1370 feet

The shortest ride on this Olympic Peninsula alternate route is designed that way for a reason. Today you have a stunning destination to explore and enjoy. You also might get a little beach time before heading off down the road.

And you travel just one road, US Highway 101, which veers inland south of the Queets River Bridge, cutting through the trees across the Quinault Indian Reservation. You'll experience an intermittent road shoulder but it is not a winding, curvy road, nor are there momentous climbs or descents.

What today's ride lacks in drama is made up for at the destination: Lake Quinault. Approach the lake's south shore from the burg of Amanda Park. A narrow, low-speed side road delivers you to Willaby Campground, then to the grand Lake Quinault Lodge, and then to a couple of small groceries, one with a short-order café. Beyond that are Falls Creek Campground and a few privately run inns.

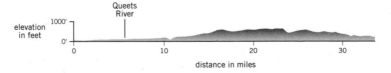

The tide flats at Kalaloch

Willaby and Falls Creek are operated by the National Park Service, head-quartered at the lodge. There are no hiker-biker sites and both campgrounds are small; advance reservations can be made for Willaby, but not for Falls Creek. Showers and access to the lodge's indoor swimming pool and sauna can be purchased for a day-use fee.

Lake Quinault is a pristine, glacier-fed wonder. "The lake is so calm, the scenery is so beautiful," raved Shuhei Akayoshi, a cyclist from Hiroshima, Japan, on tour down the coast in 2016. "It was my favorite place in Washington." Many visitors would concur.

A dense evergreen forest marches down from 3000-foot-high ridges. Elk roam and waterfowl splash about. The icy water provides a refreshing swim on a hot day, and the lake is a constant source of calming reflection. Sunsets can be stunning.

The forest offers further natural sedation. Some of the largest old-growth evergreens are here, including Douglas-fir, western red cedar, western hemlock, and Sitka spruce. The area claims the world's largest spruce tree, a quarter-mile walk from the road. It's 191 feet tall with a circumference of 58 feet, 11 inches.

The understory is replete with plants thriving in the moist rain forest environment. Fifteen miles of hiking trails are accessible from the camp-grounds, and even a short walk into the forest delivers the feeling of its gran-deur. A lakeside hiking trail links Willaby Campground to the lodge, and a quarter-mile trail from Falls Creek Campground leads to scenic waterfalls.

Take a hike. Splash in the water. Take the afternoon off. You've earned it.

MILEAGE LOG

0.0 Depart Kalaloch Campground, turning right onto US 101 S.

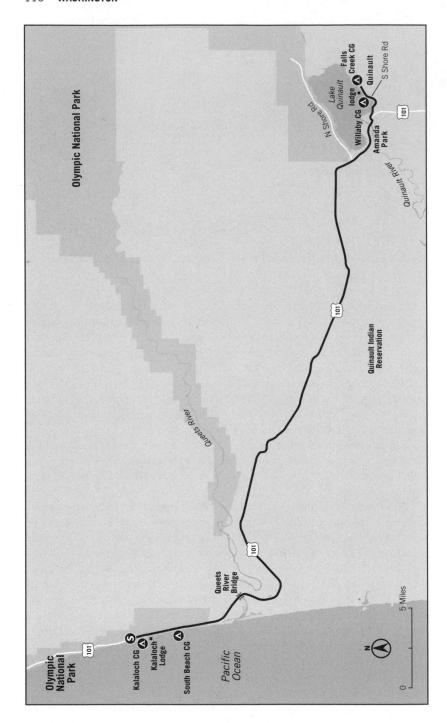

0.5   Pass Kalaloch Lodge.
3.2   Pass South Beach Campground.
5.6   Cross Queets River.
28.9 Pass N. Shore Rd.
30.4 Enter Amanda Park.
30.9 Cross Quinault River.
31.1 Left onto S. Shore Rd.
32.8 Pass Willaby Campground.
33.5 Pass Lake Quinault Lodge.
33.7 Arrive at Falls Creek Campground.

Lake Quinault to Westport
Distance: 63.6 miles
Elevation gain: 1740 feet

Two-thirds of today's ride will feel like yesterday's ride, as the highway continues to wind its way south through the timber companies' managed forests. You might see a wall of trees or maybe an area that's been clear-cut, leaving snags and lumber debris, plus room for opportunistic weeds like spiky pink fireweed to sprout and new trees to eventually be installed. The shoulder is intermittent on all roads in this area.

You could stay on US Highway 101 into the town of Aberdeen, which marks the return to coastal cycling, but I prefer the quieter side roads along the Wishkah River. Turn off after the village of Humptulips, which has the only grocery provisions before Aberdeen at a small store, and head east a bit, then trace the winding Wishkah south. The two routes offer virtually the same distance, and elevation change is minimal. The US 101 route takes you through the town of Hoquiam, which is connected to Aberdeen, so you spend the last 4 miles on town streets rather than rural road. The area's only bike shop is in downtown Hoquiam.

Aberdeen's most famous son was Kurt Cobain, guitarist and vocalist for the '90s grunge-rock band Nirvana. He spent a lot of time by the muddy banks of the Wishkah and is rumored to have been homeless for a time, living under a river bridge. Cyclists on an unlucky streak might be able to relate to lyrics from his song "Something in the Way," where he sings about his tarp springing a leak and his only sustenance being grass and rain. Let's hope it does not come to that on your visit to his hometown.

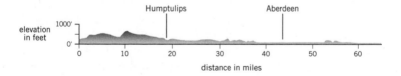

Westport harbor

Fans of the late rock star can visit his memorial park seven blocks off the route; turn left at East Second Street and take it to the river. Sculptures, plaques, song lyrics, and plenty of graffiti memorialize Cobain, whose child-hood home is two blocks away on East First Street and Chicago Avenue. Cafés are found in the neighboring downtown area.

Cross the bridge over the Chehalis River, just beyond where the Wishkah joins it. The bridge is a busy four-laner with an unprotected sidewalk that makes it safer to bike on the car deck. You'll spy a bike trail below on the dike next to the river. Navigate to it and head west out of town, picking up the road to Westport as the trail ends at an athletic complex. A causeway separating Grays Harbor from Beardslee Slough delivers you to the south edge of Westport and Twin Harbors State Park with its large, well-appointed campground. The park does not offer hiker-biker sites, so reserve a spot in advance.

Westport, sitting on Point Chehalis, marks the south edge of the twin bays of Grays Harbor. A lighthouse dating from 1898 sits restored in Westhaven State Park, between Twin Harbors State Park and the village waterfront. Ride north into town on South Forrest Street, then turn west onto West Ocean Avenue to access the lighthouse.

The octagonal lighthouse, at 107 feet, is the tallest such structure in the state of Washington and the third tallest on the West Coast. It has another unique feature: the seashore is no longer at its side. When built, it sat 400 feet from the high-tide line, but today it's 3000 feet from shore, due to accu-mulation of material that extended the land, largely because of huge jetties installed at the somewhat treacherous narrow mouth of the harbor.

Provisions can be found on the turn toward Twin Harbors State Park, and a restaurant sits at the edge of the park at the corner of South Forrest

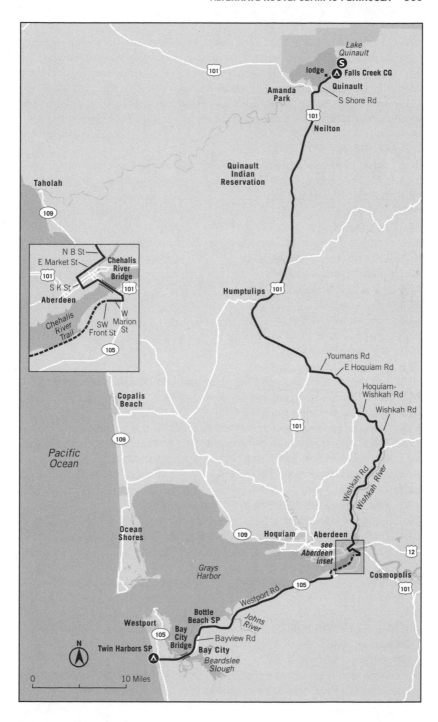

Street, where State Route 105 turns south. More services are found on South Montesano Street in town, with a large grocery at the West Grant Avenue intersection. Cafés and tourist shops line up at the marina at the end of North Forrest Street, which still hosts a small fishing fleet. The Westport Maritime Museum and a unique viewing tower round out a side trip. A bike trail through Westhaven State Park connects the tower with the lighthouse.

MILEAGE LOG

0.0   Depart Falls Creek Campground, turning right onto S. Shore Rd.
1.4   Left at Y to continue on S. Shore Rd.
2.4   Left onto US 101 S.
4.8   Pass Neilton.
18.6 Pass Humptulips.
26.0 Left onto Youmans Rd., which becomes E. Hoquiam Rd.
31.2 Left onto Hoquiam-Wishkah Rd.
32.2 Cross Wishkah River.
32.9 Right onto Wishkah Rd.
41.7 Enter Aberdeen.
42.7 Bear left onto N. B St.
43.5 Cross E. 2nd St.
43.7 Right onto E. Market St.
44.3 Left onto S. K St.
44.5 Left onto W. State St.; in ½ block, bear right onto US 101 bridge on-ramp.
44.8 Cross Chehalis River. Caution: merge with traffic.
45.4 Right onto W. Marion St.
45.6 Forward onto Chehalis River Trail on top of dike as Marion ends.
47.8 Cross Charley Creek, then immediate left at Y to stay on trail.
48.3 Left into Bishop Athletic Complex parking lot as trail ends.
48.5 Right onto Westport Rd. (SR 105).
56.7 Cross Johns River.
59.1 Pass Bottle Beach State Park.
59.8 Right onto Bayview Rd.
61.4 Right onto Westport Rd. (SR 105) into Bay City.
61.5 Cross Beardslee Slough.
63.3 Cross S. Montesano St.
63.6 Left into Twin Harbors State Park.

Westport to Bruceport

Distance: 41.1 miles
Elevation gain: 1180 feet

Yesterday's ride from Aberdeen offered a look at Grays Harbor, a large bay at the mouth of the Chehalis River. But today's outing begins a two-day route

Cycling along the Willapa River

that examines the shoreline of Willapa Bay, a much larger, verdant, and fertile ecosystem.

Ride south through Grayland and North Cove before the road turns east, which marks the entrance to the bay. The Shoalwater Bay Indian Reservation borders the North Cove waters, and a modest casino with a whimsical bear-and-eagle statue beckons at the Tokeland Road intersection.

Here the road turns east, skimming the tidelands with foothills to the north and marshland to the south. Trees interrupt the view to the bay as the road winds along its many undulations; however, there are mile-long stretches of waterfront pedaling. Look for kayakers at the mouth of Smith Creek, where an access road marked "public fishing" gets recreationalists

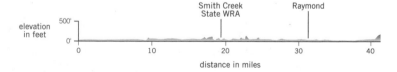

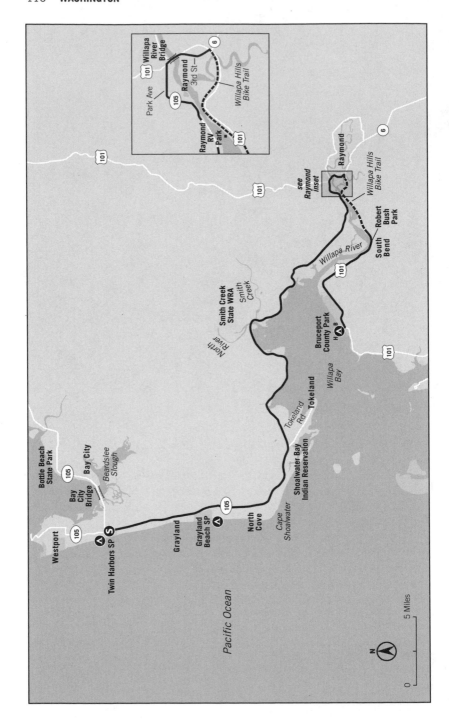

Willapa River Bridge

101

105

Park Ave

Raymond

3rd St

6

Willapa Hills Bike Trail

Raymond RV Park

101

101

101

6

see Raymond inset

Raymond

Willapa Hills Bike Trail

Robert Bush Park

South Bend

101

Willapa River

Smith Creek State WRA

Smith Creek

North River

Bruceport County Park

101

Willapa Bay

Tokeland Rd

Tokeland

Shoalwater Bay Indian Reservation

Cape Shoalwater

North Cove

105

Grayland Beach SP

Grayland

Bottle Beach State Park

Bay City

105

Beardslee Slough

Bay City Bridge

Westport

105

Twin Harbors SP

Pacific Ocean

5 Miles

0

N

to the water's edge. Its driftwood-littered beach provides a relaxing stop. Bird-watching is a sport here, but along with waterfowl you may see elk or deer in the state wildlife preserve adjacent to the creek.

The road continues to hug the water's edge until reaching the mouth of the Willapa River, where it angles inland at the area's airport, adjacent to the town of Raymond. You'll join the main route at US Highway 101 in Raymond (see the main route description from Raymond on a bike trail and US 101 west to Bruceport County Park in the Elma to Bruceport segment).

MILEAGE LOG

0.0   Depart Twin Harbors State Park campground, turning left onto S. Forrest St. (SR 105).

2.8   Enter Grayland.

4.4   Pass Grayland Beach State Park.

8.1   Pass North Cove.

11.2   Pass Shoalwater Bay Indian Reservation.

11.4   Pass Tokeland Rd.

13.8   Cross Cedar River.

19.5   Cross North River.

19.8   Enter Smith Creek State Wildlife Recreation Area.

29.4   SR 105 becomes Park Ave. as it enters Raymond.

30.1   Turn right onto US 101 to join the main route and cross North Fork Willapa River (see map of Raymond area for main route's segment from Elma to Bruceport).

30.4   Right onto 3rd St. into downtown Raymond.

30.7   Left onto Alder St., then immediate right onto Willapa Hills Bike Trail in park at Willapa Seaport Museum.

30.8   Bear right at Y, then keep left to continue on trail behind Northwest Carriage Museum. Bike trail curves right and parallels US 101.

30.9   Continue in protected bike lane on bridge over South Fork Willapa River.

31.1   Bear right to stay on trail at end of bridge.

31.2   Bear left onto Ocean Ave. as trail ends.

31.4   Right onto trail on south side of Willapa Pl. Wy.

31.5   Forward on trail on south side of Willapa Pl. Wy. in front of gas station.

31.6   Cross parking area beyond businesses to continue on trail next to US 101.

32.0   Right onto Wilson Ave., then immediate left on Peters St. to continue on trail.

32.7   Left onto Sherman Ave. as Peters ends, then slight right onto trail as Sherman ends.

32.8   Pass Raymond RV Park.

34.4   Right onto US 101 as trail ends at Monroe St. N.

34.9   Enter South Bend.

36.0   Pass Robert Bush Park on South Bend's waterfront.

41.3   Right into Bruceport County Park.

BRUCEPORT TO ASTORIA
Distance: 66.2 miles
Elevation gain: 1990 feet

Whether you cycled the main route, inland along Hood Canal, or the Olympic Peninsula alternate route, both routes now lead to Astoria and the excellent Oregon Coast. (You can also detour to Portland on this day's ride—see Side Trip: Bruceport to Portland later in this chapter.) But before we wax too poetic about that state, take a day (or maybe two) and sample a bit of Washington's southern coast.

Today's ride begins with a long trek along a beautiful wildlife preserve (with few services), followed by your arrival at the welcoming Long Beach Peninsula. Narrow tourist towns, a wide beach, a beachfront trail, and a historic park are waiting to be explored. Hence the suggestion of an extra day, breaking this 66-mile route into two days of 44 and 26 miles (a bit longer than the one-day route due to the location of the overnight stay).

At Bruceport, we left behind the Willapa River and now are cycling along wide, wild Willapa Bay. A roadside plaque indicates that the bay, at 1040 square miles, is larger than Rhode Island. A series of rolling hills guides you south above the bay, but you drop down to cross some of its rivers; bridging the Bone, the Niawiakum, and the Palix offers glimpses of the complex ecosystems feeding into and off of the bay.

As the hills flatten into river valleys nearing the bay, the sprawling rivers feed lowland forests, grasslands, and freshwater marshes, then tidelands, salt marshes, and beaches. Among all these acres of rain-fed nature live creatures great and small, many of which are visible to the cyclist who is not too focused on the path. Shorebirds and migratory waterfowl are among the most noticeable, but look for elk browsing, an eagle dining on salmon, or a snake crossing the road (or, having tried and lost, one that has become part of the road). As you track one road for three dozen miles with few roadside attractions, you can spend plentiful time on your game of spot-the-wildlife.

Two-thirds of the way along the bay, cross the Naselle River on a wide, modern bridge and then make a stop at the Willapa National Wildlife Refuge visitors center. Established in 1937 by President Franklin D. Roosevelt to protect migrating birds, the refuge has grown to shelter wildlife of all sorts among the many ecosystems that flow from the hills to the Pacific. Interpretive signage, hiking trails, and artistic touches help visitors gain appreciation

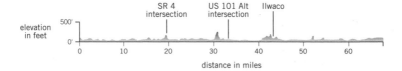

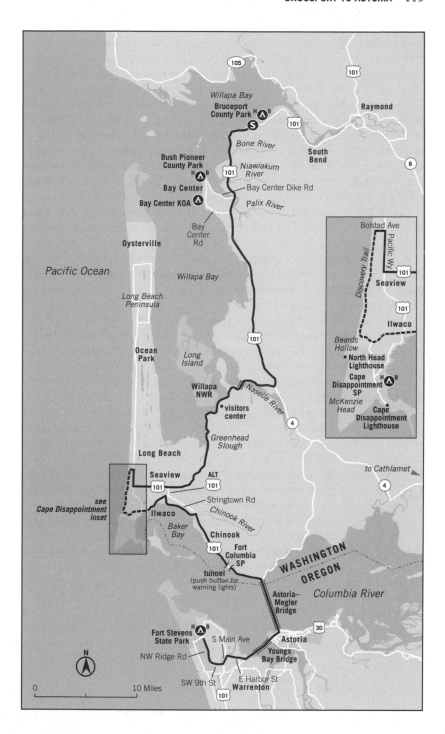

for a vast area that can necessarily be viewed only in microcosm as you travel through it. The visitors center has few open hours, but there are restrooms available at its parking lot.

Head west for the last few miles to reach the Long Beach Peninsula. There are only four traffic lights on the 20-plus miles connecting the handful of peninsula towns, but there can be plenty of slow traffic through the center of the towns on busy summer weekends. US Highway 101 brings you into Seaview, and a right here takes you to Long Beach. These two towns comprise the commercial heart of the area, with plenty of motels if you want a night off from the sleeping bag, as well as cafés, shops, and the ubiquitous saltwater taffy and T-shirts.

Long Beach hosts the north terminus of the Discovery Trail, noted by trailheads emblazoned with "1805." That, of course, is the year of "discovery" by Meriwether Lewis and William Clark. They made it to the south end of this peninsula in the fall of 1805 before overwintering south of the Columbia River at a spot that became Fort Clatsop, now part of Lewis and Clark National Historic Park, which you'll pass (and hopefully visit) on your first Oregon day.

Today's route guides you to the beachfront trail, a ribbon of smooth asphalt snaking between beach grass–covered dunes. The wide, drive-on-it beach is just beyond the dunes. Interpretive signage interrupts the 6-mile ride south, which is mostly free of evidence of human habitation.

Beach grass gives way to scrubby forest, then taller trees as you turn inland to Beards Hollow. You're on the edge of Cape Disappointment, the southernmost point on Washington's coast. Cycle across the road and onto the last section of the Discovery Trail, a steep, winding, 1-mile portion down into Ilwaco. But a diversion here, especially if you want to spend the night, is advised.

Turn right to go south on North Head Road to North Head Lighthouse. Cape Disappointment is the only place on the West Coast to have two lighthouses within 2 miles of each other. North Head Lighthouse, the older of the two by some 40 years, is being restored by the state parks department.

Bike out on the lower trail along the bluff to the lighthouse, and then take the short, steep uphill to Bells Overlook. You'll learn that during World War II this was the Triple Base Watch Station, protecting the mouth of the Columbia. It naturally had three functions: the newly available radar scanned for ships, searchlights would shine blinding lights on the ocean, and crews watched and reported the weather.

Inland from McKenzie Head, on the shark's-tooth point of land that terminates the peninsula, is Cape Disappointment, which houses the state park, camping, Fort Canby, and an extensive Lewis and Clark Interpretive Center.

Continue south after intersecting with State Route 100 to Cape Disappointment State Park, which has a small number of hiker-biker sites.

SIDE TRIP: BRUCEPORT TO PORTLAND

Including Portland as a side trip on your coastal adventure requires a significant diversion. Plan on covering 100-plus additional miles and adding one or two nights. The preferred option (honestly, second to the easy bus option), although long, is to follow this book's main route from Bruceport to the intersection with State Route 4 and take that to Cathlamet, then reverse the Stub Stewart to Astoria segment of the Portland to Astoria alternate route as far as Westport, Oregon, and Cathlamet, Washington, and also follow the Portland to Stub Stewart segment in reverse.

Day one: At 20 miles from Bruceport, turn southeast on SR 4 and cycle another 36 miles to Cathlamet. There's a cute little marina campground in that town. Total elevation for this 56-mile day: 2900 feet.

Day two: Take the tiny ferry across the Columbia River to Westport, Oregon (part of the Adventure Cycling Association route), and then head east on US Highway 30. At Clatskanie, turn south off US 30 and head for Stub Stewart State Park, where you'd camp after a 52-mile ride with 2250 feet elevation gain, including a couple of significant climbs.

Day three: Follow the Portland to Stub Stewart segment in reverse, and you'd arrive in Portland after a 41-mile ride with 2100 feet elevation gain.

It also houses the second lighthouse. The Cape Disappointment light was lit in 1856 after a disastrous year when four ships were ruined in the waters here at the treacherous mouth of the Columbia. The area was fraught with nautical danger. In 1853 a ship that had material to build this lighthouse and three in California crashed on a sand spit and went down in sight of the location where the lighthouse would be built.

On a clear day, look south across the 100-year-old jetty to the big Astoria bridge. You might even get views of the Oregon Coast. Clark finished his reconnaissance of the peninsula and headed south, noting in his journal that his crew left "satisfied with their trip beholding with estonishment the high waves dashing against the rocks & this emence ocean." May this side trip treat you as well.

Rejoin the main route at Ilwaco, a small town with a café and grocery at a turn in US 101. Turn off the big highway onto Stringtown Road to ride along a fine stretch of beachfront homes along Baker Bay. Cross the Chinook River and continue south on US 101 into the town of Chinook, the site of Washington's first salmon hatchery and today home to roadside smoked-salmon sales. Chinook County Park just off the highway on the edge of town has services and picnic tables overlooking the water.

One last stop before Oregon is Fort Columbia State Park, which held one of three gun batteries used by the US Army to protect the mouth of the river (the other two were at Fort Canby and Oregon's Fort Stevens, tonight's destination). However, it dated to 1792, the year Captain Robert Gray dropped

Approaching the 4-mile-long Astoria Bridge into Oregon

anchor here after discovering the Columbia River. It's a heckuva climb to get to the park overlook, where you can see the gun emplacements and restored fort buildings. To safely navigate the short tunnel east of the park on US 101, press the button for flashing "bikes in tunnel" lights.

The Columbia River bar is considered by professional mariners to be the most dangerous bar crossing on the planet, according to a plaque on Astoria's waterfront. But for two-wheeled tourists, it's a simple, if a bit terrifying, 4-mile ride across the Astoria–Megler Bridge.

The big bridge comes into sight soon after the tunnel. For the first few bridge-miles, it's a long, flat ride over the water on a narrow but navigable shoulder. Then you see the half-mile climb, which approaches a 7 percent grade up the green steel–peaked suspension bridge. If you can tear your eyes from the road, there's an amazing view down into Astoria Harbor; more visible are the colorful homes set into the hillside in front of the bridge.

Curve down the narrowing shoulder lane on the bridge off-ramp, navigating to the left lane for downtown Astoria or to the right lane to continue directly on to tonight's camping spot at Fort Stevens State Park. A visit to

Astoria is recommended. Its large downtown offers numerous diversions, including historic buildings, a waterfront bike path, and a grand maritime museum. It also hosts a big bike shop, bookstores, microbreweries (you are in Oregon now, after all), and many shops and cafés.

To reach Fort Stevens, travel south on US 101 over a low bridge and causeway (with a fine shoulder) into Warrenton, then up town streets to the park on the hill overlooking the harbor. For provisions, a small grocery sits on the South Main Avenue turn in Warrenton, and a KOA store sits across from the park campground entrance.

MILEAGE LOG

0.0 Depart Bruceport County Park campground, turning right onto US 101 S.

3.5 Cross Bone River.

4.9 Cross Niawiakum River.

6.0 Cross Palix River.

6.2 Pass Bay Center Dike Rd. (detour right for Bay Center KOA, Bush Pioneer County Park; camping).

7.1 Pass Bay Center Rd. south crossing.

11.2 Pass N. Nemah Rd.

13.0 Pass N. Nemah Rd. south crossing.

19.7 Right at intersection with SR 4 to stay on US 101 to Long Beach.

22.0 Cross Naselle River.

24.5 Pass Willapa National Wildlife Refuge visitors center (restrooms).

28.5 Cross Greenhead Slough.

33.0 Pass US 101 Alt. route (detour for shortcut to Astoria that cuts 11 miles and 300 feet elevation off main route).

35.3 Right onto Pacific Wy. in Seaview.

36.7 Left onto Bolstad Ave. in Long Beach.

37.0 Forward onto Discovery Trail at street end. In ½ block, left onto Discovery Trail.

37.8 Pass 17th St. trailhead.

38.7 Pass 38th St. trailhead.

41.4 Arrive at Beards Hollow trailhead. Forward through parking to road.

41.5 Left onto N. Head Rd. (detour right on N. Head Rd. to Cape Disappointment).

41.9 Right onto Discovery Trail.

42.9 Forward to exit trail onto Main St. in Ilwaco.

43.1 Left onto Williams Ave. SE.

43.2 Right onto Spruce St. E. (US 101 S.).

45.1 Right onto Stringtown Rd.

47.8 Right onto US 101 S. as Stringtown ends.

50.3 Pass Chinook town center.

51.1 Pass Chinook County Park.

52.0 Pass Fort Columbia State Park. Note: Push button for "bikes in tunnel" light.

52.1 Pass through tunnel.

54.5   Right onto Astoria–Megler Bridge.
58.7   Merge to right lane on bridge off-ramp (detour, merging to left lane, for Astoria).
58.8   Right onto W. Marine Dr. (US 101).
59.1   Bear right onto short trail at roundabout leading to bridge.
59.3   Forward onto Youngs Bay Bridge (US 101).
61.5   Right onto E. Harbor St. in Warrenton.
62.9   Left onto S. Main Ave.
63.5   Right onto SW 9th St.
64.4   Right onto unsigned NW Ridge Rd.
66.2   Left into Fort Stevens State Park.

Opposite: *Nicknamed "The People's Coast," the entire Oregon seashore and all its ocean beaches are open to the public by law.*

OREGON

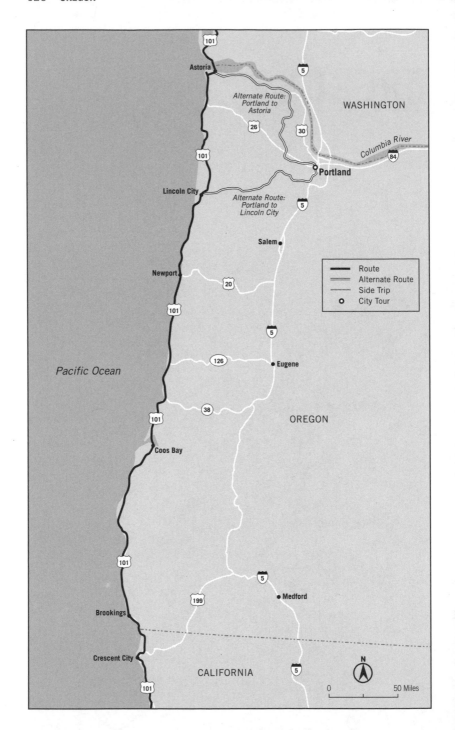

Route
Alternate Route
Side Trip
City Tour

SEA STACKS—CRAGGY ROCKS WITH WAVES crashing against them—dot the scenery of the Oregon Coast. A pale blue mist obscures the horizon line between sea and sky. The twisting road glints silver, rising and falling like your pulse. You are in and out of tourist towns, chewing saltwater taffy and counting seagulls.

Oregon's coast highway provides nearly uninterrupted coastal cycling, while nearby, the entire expanse of beach, all 350-plus miles, is free and open to the public, by legislative decree. As you bike down "the People's Coast," you'll find plentiful campgrounds, historic bridges, and scenic lighthouses.

The road traces hills and bluffs above the shore, leading one cyclist to comment that if you aren't pedaling uphill, you aren't pedaling at all: "flat" can be missing altogether from the long stretches of rolling hills.

Oregon cycling is not just about the seashore. Take an urban break in Portland, considered to be among the best American cities for bicycling. It's a two-day ride between the coast and the city, but transit can make it a few-hour jaunt that is efficient and inexpensive: from Astoria, you can take a bus (operated by Amtrak) to the Portland bus station. Or you can ride into Portland by detouring from the main route at either Elma or Bruceport, Washington (described in the Washington chapter). On the coast close to Portland, vacation towns are plentiful and frequent. Along the southern Oregon Coast, burgs are smaller and tourists are fewer, preparing cyclists for the wilds of Northern California.

CITY TOUR: PORTLAND
Distance: 21.3 miles
Elevation gain: 1280 feet

Portland calls itself "the City that Works," and that's certainly true for cyclists. Transportation planners and activists led this progressive city to becoming the trendsetter in cycling infrastructure and lifestyle. A stop here on your West Coast tour will help you enjoy and conjure the vibe of Pacific-edge cycling culture. Plus, it's a darn fine place to eat, drink, tour, cross bridges, and meet friendly locals.

In this hammer-shaped 20-mile loop tour, you pedal from edgy, glass-and-steel urbanity to front-porch relaxation, Portland style. Toss in a few fine parks, two excellent riverfront trails, and an iconic bridge, and you will

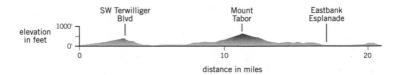

The Tilikum Crossing Bridge

experience much of the city's diversity. Of course, this short route still leaves much of the city to explore.

The tour starts and ends at Union Station, the transportation hub. Not that you'll be using it, unless you decide to take a bus out to Astoria to get back on the coastal route or take a shortcut into the city from Washington State on Amtrak (see the Side Trip: Elma to Portland sidebar in the Washington chapter). No demerits for using either transit option. If it helps you include Portland on the tour, who could criticize?

Head south and west in this counterclockwise route, through the upscale Pearl District. Make note of attractive restaurants, shops, and brewpubs for later. A stop at venerable Powell's Books at Burnside and 10th is just a half mile into the ride, but make the detour. Powell's "City of Books" main store is a collection of linked buildings that houses much of its two million volumes of new and used books for sale. Hitch your ride to a book-inspired bike rack, grab a map of the mazelike store, and navigate to their espresso stand; book shopping always goes better with caffeine in hand.

Next, head south along the city's downtown living room, the Park Blocks, connected greenspace that fronts the art museum, theaters, commerce, and a university. Portland Art Museum is worth a stop too, with its excellent collection of Northwest art and innovative traveling shows. Perhaps plan it for after the ride, or you'll never get anywhere.

Bike through Portland State University, which trains a lot of educators and embodies its mission statement: "Let knowledge serve the city." You'll buzz along a paved path and turn at the PSU Library's distinctive curved-glass wall, providing the south bookend (pun intended) to your trip through central Portland that began at Powell's.

Climb out of downtown along Terwilliger Boulevard, a tree-lined parkway. Look up to Oregon Health and Science University on the right and see the upper terminus of the Portland Aerial Tram, which helps people get up the hill from the South Waterfront neighborhood and delivers a stunning view of the city from its glass-walled cages.

The route drops down to that neighborhood with the use of another cage: an elevator at the end of the Gibbs Street Pedestrian Bridge over Interstate 5.

Punch the Level 1 button to access the bike path across from the tram terminal, and pedal just one block north to cross the Willamette River on the innovative Tilikum Crossing Bridge. The river span opened to much fanfare in 2015 because it was built to serve every transport mode except one: automobiles. You can bike, walk, or take bus or train transit over the "Bridge of the People," the largest car-free bridge in the United States.

On the big river's opposite shore, head north along the Vera Katz Eastbank Esplanade, named for the former mayor who championed neighborhoods and bicycle transportation. Pass the Oregon Museum of Science and Industry, then exit the trail and climb to a street-level bike lane on Hawthorne Boulevard. This takes you into Southeast Portland on the way to a green jewel: Mount Tabor Park. Pedal through quirky Ladd's Addition, whose easily confusing streets are centered in an X around four pocket parks and a rose-filled central roundabout. Well-marked bicycle "greenway" signs offer gentle guidance.

Pedal up the curving parkway roads to Mount Tabor, an ancient volcanic cinder cone. A perfect place for city water reservoirs, it has hosted two. When workers began sculpting it into a park in 1912, they unearthed volcanic cinders, which were then used in the park roads. The naturalistic park was designed by New York's Olmsted firm, and at its peak is a statue of Henry W. Scott, 19th-century editor of the *Oregonian* newspaper. More famed than Scott is the sculptor, Gutzon Borglum, who created the piece in the early 1930s while he was also at work carving four giant presidential heads into Mount Rushmore in South Dakota.

Return to the central city through the Laurelhurst and Buckman neighborhoods, where Portland's laid-back lifestyle is on full view. Skirt Laurelhurst Park, or wind through on its verdant pathways, then do the same at the Lone Fir Pioneer Cemetery, on the National Register of Historic Places. Where once a lone fir shaded the remains of city residents, now a verdant arboretum canopies the dead.

Return to the Eastbank Esplanade and travel north under another of Portland's many bridges, Burnside, to the Steel Bridge, where a cleverly attached lower level provides a comfortable bike ride next to rail lines across the bridge. This unusual arrangement is made more unusual by this being a "double lift" bridge, where the entire center section between two vertical trusses is lifted to allow boat passage beneath. It's one of few such bridges in the United States; another, Hawthorne Bridge, is visible just downriver.

Enter the city's Old Town neighborhood, but depart south along the Waterfront Park Trail. If you're making this trek on a weekend, expect to walk your bike through the Portland Saturday Market, where local arts and crafts are the stars. Cross under the Morrison and Hawthorne bridges (so many!), and head west once again into the heart of the city's downtown. Return to the other side of the Park Blocks and then pass Pioneer Courthouse Square, a central gathering place for downtown workers that's one block off the route

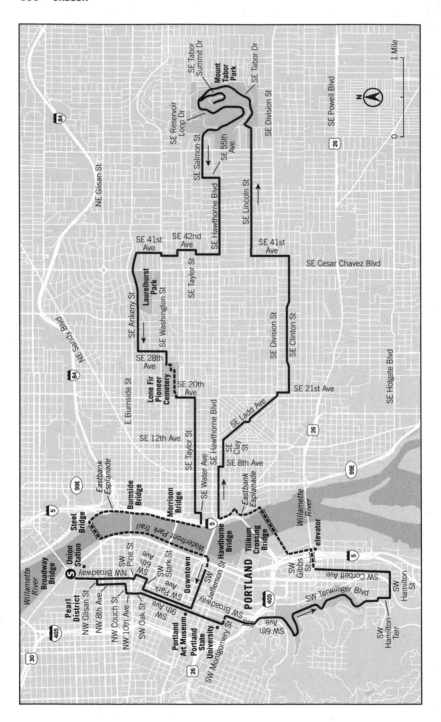

at Yamhill Street. Rows of the city's famous food trucks, also early pioneers of that gastronomical craze, beckon from a nearby side street.

End the tour by crossing Burnside again and pedaling up Broadway to Union Station. If you miss the station or desire a little longer ride, dead ahead sits yet another bikeable bridge. You can continue your own exploration by crossing the Broadway Bridge into the northeast neighborhoods.

CONNECTIONS: PDX AND AMTRAK

Want to begin or end your trip in Portland? **Portland International Airport (PDX)** is an easy 45-minute ride from downtown Portland on the MAX light rail ($2.50 at time of publication).

To bicycle to the airport from downtown, ride 10 miles northeast through the city. From Union Station (see below), go north on Broadway over the Broadway Bridge. Turn left onto North Williams Avenue, cross over Interstate 5, and continue north. At 2.2 miles, turn right on NE Going Street, jog left a bit to stay on Going on NE 33rd Avenue, then turn left onto NE 37th Avenue. Turn right onto NE Holman Street, then left onto NE 42nd Avenue and cross over US Highway 30. Turn right on NE Cornfoot Road, then left on NE Alderwood Road and left again at NE 82nd Way. Finally, turn left at NE Airport Way Frontage Road and proceed to the main terminal.

Amtrak stops at Portland's transportation hub, Union Station, at NW Broadway and NW Hoyt Street. The Cascades line runs daily between Seattle and Portland. Bicycles can be simply loaded into the baggage car, not boxed, for a small fee.

The **Portland Transportation Center,** from which buses arrive and depart, is adjacent to Union Station. It's also inexpensive to take your bike on the bus to Astoria; you load your bike into the large luggage compartment under the bus for a small additional fee. Advanced reservations are recommended for either bus or train, as their bike-storage capacity is limited.

MILEAGE LOG

0.0   Depart Union Station, turning left onto NW Broadway.

0.1   Right onto NW Glisan St., then in 1 block left onto NW 8th Ave.

0.3   Right onto NW Couch St.

0.5   Left onto NW 10th Ave. In 1 block, cross W. Burnside St., then angle left onto SW Oak St.

0.6   Right onto SW 9th Ave.; in 1 block, slight right at SW Stark St. to stay on 9th, which becomes SW Park Ave.

1.3   Forward at SW Montgomery St. onto pedestrian trail, then left in 1 block at Portland State University Library to stay on trail.

1.5   Right onto SW Broadway as trail ends at SW Harrison St.

1.6   Bear left to stay on SW Broadway over I-405.

1.8   Slight right onto SW 6th Ave., which becomes SW Terwilliger Blvd.

2.2   Left to stay on SW Terwilliger Blvd. at SW Sam Jackson Park Rd.

3.2   Left onto SW Hamilton Terr.

3.4   Left onto SW Hamilton St.

3.5   Cross SW Barbur Blvd. (Pacific Hwy. W.).

3.5   Right onto SW Hamilton St.

3.6   Left onto SW Corbett Ave.

4.2   Right onto SW Gibbs St., then in 1 block slight left onto Gibbs St. Pedestrian Bridge.

4.3   After crossing bridge, take elevator down to street.

4.4   Left onto trail at SW Moody Ave.

4.7   Right onto Tilikum Crossing Bridge.

5.2   Left onto SE 2nd Pl., then immediate left toward Vera Katz Eastbank Esplanade.

5.3   Right onto Eastbank Esplanade.

5.7   Right toward SE Hawthorne Blvd. At top of ramp, right onto SE Hawthorne Blvd.

6.2   Right onto SE 8th Ave.

6.3   Left onto SE Clay St.

6.5   Slight right onto SE Ladd Ave.

6.7   At traffic circle, continue straight to stay on Ladd.

7.1   Left onto SE Division St. In ½ block, right onto SE 21st Ave.

7.2   Left onto SE Clinton St.

7.5   Jog left at SE 26th Ave. to stay on Clinton.

7.8   At traffic circle, continue straight to stay on Clinton.

8.4   Left onto SE 41st Ave.

8.5   Jog right at SE Division St., then immediate left to stay on 41st.

8.8   Right onto SE Lincoln St. In 1 block, jog right at 42nd to stay on Lincoln.

9.9   Left to stay on SE Lincoln St. at entrance to Mount Tabor Park.

10.2   Bear left onto SE East Tabor Dr.

10.6   Slight left onto SE North Tabor Dr.

10.8   Sharp left onto SE Tabor Summit Dr.

11.1   Continue onto SE Harvey Scott Cir.

11.3   Arrive at park summit. Retrace route to depart.

11.7   Slight left onto SE Reservoir Loop Dr.

12.6   Continue onto SE Salmon St. at park exit.

13.0   Left onto SE 55th Ave.

13.1   Right onto SE Hawthorne Blvd.

13.4   Right to stay on SE Hawthorne Blvd. at SE 50th Ave.

13.8   Right onto SE 41st Ave.

14.0   Right onto SE Taylor St. In 1 block, left onto SE 42nd Ave.

14.1   Right onto SE 42nd Ave.

14.2   Left onto SE Morrison St. In 1 block, slight right onto SE 41st Ave.

14.4   Right onto SE Stark St. In ½ block, left to continue on 41st.

14.6   Left onto SE Ankeny St.

15.5   Left onto SE 28th Ave.

15.7   Left onto SE Stark St., then immediate right to stay on 28th. In 1 block, right onto SE Washington St.

15.8   Left onto SE 26th Ave. In ½ block, right onto Lone Fir Pioneer Cemetery Trail.

16.2   Right onto SE Morrison St. to exit cemetery.

16.3   Left onto SE 20th Ave.

16.4   Right onto SE Taylor St.

16.7   At traffic circle, continue straight to stay on Taylor.

17.4   Left onto SE Water Ave. In 1 block, right onto SE Salmon St.

17.5   Right onto Eastbank Esplanade.

18.1   Left to stay on Eastbank Esplanade.

18.6   Continue onto Steel Bridge Lower Deck.

18.7   Steel Bridge Lower Deck turns left and becomes Waterfront Park Trail.

19.7   Right toward SW Naito Pkwy. after passing under Hawthorne Bridge.

19.9   Cross Naito Pkwy. onto SW Jefferson St.

20.3   Right onto SW Park Ave.

20.7   Right onto SW Stark St.

20.8   Left onto SW 6th Ave.

20.9   Left onto SW Pine St. In 1 block, right onto SW Broadway, which becomes NW Broadway.

21.3   Right onto NW Hoyt St. to return to Union Station.

ALTERNATE ROUTE: PORTLAND TO ASTORIA

Fortunately, there are interesting options for leaving Portland. If you don't want to skip any of the Oregon Coast tour, from Portland head northwest to Astoria with one or two overnights on a 124-mile route that includes a wonderful wooded rail trail followed by some challenging hill-country roads. (You can also take Portland's light rail partway on that route. Or, of course, you could just take the bus all the way from Portland back to Astoria and resume your trip.)

If you ride to Astoria, you'll travel northwest via the Banks-Vernonia State Trail to L. L. "Stub" Stewart Memorial State Park on a fairly mellow 40-mile ride the first day. The second day (which can be split with camping at the Cathlamet marina campground) is 82 miles with significant climbing on a rural road.

Portland to Stub Stewart

Distance: 40.8 miles
Elevation gain: 2110 feet

From Union Station in downtown Portland, climb out of the city via hilly Washington Park and combined city streets and trails that roughly parallel US Highway 26 to the small town of Banks. (Or take Portland's light-rail service to the western suburb of Hillsboro and bike north to Banks from there.)

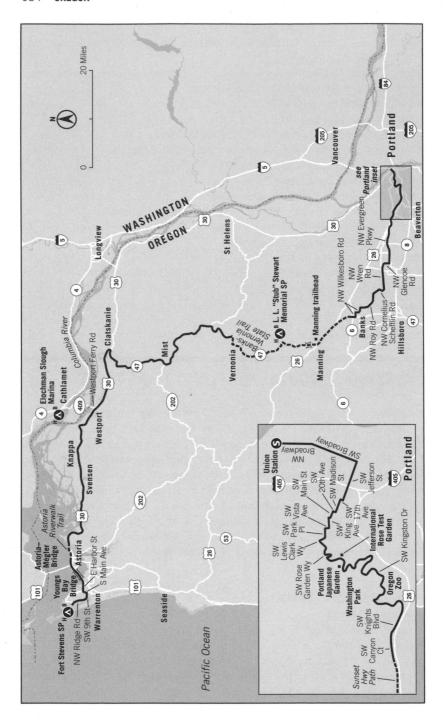

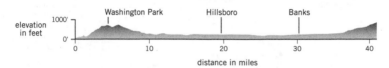

Banks, at 30 miles, is a good place to provision for the night. At Banks, pick up the Banks-Vernonia State Trail, a scenic rail-trail bikeway. The wooded trail is flat and secluded, making a moderate climb at about 40 miles into L. L. "Stub" Stewart Memorial State Park, which has inexpensive walk-in-style hiker-biker camping.

MILEAGE LOG

0.0 Depart Union Station, turning left onto NW Broadway, which becomes SW Broadway.

1.0 Right onto SW Jefferson St.

1.5 Right onto SW 17th Ave. In 1 block, left onto SW Madison St.

1.7 Right onto SW 20th Ave. In 1 block, left onto SW Main St.

1.9 Right onto SW King Ave., then immediate left back onto SW Main St.

2.0 Right onto SW Vista Ave. In 1 block, left onto SW Park Pl.

2.2 Right onto SW Lewis Clark Wy. to climb through Washington Park.

2.4 Right onto SW Sacajawea Blvd. (unsigned; follow Rose Garden sign).

2.5 Left onto SW Rose Garden Wy (unsigned; follow Rose Garden sign).

2.9 Forward at stop sign onto SW Kingston Dr.

4.4 Left onto SW Knights Blvd.

4.9 Right when exiting park onto SW Canyon Ct. at on-ramps to Sunset Hwy. (US 26).

5.6 Forward onto Sunset Hwy. Path as road curves right; continue to parallel US 26.

5.8 Path crosses under SW Skyline Blvd.

6.5 Left to cross over Sunset Hwy. on SW Camelot Ct., then right onto SW Pointer Rd., which merges into Sunset Hwy. Path.

7.8 Left onto SW Knollcrest Dr. as path ends.

7.9 Right onto SW Wilshire St.

8.4 Right onto SW Marlowe Ave., which becomes SW Butner Rd.

8.5 Right onto path to bridge over Sunset Hwy., then left onto Sunset Transit Center Rd.

8.9 Left onto SW Barnes Rd., which becomes NW Barnes Rd.

10.4 Left onto NW Cornell Rd.

13.4 Right onto NW Evergreen Pkwy., which becomes NW Evergreen Rd.

20.6 Right onto NW Glencoe Rd. as Evergreen ends. (Hillsboro MAX light rail station to left on NW Glencoe Rd.)

21.6 Left onto NW Wren Rd. as Glencoe curves right.

24.2 Right onto NW Cornelius Schefflin Rd.

24.6 Left onto NW Roy Rd.

27.5 Left onto NW Wilkesboro Rd. at NW Harrington Rd.

29.7 Right onto Nehelem Hwy. (SR 47). Enter Banks.

The Banks-Vernonia State Trail

30.7 Left onto Banks-Vernonia State Trail.

32.6 Trail crosses under US 26.

34.7 Pass Manning trailhead.

35.9 Cross NW Pongratz Rd. and continue on trail.

37.4 Cross Buxton Trestle.

40.8 Right into L. L. "Stub" Stewart Memorial State Park.

Stub Stewart to Astoria

Distance: 82.4 miles
Elevation gain: 3600 feet

The next leg continues on the Banks-Vernonia State Trail to Vernonia in 11 miles, a great place for breakfast or coffee, and then switches to hilly, winding State Route 47 to Clatskanie, Oregon, at 39 miles, where you join the ACA route on US Highway 30. It's another 43 miles to the campground at Warrenton, just beyond Astoria, or you can stop at Westport and take the small ferry across the Columbia into Washington and camp at the quaint marina at Cathlamet for the night, the last Washington stop on the ACA map route.

MILEAGE LOG

0.0 Depart L. L. "Stub" Stewart Memorial State Park, turning right onto Banks-Vernonia State Trail.

10.7 Left onto Jefferson Ave.; enter Vernonia.

10.8 Right onto Bridge St., which becomes Nehelem Hwy. N. (SR 47).

27.3 Pass Mist and junction with SR 202.

38.7 Enter Clatskanie.

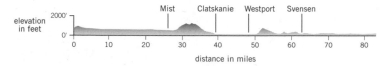

39.1 Left onto US 30.

47.8 Enter Westport.

48.1 Pass Westport Ferry Rd. (detour on short ferry and 3-mile ride on SR 409 to Cathlamet, optional camping).

58.7 Enter Knappa.

63.2 Pass Svensen.

68.1 Cross John Day River.

71.6 Right on 45th St. in Astoria, then left on Astoria Riverwalk Trail at street end.

74.3 Left onto 3rd St. in downtown Astoria. In 1 block, right onto Marine Dr.

74.8 Cross under Astoria–Megler Bridge.

75.0 Pass bridge off-ramp.

75.3 Bear right onto short trail at roundabout leading to bridge.

75.5 Forward onto Youngs Bay Bridge (US 101).

77.8 Right onto E. Harbor St. in Warrenton.

79.1 Left onto S. Main Ave. Last provision shopping before campground.

79.7 Right onto SW 9th St.

80.7 Right onto unsigned NW Ridge Rd.

82.4 Left into Fort Stevens State Park.

ALTERNATE ROUTE: PORTLAND TO LINCOLN CITY

When leaving Portland, you must decide whether you can skip part of the Oregon Coast. If you are OK with omitting about one-third of it (115 miles and two nights), you can head south toward a historic park outside of Portland, then bike through the Willamette wine country and out west along a big, flat road to the coast at Lincoln City. This is a two- to three-day excursion with good campground options, via Champoeg State Heritage Area on a 105-mile route.

Portland to Champoeg
Distance: 34.6 miles
Elevation gain: 1250 feet

If you start this mellow route out of Portland early, you'll have the afternoon to explore the Willamette Valley wine country surrounding the historic park that is your night's destination. Depart from Portland's Union Station on the Vera Katz Eastbank Esplanade, which traces the river south. This merges into the Springwater Corridor Trail, which then joins the Trolley Trail. By the time

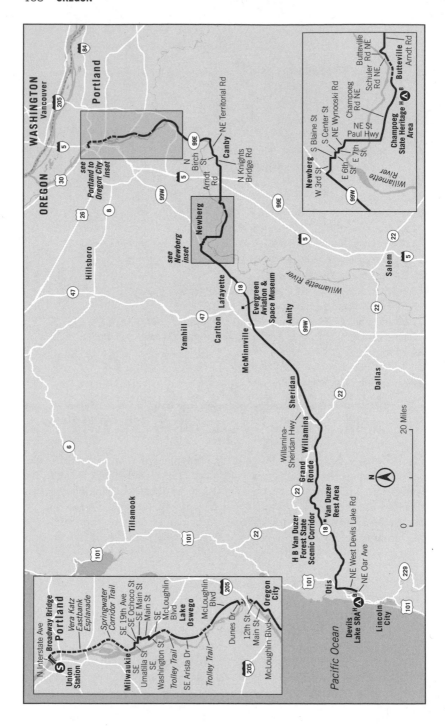

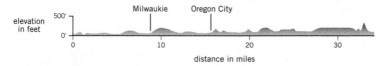

you exit the trails, you're in Oregon City, on the edge of the south suburbs. Well done, Portland planners! Continue along the river until it turns west, then trace a path across farm roads to rejoin the river, where you reach a lovely park.

Champoeg State Heritage Area holds much significance for Oregon. It was the site where the state's first provisional government was formed, in 1843. Pioneer cabins and reconstructions showcase life of those days. Today, Champoeg (pronounce it like a local: *sham-POO-ee*; you're welcome) is the northern terminus of the Willamette Valley Scenic Bikeway, which roughly tracks the river south to Springfield, some 130 miles away. You can enjoy the verdant farming area, replete with wineries, on the roads south toward Salem, or head west into Newberg for plentiful shops, cafés, and, yes, wineries.

MILEAGE LOG

0.0   Depart Union Station, turning right onto NW Broadway.

0.2   Merge onto Broadway Bridge in bike lane.

0.5   Right onto N. Interstate Ave.

1.0   Right onto Vera Katz Eastbank Esplanade.

2.7   Left onto SE Caruthers St. at Tilikum Crossing Bridge.

2.8   Right onto SE 4th Ave.

2.9   Continue on Springwater Corridor Trail.

6.1   Left onto SE Umatilla St.

6.8   Right onto SE 19th Ave.

7.1   Left onto SE Ochoco St.

7.4   Cross SE McLoughlin Blvd. (SR 99E), then immediate right onto Main St., which becomes SE Main St.

8.1   Cross under SR 224.

8.6   Right onto SE Washington St.

8.7   Left onto SE McLoughlin Blvd.

9.1   Bear right onto Trolley Trail under bridge after SE River Rd. intersection.

10.2   Forward onto SE Arista Dr. at SE Courtney Rd. as trail ends.

10.9   Bear left onto Trolley Trail.

12.9   Left onto SE Jennings Ave., then immediate right onto McLoughlin Blvd.

14.7   Right onto Dunes Dr. In 1 block, left onto Clackamette Dr.

14.9   Continue on trail under I-205.

15.3   Left onto 12th St. In ½ block, right onto Main St.

15.8   Left onto McLoughlin Blvd., which becomes SR 99E.

22.6   Right onto NE Territorial Rd. at Fish Eddy Landing.

The world's largest airplane, the "Spruce Goose," sits roadside in the Evergreen Aviation & Space Museum at McMinnville.

24.6	Left onto N. Birch St.
25.0	Right onto N. Knights Bridge Rd.
25.3	Cross Molalla River.
26.4	Road curves right and becomes S. Arndt Rd.
27.1	Cross Pudding River.
29.5	Cross under I-5; road becomes Arndt Rd. NE.
32.2	Left onto Butteville Rd. NE.
32.4	Right onto Schuler Rd. NE.
32.9	Bear left uphill onto Champoeg Bike Path as Schuler ends.
34.6	Arrive at Champoeg State Heritage Area campground.

Champoeg to Lincoln City
Distance: 70.2 miles
Elevation gain: 2240 feet

The second day of this route is quite a bit longer, but its main difficulty lies in noisy highway riding. Cycle 6 miles into Newberg on side roads, and then hop on bigger roads (state routes 99W and 18) to McMinnville, the area's largest town. Explore the town or take the faster southeast bypass route, and then continue west on SR 18, which takes you to the coast on the generous shoulder lane of this big, busy road.

One significant climb comes shortly after passing through Grand Ronde at about 48 miles. After the climb, enjoy 5 miles of H. B. Van Duzer Forest State Scenic Corridor, a heavily wooded corridor along the Salmon River with

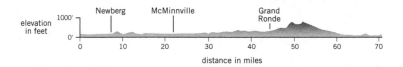

a roadside rest stop. The route ends at Devils Lake State Recreation Area, which offers hiker-biker sites and nearby shops for provisions. There are also plentiful cafés and motels in Lincoln City, the area's largest town. You'll rejoin the main route from Cape Lookout as it passes through Lincoln City on the way to Otter Rock.

MILEAGE LOG

0.0 Depart Champoeg State Heritage Area campground, turning right onto Champoeg Rd. NE.

2.6 Right onto River Rd. NE, which becomes NE St. Paul Hwy.

3.3 Cross Willamette River.

4.6 Left onto NE Wynooski Rd.

5.8 Left onto E. 7th St. into Newberg.

6.1 Right on S. Center St.

6.2 Left onto E. 6th St.

6.5 Right onto S. Blaine St.

6.7 Left on E. 3rd St., which becomes W. 3rd St.

7.2 Left onto Pacific Hwy. W. (SR 99W).

13.0 Left onto SE Dayton Bypass (SR 18).

21.9 Merge onto Salmon River Hwy. (SR 18) at junction with SR 99W south of McMinnville.

31.5 Pass exit to Sheridan.

32.0 Cross South Yamhill River.

38.3 Pass exit to Willamina.

42.6 Pass intersection with SR 22 at Valley Junction.

44.4 Pass Grand Ronde.

51.3 Enter H. B. Van Duzer Forest State Scenic Corridor.

55.6 Pass Van Duzer Rest Area (restrooms).

59.1 Cross Salmon River.

64.1 Pass intersection with N. Old Scenic Hwy. 101 at Otis.

65.4 Merge left onto US 101 southbound at overpass.

67.6 Left onto NE West Devils Lake Rd., which becomes NE 14th St.

69.7 Left onto NE Oar Ave.

69.8 Right onto NE 10th St.

69.9 Left onto NE Mast Ave.

70.0 Right onto NE 6th Dr.

70.2 Left into Devils Lake State Recreation Area.

ASTORIA TO MANZANITA
Distance: 46.3 miles
Elevation gain: 3070 feet

After riding through inland Washington and possibly taking an urban side trip to Portland, your wheels might be itching to try out more coastal roads. Today they get their wish.

Depart the campground early to take in the plentiful stops on today's 46-mile ride: a significant historical site and two charming coastal towns. Not to mention traversing a tunnel and climbing a few healthy hills.

Cycle back through Warrenton, past a small breakfast café on the route. Practice your Shakespeare as you cross the bridge over the Skipanon River: "Prithee, I will skipanon to yon historic site!" The bicycle-friendly roads take you across the Oregon Coast Highway (US Highway 101), yet again delaying the gratification of a coastal destination. But it's worth the wait.

Astoria and its grand bridge are in view across the fields and airport to the left as you head down the hill toward Fort Clatsop and the Lewis and Clark National Historical Park. At 5.9 miles, rejoin the ACA mapped route (the turn marked at 7 miles on section 2, map 14). Shortly you are riding Lewis and Clark Road through the park, which sits along a stretch of the Lewis and Clark River. Even if your name is not Lewis or Clark, you can probably begin to sense the significance of this location.

The nation's most famous western explorers wintered here, upriver from the mouth of the mighty Columbia, in the winter of 1805–1806. It was their final camp before beginning the long trek back to European-settled civilization, which extended at that time only to St. Louis, Missouri. The 33-man Corps of Explorers established the perimeter walls and log-cabin barracks that became Fort Clatsop, which succumbed to the soggy environment (the area gets an average 70 inches of rain a year) by the 1850s. The fort's accurate reconstruction is enhanced by interpreters in period costume who share historic details on busy days. A well-appointed visitors center and marked trails encourage self-touring. Plan an hour if you can, even though you have much cycling ahead.

Depart south through a moist rural valley with cattle grazing on the rangeland and the river visible. There are no services along this stretch, and at 15 miles you encounter the day's first climb, 2 miles of gradual ascent, followed by a winding, scenic drop to the coast, finally, at the town of Seaside.

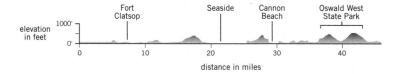

Impressive stone work on the highway in Oswald West State Park

The route comes in just south of the Necanicum River, north of which is Seaside's sister town of Gearhart. This is really where the coast highway gets close enough to the water that you can feel connected to the Pacific. And Seaside, the largest town between Astoria and Lincoln City, also has a couple of creeks that parallel its north-south streets, creating a riverine delta feel as you bike in.

At Seaside, pedal the trail along the Promenade, which dates from 1920 and borders sandy trails and a wide beach. Tufts of golden grass wave atop the dunes. As enjoyable as it is, expect the Promenade also to be touristy, with candy shops, bingo parlors, bumper cars, and a quaint aquarium. Gawking families move unpredictably across your path, as they will at popular tourist spots all along the coast. Take it slow and join the parade. Have lunch. Visit Lewis and Clark one final time at a statue in their honor at the Promenade's center. On South Prom, ogle wonderful big old homes facing the water, which you can safely do, as walking tourists don't get down that far.

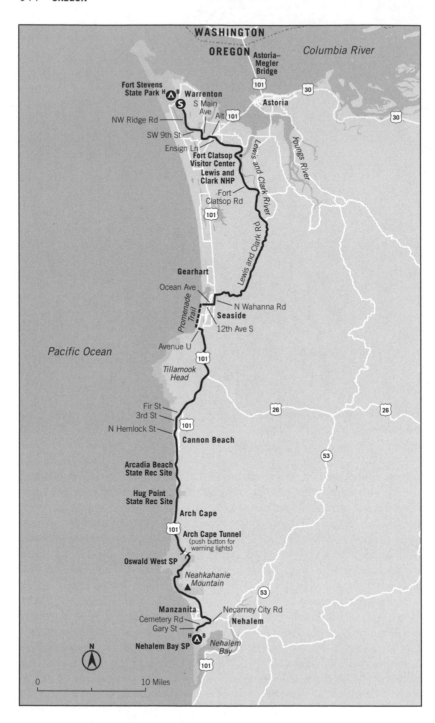

Exiting Seaside, you also leave the shore for a few miles, as US 101 shoots due south and avoids hilly Tillamook Head. It's 7 miles to the next town, and halfway there you'll meet hilly US 26 coming in from Portland. After another significant climb, you drop back to the coast at Cannon Beach, a town with a bit less of a carnival nature. In fact, upscale cafés beckon for a midafternoon break. Expect slow, heavy traffic on the main lane, North Hemlock Street. Out in the bay, Haystack Rock and the Needles rise craggily from the surf, the first sighting of so many sea stacks you'll see by the seashore as you cycle south.

Enjoy a 5-mile stretch of glittering coastline before the views turn into a wall of evergreen trees as you enter Oswald West State Park, which contains the day's two biggest climbs and the Arch Cape Tunnel. The park's namesake, Oswald West, should be given significant deference by every visitor to the Oregon Coast, for it was he who saved the coastline for the public. He became the governor of Oregon in 1911 and established a law mandating that Oregon's coastline, to the high-tide line, be considered a state highway. This preserved all the beaches along the coast for public use. The beaches themselves were formally protected by Governor Tom McCall's Oregon Beach Bill in 1967 that mandated the public's "free and uninterrupted use" of the seashore and ocean beaches. That is why today Oregon's coastline is commonly known as "the People's Coast."

High above the coast is the approach to the Arch Cape Tunnel. Stop and press the button to warn vehicles that bikes are coming through. Lights go on at each end over signs that say "bikes in tunnel," and drivers are told to slow to 30 miles per hour. Turn on your own lights and bike quickly along the narrow lane edge through the dark quarter-mile tunnel. As you exit, take a look south to Neahkahanie Mountain and say a silent thanks for the boring passageway; prior to its opening in 1940, the coast highway drive was interrupted by a detour many miles inland.

Catch your breath and head up the hills that define the last 10 miles of today's ride. Here you'll have another chance to thank road engineers, as the climb is made much more comfortable by the extensive—and recently renovated—concrete and stone walls that help the snaking road safely hug the mountainside. Rock was blasted away from the mountain's edge and masons reassembled it into protective walls edged with concrete. Two sections of the walls were restored between 2005 and 2014. As your counter hits 41 miles, Neahkahanie Viewpoint marks the top of the second, and largest, climb in the park. From here, it's downhill to Manzanita and a sandy overnight park.

The campground at Nehalem Bay State Park is 2 miles south of the town of Manzanita, which has a grocery store, motels, coffee shops, and cafés. A half mile south of the park turnoff from US 101 is a coin-operated laundry. The park is a long, narrow sand spit, with a trail exploring the jetty south of the campground. There are also views north to Neahkahanie Mountain, but very likely you will have seen quite enough of that, so look forward to gazing south toward tomorrow's oceanfront ride, featuring capes and cheese.

A DEFENSIVE HIGHWAY

The rugged Oregon Coast hardly seems as though it's a likely point of attack from an enemy power. However, before there was a highway along the coast, there was no way to see hostile forces approaching or to police the entry of foreign troops onto US soil. Thus the coast was called one of the weakest links in the US national defense system. As World War I approached, a savvy state legislator, Ben Jones, used the "weak link" argument to push through legislation funding a coastal highway.

Work began in 1919, and a coastal highway was basically complete by 1931. It would take another six years to build all the bridges along the route, many of them done by the Civilian Conservation Corps, a cadre of workers hired by the government to offset massive job losses during the Great Depression. The CCC turned out to be hardworking and creative, completing many difficult public works projects like this coastal road.

The road was first known as the Roosevelt Military Highway before being christened US Highway 101, then the Pacific Coast Scenic Byway.

MILEAGE LOG

0.0   Depart Fort Stevens State Park, turning right onto NW Ridge Rd.

1.8   Left on SW 9th St.

2.7   Right on S. Main Ave.

3.3   Left onto Alternate Hwy. 101. Ignore signage to Fort Clatsop and Seaside.

3.6   Right onto Ensign Ln. (BUS 101).

3.8   Continue straight through intersection.

4.0   Cross Oregon Coast Hwy. (US 101).

5.9   Right onto Fort Clatsop Rd.

6.5   Left into Fort Clatsop.

9.1   Left to stay on Fort Clatsop Rd.

9.7   Right onto Lewis and Clark Rd. as Fort Clatsop Rd. goes left at bridge over Lewis and Clark River.

10.8   Cross Lewis and Clark Mainline.

11.7   Left at intersection with Wadsworth Rd.

12.3   Continue straight at intersection with Logan Rd.

19.3   Left onto N. Wahanna Rd. just before US 101, which is visible on the right after the Y.

19.9   Right on Ocean Ave., which becomes 12th Ave. S., into Seaside.

20.3   Pass Prom Bike Shop on right.

20.7   Left onto Promenade Trail as road ends.

21.2   Pass Lewis and Clark statue at intersection with Broadway St.

22.2   Left onto Avenue U.

22.5   Right onto US 101.

25.3   Pass intersection with US 26. Caution: fast traffic.

28.3   Exit US 101 to Cannon Beach at city center off-ramp. Exit becomes Fir St.

29.1   Right onto 3rd St., which curves left in 1 block onto N. Spruce St.; in 200 yards, right again onto 3rd, which becomes N. Hemlock St.

31.9   Right onto US 101 as Hemlock ends.

33.0   Pass Arcadia Beach State Recreation Site.

34.3   Pass Hug Point State Recreation Site.

34.7   Pass Arch Cape.

36.2   Arrive at Arch Cape Tunnel in Oswald West State Park. Press button to activate tunnel lights.

41.7   Reach peak of Neahkahanie Mountain climb.

43.7   Pass Landeda Ave., entrance to Manzanita town center.

44.4   Right onto Necarney City Rd., which becomes Cemetery Rd., then Necarney City Rd., then Gary St.

46.3   Arrive at Nehalem Bay State Park campground.

MANZANITA TO CAPE LOOKOUT
Distance: 39.3 miles
Elevation gain: 1430 feet

The northern Oregon Coast is a meander through small beach-cottage towns and along beautiful stretches of rugged, hilly coastline dotted with campgrounds. The combination makes for a heady mix of traffic and tourist attractions.

Depart Nehalem Bay State Park by retracing the route back to the Pacific Coast Highway (US Highway 101). A scant 2 miles east is Nehalem, which offers grocery stores and cafés if you didn't have breakfast at the campground. The first section of the ride today is rolling climbs, with a steady rise to the big town of Tillamook, followed by this modest ride's only significant climb as you skirt the Three Capes Scenic Route, where you discover that you'll get to experience only two of the three scenic capes.

As the road skirts the inlet for Nehalem Bay, pass a long stretch of homes but no roadside services at Wheeler, then come upon the two linked burgs of Manhattan Beach and Rockaway Beach, where the scattered shops call out for a coffee stop. In Rockaway Beach, visit the Oregon Coast Scenic Railroad, dating to 1925, across the street from a welcoming café. If you are lucky, they will be firing up the steam-powered locomotive.

At Barview, begin a nice ride along Tillamook Bay, with the Bayocean Peninsula in view. In Garibaldi, pass a small museum fronted by a jaunty

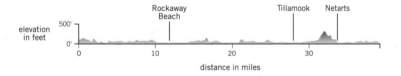

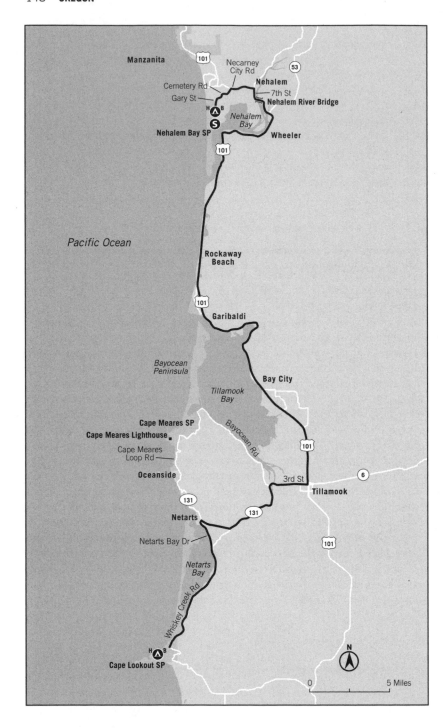

Secluded Netarts Bay Drive

statue of Captain Robert Gray, the first European to discover the Columbia River, in 1792. The Garibaldi Maritime Museum tells the story of Gray and his renowned ships, one of which was the *Columbia Rediviva*; the museum sits at the base of Captain Robert Gray Mountain.

Fifteen miles around the bay is Tillamook, famous for its cheese, made in a cooperative dairy. A tour of the big factory is enjoyable, as is a stop at another local cheese maker, Blue Heron, a bit farther toward town. Bike lanes provide comfortable riding through this regional commerce center.

Tillamook is the terminus of the Wilson River Highway (State Route 6), which is a 75-mile ride due east to Portland, with a 1600-foot climb in the middle. It's about 60 miles to the intersection of US 26 at Portland's westernmost suburb, Hillsboro, which has a light rail connection into the city. Not that you'd want to depart the coast here—the riding is just getting good.

From Tillamook, you'll need to cut across the Cape Meares Peninsula due to unstable soil. The narrow, winding road up to Cape Meares has been closed since 2013 due to landslides. The Oregon Department of Transportation had been monitoring (and repairing) landslides for some time on this little-used road, but has not repaired the road after a particularly heavy storm in November 2012.

Although you can't ride the entire loop, you can still detour up Bayocean Road on the north side of the cape or up to Oceanside and Cape Meares on the south side, but it makes little sense to do so for Pacific Coast cyclists. Although the views are indeed scenic, the road is narrow, winding, and steep. The landslide is the reason that today's ride is reduced by 10 miles and 700 feet of elevation.

Instead, continue on Netarts Bay Drive (SR 131) to the waterfront village of Netarts, which has full services (and your last opportunity for provisions), and then along Netarts Bay to the night's retreat at Cape Lookout State Park, the highlight of which is a 2-mile trail along the headland with consistent ocean views. The campground is a half mile from the highway, and the hiker-biker camp straddles an open wooded glade.

MILEAGE LOG

0.0   Depart Nehalem Bay State Park onto Gary St., which becomes Necarney City Rd., then Cemetery Rd., then Necarney City Rd. again.

1.3   Right onto US 101 S.

2.4   Right onto 7th St.

3.0   Cross Nehalem River.

4.8   Pass Wheeler.

12.3   Pass Oregon Coast Scenic Railroad in Rockaway Beach.

17.5   Pass Garibaldi Maritime Museum.

21.5   Continue forward through Bay City.

25.2   Pass Tillamook Cheese Factory Visitors Center.

27.1   Pass intersection with SR 6.

27.2   Right onto 3rd St. (SR 131).

28.9   Pass Bayocean Rd.

32.1   Bear right to stay on SR 131.

33.6   Left onto Netarts Bay Dr.

35.9   Continue straight as road becomes Whiskey Creek Rd.

38.9   Right into Cape Lookout State Park.

39.3   Arrive at Cape Lookout campground.

CAPE LOOKOUT TO OTTER ROCK
Distance: 61.4 miles
Elevation gain: 3770 feet

Persistence might be the watchword of the day as you traverse two long climbs—one right out of the Cape Lookout campground and another at the halfway point—and then tackle a third, somewhat smaller, climb right at the end of this full day's ride.

You're barely off the access road before starting the day's big climb to Cape Lookout, and it's here that you discover that "cape" is a four-letter word

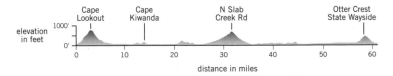

This cyclist is on a fast ride over Rocky Creek Bridge, also known as Ben Jones Bridge, on his way to a new job in San Francisco. He shipped everything but his bike.

for "hill." Start the climb early, and you will see little traffic on the long, slow, 6–8 percent grade. A decent shoulder makes for a comfortable pedal, but there are many twists and turns on the tree-lined road.

At about 300 feet, look for crazy people jumping off the cliff. Hopefully, they will be using hang gliders or paragliders, as this is a popular site for the sport. The launch site is dedicated to Dick Gammon, a pioneer hang glider pilot, 1943–2009. The landing zone is on the beach just west of Cape Lookout State Park's day-use area.

The top of the climb is at the Cape Lookout trailhead parking. This is followed by a screaming, curvy downhill to Sandlake Road, and then a jaunt along the coast to Cape Kiwanda, the third in the Three Capes Scenic Route.

Enter Pacific City, with full services. An RV park on the north edge of town offers tent camping, conveniently located across from a microbrewery. On a spit at the turn to cross the Nestucca River sits Bob Straub State Park (day use only). After crossing the river, the route continues south, but a turn north here brings you in two blocks to the town center, with a bakery and coffee shops.

Farmland and the Nestucca Bay National Wildlife Refuge flank the road south, followed by wooded riding to Neskowin, reached at 25 miles. On summer Saturdays, there is a farmers market in the convenient parking area at the turn to the small, scenic beach. Restrooms and water are here too, and a well-stocked grocery is across the street.

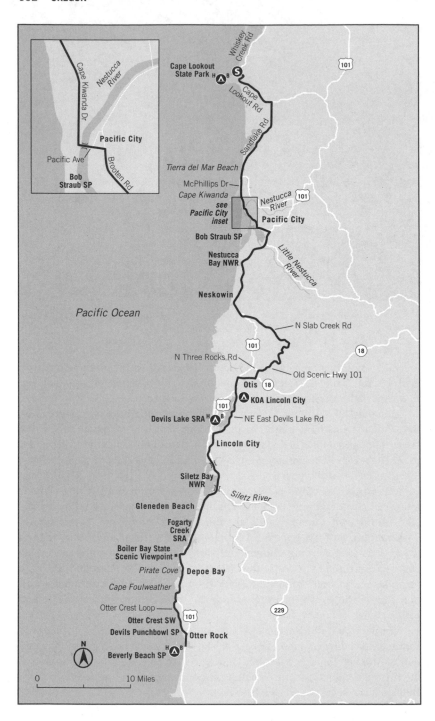

Whiskey Creek Rd

101

Cape Lookout
State Park H ▲ B S

Cape
Lookout Rd

Sandlake Rd

Cape Kiwanda Dr

Nestucca River

Pacific City

Pacific Ave

Pacific Ave

Brooten Rd

**Bob
Straub SP**

Tierra del Mar Beach

McPhillips Dr

Cape Kiwanda
see
Pacific City
inset

Nestucca River

101

Pacific City

Bob Straub SP

**Nestucca
Bay NWR**

Little Nestucca River

Neskowin

N Slab Creek Rd

101

18

N Three Rocks Rd

Old Scenic Hwy 101

Otis 18

▲ **KOA Lincoln City**

101

Devils Lake SRA H ▲ B   NE East Devils Lake Rd

Pacific Ocean

Lincoln City

**Siletz Bay
NWR**

Siletz River

Gleneden Beach

**Fogarty
Creek
SRA**

**Boiler Bay State
Scenic Viewpoint** ■

Pirate Cove **Depoe Bay**

Cape Foulweather

Otter Crest Loop

229

Otter Crest SW

101

Devils Punchbowl SP

Otter Rock

N

Beverly Beach SP H ▲ B

0   10 Miles

A stretch of remote rural road comes next, so fuel up in Neskowin, then continue on the highway just over a mile to a left onto North Slab Creek Road, also sporting the Oregon Scenic Bike Route sign. Prior to this turn, you will see two "Slab Creek" road signs, but do not take them; they mark a side-road loop that adds unnecessary climbing.

The Neskowin Valley is beautiful, wooded, and quiet. You might see goats or llamas on a modest farm or a home sporting many cords of firewood stacked to create imposing garden walls. Wave to the local cyclists enjoying its old-growth forest shade and to the very few cars you will see. Then get ready for a long, winding climb. The significant hill is worth the effort; it contains the same elevation gain as the newer US Highway 101 to the west, but it's spread out over a longer route to ease the challenge.

Spin down and out of the forest into a farmland plain at Otis, where a stellar country café sits roadside at the turn into Lincoln City. Here you meet State Route 18, which comes to the coast southwest from Portland. (If you desire a side trip to the Willamette Valley wine country, this busy highway will take you 44 miles inland to McMinnville, the center of pinot noir territory. That route, with a fine shoulder, sports another major climb to 800 feet and 1500 feet of overall elevation gain. See Alternate Route: Portland to Lincoln City at the start of this chapter for this alternate route from the city that connects to the main route here.)

The main route stays on the coast here. The last miles into Lincoln City on SR 18 are loud and busy, but a decent shoulder keeps you clear of the heavy traffic. The ACA map route has you skirt the worst of the stop-and-go city driving (which has no shoulder or bike lane) by turning left onto a road around long, narrow Devils Lake, with a state park and hiker-biker campsites very near the town center, should you desire it.

Despite the voluminous shopping and even an outlet mall, the town lets you know that you're passing through its Historic Lake District. Then comes the Historic Taft District, which hosts the North Coast Historical Museum, and then the Historic Cutler District at the very south end of town. As you exit Lincoln City, enjoy the historic marshy areas and historic driftwood washed up by the big highway at the mouth of (historic?) Siletz Bay.

Restrooms, picnic tables, and lots of space to spread out and view the rocky coast greet you at Boiler Bay State Scenic Viewpoint, where perhaps you'll see gray whales among the glittering waves. Washington's orca whales are not often spotted along this part of the coast. You're nearing the end of today's ride when you reach Depoe Bay, which may cause you to stop and browse the tourist shops or provision for tonight's camp dinner.

A welcome side road at Rocky Creek lets you escape the busy highway. Follow the bike signs to Otter Crest Loop, a nearly car-free zone that parallels the highway. It's the old highway, actually, and it gets close to Cape Foulweather and then sports a significant climb in a very nice bike lane. Stop to admire the historic Ben Jones Bridge and the excellent rehabilitation it's received to combat degradation from the coastal air. The moist, salty air seeps into the concrete and rusts the rebar that holds it together. This causes cracks and makes the bridge lose structural integrity, hence the restoration.

Returning to the highway, you have a scant mile to cover before the campsites at Beverly Beach State Park. If you're not out of gas, you could continue another 10 miles to South Beach State Park campground just beyond Newport or even Beachside State Park, 18 miles south of Newport outside the burg of Waldport. But Beverly Beach is a delightful stop, with a walkway under the highway that connects the campground to the beach. There you can see north to the Otter Rock headlands and south to the Yaquina Head Lighthouse and experience a stunning sunset. A boardwalk guides you through a birder's paradise along Spencer Creek. The crashing waves nearby blend with the diminishing highway traffic to form a pleasant background to the night's sleep.

MILEAGE LOG

0.0   Depart Cape Lookout campground, turning left onto park access road.

0.4   Right onto Cape Lookout Rd.

3.1   Pass Cape Lookout trailhead, top of climb.

6.4   Right onto Sandlake Rd., toward Pacific City.

7.4   Pass Sandlake Store.

9.9   Pass Whalen Island Rd.

12.1   Pass Tierra del Mar Beach.

12.8   Forward onto McPhillips Dr.

14.3   Forward as McPhillips becomes Cape Kiwanda Dr. (grocery store on left at beach).

15.2   Left onto Pacific Ave., cross Nestucca River.

15.5   Right onto Brooten Rd.

18.3   Right onto US 101.

24.7   Pass Neskowin (restrooms, water at Hawk St. on right).

25.9   Left at signs for Old Hwy. Rd., Neskowin Valley Rd., N. Slab Creek Rd., Oregon Coast Scenic Bike Route.

30.4   Curve right to stay on N. Slab Creek Rd.

31.8   Crest climb at intersection with unpaved Forest Service roads. Road becomes Old Scenic Hwy. 101.

35.2   Curve left at intersection with N. Three Rocks Rd.

35.7   Road becomes N. Old Scenic Hwy., with SR 18 ahead across a small valley.

35.8   Right onto SR 18 at Otis.

37.0   Merge left onto US 101 southbound at overpass.

38.2   Left onto NE East Devils Lake Rd.

42.7   Left onto US 101 at SW 12th St. in Lincoln City. (Detour right and travel 1 mile north on US 101 to a right onto NE 6th Dr. to Devils Lake State Recreation Area; camping.)

45.3   Cross Siletz River.

46.3   Cross second Siletz River bridge.

49.4   Pass Gleneden Beach.

52.2   Pass Fogarty Creek State Recreation Area.

53.2   Pass Boiler Bay State Scenic Viewpoint.

53.9   Pass Pirate Cove.

54.1   Enter Depoe Bay.

56.7   Curve right onto Otter Crest Loop. Follow sign for Oregon Coast Bike Route.

58.6   Pass Otter Crest State Wayside, top of climb.

59.9   Pass turnoff to Devils Punchbowl State Park, 0.5 mile west.

60.3   Merge back onto US 101.

61.4   Left into Beverly Beach State Park. Caution: beware traffic when merging.

OTTER ROCK TO WASHBURNE
Distance: 42.5 miles
Elevation gain: 2020 feet

Today's ride should be a breeze, without a large climb or great distance. Instead, hop from one scenic coastal site to the next, with a few welcoming towns, one large and a few small, to interrupt the reverie. Sure, there's a bridge to cross and a winding cape to climb, but by now that should present no more of a challenge than setting up a tent. With a little weather luck, it could be a perfect Oregon day.

Reluctantly depart Beverly Beach immediately south onto US Highway 101. Just as the leg muscles are starting to warm, take a break by visiting one of the most scenic and accessible lighthouses on the trip. The Yaquina Head Lighthouse, one of the most-photographed on the coast, is worth a detour, about a mile off the route. A short paved path leads from the large parking lot to the lighthouse. The striking white tower is topped with a matte-black gallery and cupola. It dates from 1872 and, at 93 feet, is the tallest such structure on the Oregon Coast. A 1000-watt bulb in its Fresnel lens flashes a distinct pattern every night, sundown to sunup.

It's just another mile into Newport, which generally lives up to its slogan as "the Friendliest." Although you're 140 miles into a 350-mile ride down the state, it feels like you've reached the middle of the coast. It's got everything a touring cyclist could want, including a welcoming bike shop that offers

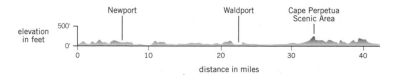

Wide "pullouts" along the highway provide convenient stops for cyclists who need a brief rest or want to let heavy traffic roll past.

services like showers and laundry, rarely found in such a setting. You'll pass a cinema multiplex on the north edge of Newport, which might make you think that you could have had some entertainment before retiring to your tent last night. It's about a half hour from the Beverly Beach campsite.

Skirting the heavily trafficked highway through town, wind your way to Nye Beach, which has a beach-town feel. There's a performing arts center here, cafés, coffee, and shops. A memorial to area fishermen marks the end of SW Elizabeth Street as it curves to head up to Yaquina Bay State Park. Situated on the north side of the mouth of the Yaquina River, the park offers stunning views of the Yaquina Bay Bridge and also contains the Yaquina Bay Lighthouse, a historic wooden home with the lighthouse popping out the top. Built in 1871 and believed to be the oldest building in Newport, it was in use for just three years. With a small donation, you can walk up to the watch room and spy the bridge and the bay.

The bridge is certainly something to behold. Along a 600-foot span, it has one large steel-girder arch that soars over the roadway, but when you look at it from the side, you'll see a number of arches belowdecks, two of steel and five of concrete. They all echo the classic arc. The bridge sports stylish pillars and decorative elements, most prominently art deco.

Again you can warn other traffic about your presence by pushing a button on the bridge approach that activates lights as you cross in the car lane. If the day is very windy or you would prefer a more sedate crossing, the pedestrian decking is wide enough to walk your bike across. On the far side sits the Oregon Coast Aquarium, a modern and well-stocked marine education center with interpretive exhibits on marine ecosystems and more than 150 aquatic animals, including a stunning shark display.

At about 15 miles sits the Beaver Creek State Natural Area at Brian Booth State Park. The small park includes trails, tables, and a grassy open area calling out for picnicking. Also, a side trip here is possible: Turn inland onto North Beaver Creek Road, then right onto South Beaver Creek Road. It offers an alternative route into Waldport that comes out right before the Alsea Bay Bridge. Adding 3 relaxing miles through a verdant farming valley, the road ends at North Bayview Road, where a right turn and a 175-foot climb brings you back to rejoin US 101 in 1 mile along the Alsea River.

Spend the afternoon cycling past glassblowing studios (where you could blow your own sea bauble and hang it off your handlebars), beaches with their siren calls (one is even called "Wakonda" in a suspiciously groan-inducing play on words), wood-carving and bric-a-brac shops, and a few more small burgs to visit. Cross the comfortable Alsea Bay Bridge into Waldport, and if you need to air up the tires, pop into the old gas station housing the Green Bike Co-Op, where locals can work on their bikes or even get a free one based on need. Note: It's not open Sundays.

Green Bike, a program of the Seashore Family Literacy Center, is a laudable community effort. Each summer the "green fleet" is deployed around town for locals to use as needed. These are serviceable, but better bikes can be borrowed or rented from the shop, where they're fixed up from donations. "It's all used parts, except for the safety items," manager Rick Hill told me on a visit a few years ago. Donations come from everywhere, including commercial crab fisherfolk, who snag old bikes on their crab pots, he said. "The bigger metal parts are still OK."

As we talked, a woman entered the shop with an appointment to repair her bike. "Ready to start?" Hill asked her brightly. "We have wrenches!" She was Lola Fedick of Yachats, who had moved from San Francisco a few years earlier. Although suffering from chronic knee pain, she got a bike and, along with regular exercise surfing, used it to help herself lose 80 pounds in 18 months. She beamed at her accomplishment and extolled the local cycling. "It's amazing," she said, "until you get to Perpetua!"

Don't fret over her warning right away, because it's a flat, straight ride from Waldport to Yachats after a short climb coming out of Waldport. Not much to see between the two except vacation homes, but you will understand what about the area appeals to vacationers when you pedal into Yachats. Here's a stylish, upscale, organic-farming-meets-seatown village. Pretend you're a local and pronounce it *yah-hots* (you're welcome) when you hit up the foodie stands, farmers market, or microbrewery for refreshments. Yachats State Park, just a couple of blocks from the numerous cafés, would be a nice place for a picnic.

One last bit of effort awaits, as you climb Cape Perpetua just after Yachats. It is not a wide climb, and it has a disappearing shoulder on a couple of curves, so be careful. Finally, arrive at Carl G. Washburne Memorial State Park and its open field of hiker-biker sites on the edge of a camping loop. The wide beach is a half mile away, via a brushy wood walkway under the highway.

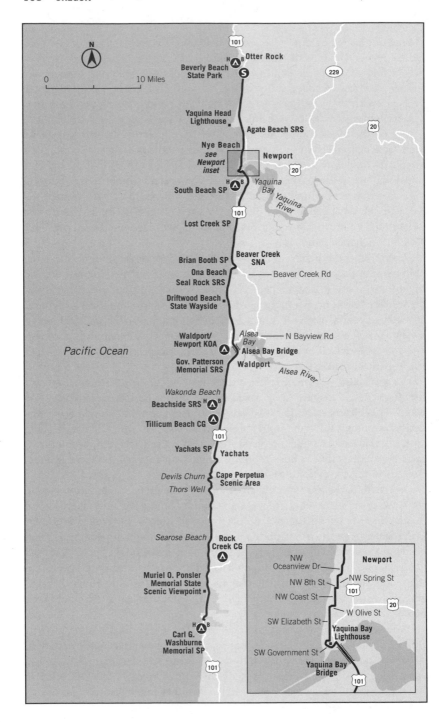

101
H **B** Otter Rock
S
Beverly Beach
State Park

229

0   10 Miles

20

Yaquina Head
Lighthouse ▪   Agate Beach SRS

Nye Beach   Newport
see
Newport   **20**
inset

H **B**   *Yaquina*
South Beach SP   *Bay*
101   *Yaquina*
River

Lost Creek SP

Beaver Creek
Brian Booth SP   SNA
Ona Beach   —— Beaver Creek Rd
Seal Rock SRS

Driftwood Beach
State Wayside ▪

Alsea   —— N Bayview Rd
Waldport/   *Bay*
Newport KOA   Alsea Bay Bridge
Gov. Patterson   Waldport
Memorial SRS   *Alsea River*

Wakonda Beach
Beachside SRS **H** **B**

Tillicum Beach CG

101

Yachats SP   Yachats

Devils Churn   Cape Perpetua
Thors Well   Scenic Area

Pacific Ocean

Searose Beach   Rock
Creek CG

Muriel O. Ponsler
Memorial State
Scenic Viewpoint ▪

H **B**

Carl G.
Washburne
Memorial SP

101

NW   Newport
Oceanview Dr
NW 8th St   NW Spring St
101
NW Coast St   **20**
W Olive St
SW Elizabeth St ⌐

Yaquina Bay
Lighthouse
SW Government St

Yaquina Bay
Bridge   **101**

MILEAGE LOG

0.0 Depart Beverly Beach State Park, turning left onto US 101 S.

3.6 Pass Lighthouse Rd., leading to Yaquina Head Lighthouse in 1.1 miles.

4.3 Right onto NW Oceanview Dr.

4.8 Pass turn to Agate Beach State Recreation Site.

5.8 Forward onto NW Spring St. as Oceanview ends at NW 12th St.

6.0 Right onto NW 8th St. as Spring ends.

6.1 Left onto NW Coast St.

6.3 Pass Nye Beach shopping area (cafés, restrooms).

6.5 Right onto W. Olive St., which passes Don Davis Park at 6.6 miles (restrooms), then becomes SW Elizabeth St.

7.3 Curve right onto SW Government St. as Elizabeth ends.

7.4 Left into Yaquina Bay State Park.

7.5 Pass Yaquina Bay Lighthouse.

7.8 Left at stop sign at approach to Yaquina Bay Bridge. In 100 yards, right at stop sign to ride the bridge. Push button to active warning lights on bridge.

8.3 Exit the bridge.

8.6 Pass SW Abalone St. (Detour and circle back under bridge approach on SE Marine Sciences Dr. and Ferry Slip Rd. to Oregon Coast Aquarium, Hatfield Marine Science Center.)

9.8 Pass turnoff to South Beach State Park (camping).

13.3 Pass Lost Creek State Park (restrooms).

14.6 Enter Brian Booth State Park.

15.6 Pass Ona Beach at Beaver Creek State Natural Area. (Detour on Beaver Creek Rd. and N. Bayview Rd. to Waldport in 4 miles.)

17.3 Enter Seal Rock.

17.5 Pass Seal Rock State Recreation Site.

18.9 Pass Driftwood Beach State Wayside.

21.8 Cross Alsea Bay Bridge into Waldport.

23.9 Pass Governor Patterson Memorial State Recreation Site (restrooms).

25.8 Pass Wakonda Beach and Beachside State Recreation Site (camping).

27.0 Pass Tillicum Beach Campground.

29.9 Enter Yachats.

30.8 Pass Yachats State Park and central shopping area.

33.1 Pass Cape Perpetua Scenic Area (US Forest Service).

33.4 Pass Devils Churn.

34.0 Pass Thors Well.

35.8 Pass Strawberry Hill overlook.

41.0 Pass Rock Creek Campground (US Forest Service).

42.2 Pass Muriel O. Ponsler Memorial State Scenic Viewpoint.

42.5 Left into Carl G. Washburne Memorial State Park.

WASHBURNE TO WINCHESTER BAY
Distance: 42.1 miles
Elevation gain 2530 feet

Today, you enter the dunes. Or, more correctly, the Dunes, because these sand dunes are no small matter. Beginning a third of the way into today's ride, the Oregon Dunes National Recreation Area stretches south forever. Or at least it seems to; the actual distance is approximately 47 miles.

First, though, there's a little matter of another stellar lighthouse to shoot (for the shutterbugs) and a visit to a very odiferous sea mammal in its natural environment. Don't worry, you won't get wet—at least, not from a visit to the Sea Lion Caves.

Begin the day with a slow, steady climb from Washburne. On a brief descent, pass the side road to Heceta Head Lighthouse. It's a short side trip with a half-mile hike to see the iconic lighthouse itself. More than a century old, it was renovated in a two-year project begun in 2011. A bit farther on the

EXPLORE PACIFIC COAST SUPPORTED RIDES AND CHARITY OUTINGS

Do you have arthritis? Many people do, and most of us have a family member or good friend afflicted by the disease. Why not bike part of the Pacific Coast route and simultaneously raise money for a cure? It can be done on rides in Oregon and California, and you'll be "riding light," because on this sort of a tour, the organizers carry your gear!

"I'm just in awe every year," says my friend Steve Cardin of Snohomish, Washington, who's ridden the Oregon version of the Arthritis Bike Classic six times. "Every year I see things I missed the previous year, taking in that incredible natural beauty every day."

Steve battles Ehlers-Danlos Syndrome, a painful chronic disease that causes hypermobile and loose or unstable joints, among other symptoms. When diagnosed in 2009, he learned that EDS can progress and severely hinder movement, but that strength from physical activity can quell the symptoms. Most exercise was out, but bicycling worked, and a few months after he bought his first bike, he rode the 350-mile Oregon Coast on the Arthritis Foundation's seven-day fund-raising ride.

He says the camaraderie fuels the fun. "We're all there for the same reason. Every year we meet new people, and that means a new group of friends." He's also inspired by other riders' stories, which often include battling some form of arthritis themselves.

The Oregon trip, which happens in mid-September, includes transfers to and from Portland, full support, many meals, camping, and lots of extras. The

highway is another side road that drops you to parking below the headlands, which offers a stunning view of the rocky promontory, with tide pools and a sandy beach at the base.

The Heceta Head Tunnel comes shortly, where you again push a button to activate lights warning other drivers of bikes in the tunnel. It's quite short with good lighting. There's little danger in the tunnel, but maybe you'll want to know that as you leave it you're just skirting the inside edge of the Devils Elbow. (Note: Perhaps this is a precursor to tomorrow's ride, in which devils play a more prominent role.)

You'll get one more chance for a postcard look at the stunning lighthouse when the road climbs around the next headland. Here is a pullout where many visitors stop and take pictures back toward the lighthouse, which beams seaward from 206 feet above the shore.

Just beyond that picture stop is a tourist attraction that vies for one of the cheesiest and also most unique on the coast. It's the Sea Lion Caves. From the promontory-perched gift shop, you do not see (or hear or smell) sea lions or

Arthritis Foundation's California coast trip departs San Francisco for Los Angeles in early September.

There are a few other big supported tours—not all are charity rides, but you could add your own fund-raising when doing any of them—that you could meld with your coast exploration. The mammoth Seattle to Portland ride, presented by Seattle's Cascade Bicycle Club, sends 10,000 riders on a two-day, 203-mile straight route to Portland in mid-July. In August, Cascade presents the 180-mile RSVP: Ride from Seattle to Vancouver (BC) and Party. Cycle Oregon plans different routes around the state each year, and often the weeklong September ride includes part of the coast. The Climate Ride offers a central California route in June and a Pacific Northwest route through the San Juan Islands in August. The California Bicycle Coalition produces the California Dream Ride in mid-October on different routes.

When I rode the Arthritis Bike Classic with Steve in 2011, the inspiration was almost on par with the scenery. A group of colleagues from sponsor Amgen, a biotech company, raised a lot of cash and had a great team-building experience. One scientist went a bit crazy and raised funds as he rode, stopping to evangelize about our cause and entering camp each night with a fistful of dollars. The brewmaster from Rogue Ales joins the ride each year, so every day ended by sampling a great beer in camp to toast the day's achievement.

As Steve says with a smile, "Come for the beer, and stay for the scenery!" Learn more: www.arthritis.org, www.cascade.org, www.cycleoregon.com, www.cadreamride.org, www.climateride.org.

caves. However, pay the fee and descend in the elevator through the rock to sea level, and your senses will be filled with the big mammals.

After the tourism early in the day, you're able to stretch out a bit into riding. The route loops and drops, then veers away from the water into an open valley, which is warmer and drier on a cool day than the exposed headlands. At nearly 9 miles, you'll pass the Twin Lakes Store, the first retail establishment since the campground. More retail lies ahead, at 15 and 30 miles. Before reaching the dunes, the route continues through Siuslaw National Forest, where you'll see turnoffs for camping and lake access.

Florence offers a good comfort stop or lunch interlude. Situated at the intersection with State Route 126, the highway to Eugene, it offers cafés roadside for a half mile and a small downtown flanking the historic bridge that crosses the Siuslaw River. (FYI, if you need to bail out of your trip here and head to the Amtrak station at Eugene, or just want to include that town in your tour, you'd face a 62-mile, 2410-foot-elevation ride up SR 126. Alternatively, you can take a 90-minute bus for about $25 that runs twice daily on weekdays, once on Sundays, and not at all on Saturdays.)

Just south of Florence, enter the Oregon Dunes National Recreation Area. It stretches from Florence to Coos Bay. The wind has sculpted some of the dunes to be nearly 500 feet tall. Others send tentacles down to meet the road. On windy days, you might experience the stinging sensation of having your face sandblasted as you pedal by the sandy hills.

An opportunity to wash the sand off comes at Jessie M. Honeyman Memorial State Park a few miles south of Florence. You can rent kayaks or canoes or go swimming at two freshwater lakes, including Cleawox, which is quite handy to the park's campground. The park is also a popular fishing spot for stocked trout and bass. Check out the 1930s-era stone-and-timber bathhouse and other park structures built by the Civilian Conservation Corps, the Depression-era public works program.

Expect crowds, because Honeyman is the state's second-largest campground. Hiker-biker sites are right at the campground entrance, but this is a place for another type of vehicle: the motorized buggies called all-terrain vehicles (ATVs) or off-road vehicles (ORVs). They have nearly unlimited access to the dunes, which are 2 miles wide from the campground to the ocean. Their frenetic noise makes it not a pleasant walk to the beach.

If exploring the dunes the ATV way interests you, commercial dune-buggy rental and tours are plentiful along the way. Or you could play in the

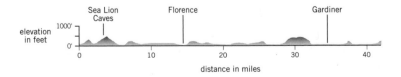

A look back at the iconic Hecata Head Lighthouse

sand on a sandboard, which is like a snowboard that you stand on to ride down the dunes. As the billboards say, just dune it!

Shops, campgrounds, and dune exploration sites dot the road, which you might just pedal by if you're not into sand-focused recreation. But one detour might be worth a look: the Siltcoos River estuary. One mile off the road is the Waxmyrtle Campground, which is hard up against the Siltcoos River estuary, with a lagoon trail that is birding heaven. You'll see signs for snowy plover protection during its mating season, and you surely will see the small shorebird with its tan tail and white underside. But you may also spot herons, bitterns, ospreys, eagles, ducks such as mergansers and cinnamon teals, and brightly colored kingfishers.

For a comprehensive overview of the dunes area, stop at the day-use area's overlook at about 25 miles. Boardwalks above the undulating sand offer a good feel for the scale of this place.

The route climbs slowly into the forest before reaching Gardiner and Reedsport, the largest towns visited today. Views of valleys to both sides, as well as forests and clear-cuts, distract you from a long, steady climb. The road tops out to a flat run before dropping back to the expansive mouth of the Umpqua River just prior to Gardiner. The Umpqua River Bridge into Reedsport is another historic (read: no shoulder) river crossing. It is not long, and its sidewalk is navigable if you are extra careful on the tight corners at each end.

This bigger town might be the provisioning spot for tonight's camp, as larger stores offer much more than the village near the Umpqua Lighthouse State Park campground. The town of Winchester Bay, which sits just before the campground, does have one small grocery and a handful of cafés, including a quaint fish-and-chips place on a floating barge.

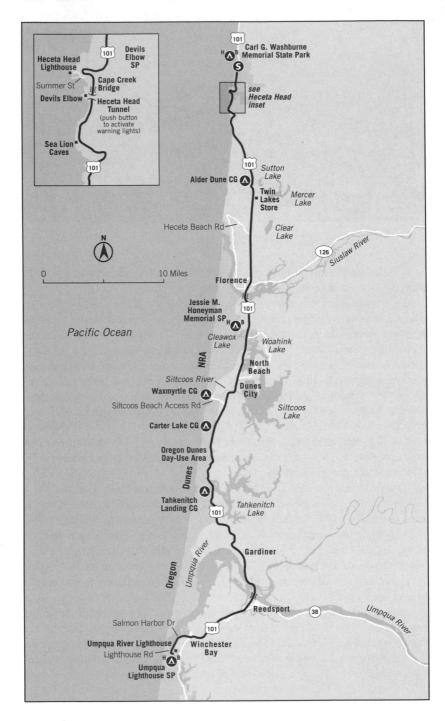

Heceta Head Lighthouse

Devils Elbow SP

Summer St

Cape Creek Bridge

Devils Elbow

Heceta Head Tunnel
(push button to activate warning lights)

Sea Lion Caves

Carl G. Washburne Memorial State Park

see Heceta Head inset

Alder Dune CG

Sutton Lake

Twin Lakes Store

Mercer Lake

Heceta Beach Rd

Clear Lake

Siuslaw River

Florence

Jessie M. Honeyman Memorial SP

Cleawox Lake

Woahink Lake

Pacific Ocean

NRA

North Beach

Siltcoos River

Waxmyrtle CG

Siltcoos Beach Access Rd

Dunes City

Siltcoos Lake

Carter Lake CG

Oregon Dunes Day-Use Area

Dunes

Tahkenitch Landing CG

Tahkenitch Lake

Gardiner

Oregon

Umpqua River

Reedsport

Umpqua River

Salmon Harbor Dr

Umpqua River Lighthouse

Lighthouse Rd

Winchester Bay

Umpqua Lighthouse SP

N

0   10 Miles

You'll see nearly all of Winchester Bay as you ride the three blocks from the highway to its waterfront on Salmon Harbor, then skirt the bay before climbing to the park near the lighthouse above. The route takes you by the lighthouse and then by Lake Marie, which gets stocked with rainbow trout and has a half-mile trail encircling it. The lighthouse is worth a stop, and maybe a return to catch the sunset after setting up camp.

Below, at the mouth of the Umpqua River, the original 1857 lighthouse was the first one built in the Oregon Territory. Its structure was undermined by flooding and it was destroyed in 1864. It was rebuilt here, 165 feet above sea level, in 1891, and the park and Coast Guard facilities around it have been in use ever since. Tours are offered daily in summer.

But settler activity occurred even before the original lighthouse. Spanish explorers first sailed by in the 1500s. The first crossing of the treacherous Umpqua Bar happened in 1791 by the English brig *Jenny*. A party of Hudson Bay Company explorers came through in 1826 looking for furs. The group included famed botanist David Douglas. The town is named for Herman Winchester, who came from San Francisco in 1850 and helped build it into the largest settlement on the river.

Across from the replaced lighthouse is the viewing platform of the Umpqua River Whale Watching Station, part of the Coastal Visitors Center. It overlooks the mouth of the river, the beaches, and the jetty that now protects the harbor. Humpback whales can be spotted from here, although not as commonly seen as gray whales. But in sun or fog you can spot the lower jawbone of a 60-foot humpback, mounted at the edge of the parking lot like a rustic hitching post.

Passing through most of Duneland today took grit, or perhaps more accurately, maybe you took on grit. Tonight it would be a very good idea to clean and oil the chain.

NAVIGATING BY DAYMARK

By night, mariners sailing along the West Coast were warned against crashing into the rocky shores by strategically placed lighthouses. Their "light signature," or the light flashing pattern, would inform sailors which lighthouse they were passing.

But by day, lighthouses could also provide an aid to navigation due to each one's unique "daymark." The daymark is a particular pattern, color, or shape of a lighthouse.

The Yaquina Head Lighthouse outside of Newport, Oregon, for instance, is a tall, tapered white building with a black cap and a wide black bar below the lens. The Umpqua River Lighthouse is broader and more squat, with a red cap and a white bar containing windows below the light.

MILEAGE LOG

0.0   Depart Carl G. Washburne Memorial State Park campground, turning left onto US 101 S.

2.0   Pass Heceta Head Lighthouse.

2.1   Pass Heceta Head Lighthouse State Scenic Viewpoint turnoff (0.25 mile to parking on Summer St.).

2.3   Cross Cape Creek Bridge.

2.5   Ride through Heceta Head Tunnel; push button to activate warning lights.

2.9   Pass viewpoint of Heceta Head Lighthouse.

3.2   Pass Sea Lion Caves.

7.5   Pass Alder Dune Campground.

8.9   Pass Twin Lakes Store.

11.2   Pass Heceta Beach Rd.

11.5   Enter Florence.

14.2   Pass SR 126 intersection.

14.8   Cross Siuslaw River Bridge.

17.2   Pass Jessie M. Honeyman Memorial State Park (camping).

19.9   Pass Clear Lake Rd. to North Beach area.

20.9   Cross Siltcoos River.

22.0   Pass Siltcoos Beach Access Rd.

22.7   Pass Carter Lake Campground and Carter Dunes trailhead.

24.6   Pass Oregon Dunes Day-Use Area.

26.1   Pass Tahkenitch Creek trailhead road.

27.3   Pass Tahkenitch Landing Campground.

33.3   Pass Gardiner.

34.9   Cross Umpqua River Bridge.

35.5   Enter Reedsport.

39.6   Enter Winchester Bay.

39.8   Right onto Salmon Harbor Dr.

39.9   Pass Beach Blvd.; cafés, shops on right in 1 block.

41.1   Left on Umpqua River Lighthouse Rd.

41.8   Arrive at lighthouse. Continue straight on road, which curves downhill.

42.1   Arrive at Umpqua Lighthouse State Park.

WINCHESTER BAY TO BULLARDS BEACH
Distance: 47 miles
Elevation gain: 2140 feet

Not every ride includes nonstop amazing sites and sights; on some days, you'll find the pleasures of the ride unfolding slowly, perhaps unexpectedly or even just in retrospect. That's the case with today's route.

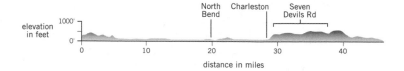

I found myself passing by or through some impressive landscapes, but maybe not quite realizing it. Then I would think, "Yeah, those dunes stretched on forever. That really was an amazingly long spit of land that protected that bay. Come to think of it, the bay itself was quite grand, as was the bridge. And I'm sure glad I stopped at the nature preserve, because I hadn't known what I was looking at when I crossed that bridge at the entrance to the slough." The message on such a day is to trust your instincts and keep your awareness level high.

Today's ride takes you through Coos County, "the Sunset Coast," and the day's ride is not too long, so you can plan to see an amazing sunset over the Pacific next to your relaxing beachside campground. Start the ride on the big highway, but shortly veer off the too-beaten path onto quiet Wildwood Drive, which takes you through a winding ravine.

Nearly 9 miles into the ride, pass the US Forest Service Spinreel Campground (no hiker-biker sites, but dune-buggy rentals). Pass a few more parks and campgrounds before crossing over Coos Bay on the McCullough Memorial Bridge into the connected towns of North Bend and Coos Bay. One of the bigger bridges on the Oregon Coast, it rises in a climb to the center of the span. If you ride the road surface, expect to take it slow and create a bit of a traffic bottleneck. It also has a sidewalk, but you must walk the bikes there.

A few turns in North Bend take you through a shopping district, past a park with restrooms, and then into a residential area as you skirt the edge of the town of Coos Bay. Views open to water and foothills. The river is wide here, and a branch of it filters into the massive South Slough.

Pass a shellfish processing operation at the next town, Charleston, and refill the water bottles because next up is a dry, hilly climb along Seven Devils Road. (That is, if you don't take a dead-end detour to a trio of ocean-side parks. In a scant 6 flat miles you'd be at Cape Arago State Park, at the end of Cape Arago Highway. A series of state parks are grouped closely along this quiet road, and one campground, Sunset Bay, has hiker-biker facilities. Shore Acres State Park, former home of lumber baron Louis Simpson, has a lush botanical garden, and all the parks in this string have stunning views, sandy beaches, tide pools, fishing, and beachcombing. If you're interested in a day off from the ride, this quiet section of coast would provide a nice escape.)

The main route turns left at Charleston onto Seven Devils Road. It is low in traffic and light on scenery, with just a couple of view spots: lots of trees,

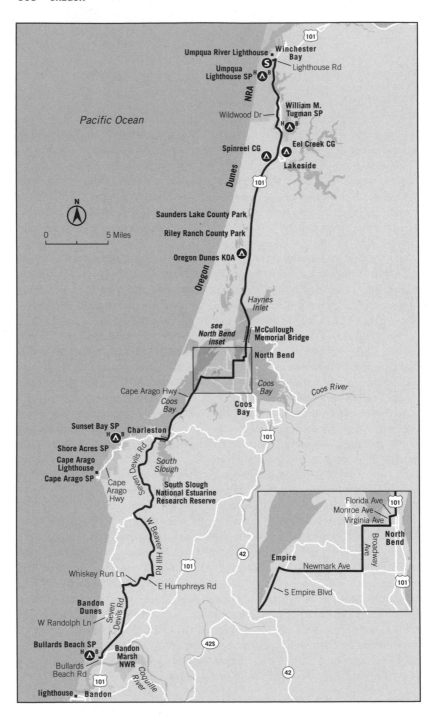

Pacific Ocean

Umpqua River Lighthouse
Winchester Bay
Lighthouse Rd
Umpqua Lighthouse SP
NRA
William M. Tugman SP
Wildwood Dr
Eel Creek CG
Spinreel CG
Lakeside

Dunes

N
0   5 Miles

Saunders Lake County Park
Riley Ranch County Park
Oregon Dunes KOA

Oregon Dunes

Haynes Inlet

see North Bend inset
McCullough Memorial Bridge
North Bend

Cape Arago Hwy
Coos Bay
Coos River
Coos Bay
Coos Bay

101

Sunset Bay SP
Charleston
Shore Acres SP
Cape Arago Lighthouse
Cape Arago SP
Cape Arago Hwy

Seven Devils Rd
South Slough
South Slough National Estuarine Research Reserve

W Beaver Hill Rd

Whiskey Run Ln
E Humphreys Rd
101
42

Bandon Dunes
W Randolph Ln
Seven Devils Rd

Bullards Beach SP
Bandon Marsh NWR
Bullards Beach Rd
101
lighthouse Bandon
Coquille River
42S
42

Florida Ave
101
Monroe Ave
Virginia Ave
North Bend
Broadway Ave
Empire
Newmark Ave
S Empire Blvd
101

A Canadian family traverses the busy McCullough Memorial Bridge at North Bend.

no coastal views. But still, Oregon Department of Transportation strongly recommends you get off US Highway 101 south of North Bend and not meet it again until nearing Bandon, which is nearly all of today's remaining route.

Gear down for an initial climb onto Seven Devils Road. Look for the demarcations of each devilish hill painted on the road surface, starting with the first one almost immediately. One has a false top, another has the wry scrolled commentary "Don't you love it?" The rural route is signed as the Charleston-Bandon Scenic Loop.

A welcome comfort stop appears at 33 miles as you pass the South Slough National Estuarine Research Reserve, nearly 5000 acres. The informative free visitors center is worth a stop, and there are trails to overlooks of the estuary, which is a regularly flooding spongeland where salt water meets fresh. A half-mile roundtrip clamber takes you down to an observation deck at Hidden Creek Marsh. Look for black-tailed deer or the somewhat rare green heron, whose home is here. Perhaps the bird's color comes from a diet of the native green crab found here. In this deep forest ecosystem, every shade of green seems represented.

The last part of Seven Devils Road is flat and rather boring. The rest is trees growing up to the road, except for the timber-company clear-cuts, where you can see distant vistas. That's one way to create views. The side road ends with a fun downhill run to the Bandon Marsh National Wildlife Refuge.

Rejoin the coast highway for the last 3 miles to Bullards Beach State Park, which has a mostly paved, bikeable trail to the beach beyond the large campground. Watch for horses, as Bullards is one of three horse campgrounds along the Oregon Coast.

To view the 1896-era lighthouse, take a 2.6-mile pedal along the Coquille River to the end of the road. The light station sits on the north jetty overlooking the mouth of the river at Bandon. From lighthouse to lighthouse, park to park, sunset awaits.

MILEAGE LOG

0.0   Depart Umpqua Lighthouse State Park campground on Lighthouse Rd.

0.1   Right onto US 101 S.

1.0   Pass second entrance to Lighthouse Rd.

3.1   Right onto Wildwood Dr.

5.8   Right onto US 101 as Wildwood ends. William M. Tugman State Park (camping) across highway.

7.6   Pass Eel Creek Campground.

8.7   Pass Spinreel Campground.

11.2   Pass Saunders Lake County Park.

12.1   Pass Riley Ranch County Park.

13.4   Pass Oregon Dunes KOA campground.

17.9   Cross McCullough Memorial Bridge across Coos Bay.

18.6   Enter North Bend.

19.5   Right onto Florida Ave. In 1 block, curve right, then left to stay on Florida.

19.8   Left onto Monroe Ave.

20.1   Right onto Virginia Ave.

20.7   Left onto Broadway Ave.

21.7   Right onto Newmark Ave. (SR 540); follow sign for Oregon Coast Bike Route.

23.5   Left onto S. Empire Blvd., which becomes Cape Arago Hwy.

28.1   Cross bridge into Charleston.

28.6   Left onto Seven Devils Rd. (Detour right to Cape Arago Lighthouse and Sunset Bay, Shore Acres, and Cape Arago state parks.)

33.1   Pass South Slough National Estuarine Research Reserve.

34.9   Curve left as paved road becomes W. Beaver Hill Rd.

39.4   Right onto E. Humphreys Rd., which becomes Whiskey Run Ln.

41.9   Left onto Seven Devils Rd.

44.1   Continue straight across W. Randolph Ln.

44.7   Bear right onto US 101.

46.7   Right onto Bullards Beach Rd.

46.9   Right into Bullards Beach State Park.

47.0   Left into campground.

BULLARDS BEACH TO HUMBUG MOUNTAIN
Distance: 37.8 miles
Elevation gain: 1780 feet

Pedal across a faded green bridge from Bullards Beach into Bandon. Below on the shores of the Coquille River sits the Bandon Marsh National Wildlife Refuge. Today's ride is a modest distance with a few stretches of landlocked valley riding and only a couple of hill climbs toward the end. It might be a

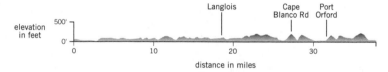

good day to take a breakfast in town. Diversions include a couple of artistic and historic sites along the way.

The town of Bandon, a scant 3 miles from the park, is known as the cranberry capital of Oregon, complete with a festival in early September that celebrated its 70th year in 2016. Some cranberry bogs are visible from the highway, and in early fall you might spot the unique harvest, where the fields are shallowly flooded and a machine skims the floating berries off the water's surface.

Bandon's historic old town centers on three blocks of shops and cafés, complete with cranberry delicacies. Public restrooms can be found in the McNair Building, under a mural of orcas. An Airstream-size yellow-and-orange sculpture of *Henry the Rockfish* points to the shop and workspace for Washed Ashore, a nonprofit beach-cleaning organization that creates such sculptures and smaller art from sea debris. Another shop offers "neat old stuff." Sidewalk murals in stone and tile decorate the Old Port Office building, which was originally a US Coast Guard station, built in 1939 and used only for six years.

Before there were settlers or sailors in Bandon, there were the Nasomah people, according to a sobering memorial in a small park across from the port building. The narrative tells that the Nasomah, "the people by the big water," lived here for 3000 years. They hunted sea lions off Coquille Point and lived in plank homes. They would celebrate with 10 nights of continuous dancing. Memorial displays share the plight of their more recent cousins, the Coquille Indian Tribe, who were persecuted for 30 years in the early 1800s by settlers and soldiers before finally moving to a reservation in 1856. Pedal somberly out of town, contemplating the rough history that's happened under the mute massiveness of the Coquille Point Rocks standing sentry in the bay.

The route continues on a beach access road and past wayside stops and marshlands before returning to US Highway 101. A dozen miles farther, pass the country studios of Art 101, housing the Washed Ashore artists. It's highlighted by the billboard-size *Avery the Eagle*, constructed of all manner of garbage, mostly plastic and Styrofoam, that humans had allowed to spill into the sea. There are often other giant flotsam-art projects under way at the site. In their first five years after opening in 2010, the art group processed 17 tons of ocean debris, 95 percent of it petroleum-based. Twelve thousand volunteers, including thousands of schoolchildren, created 65 pieces of sea-debris art.

On a recent visit, the artists showed me debris that began coming ashore in 2014 and was evidently from the 2011 Tohoku earthquake–caused tsunami

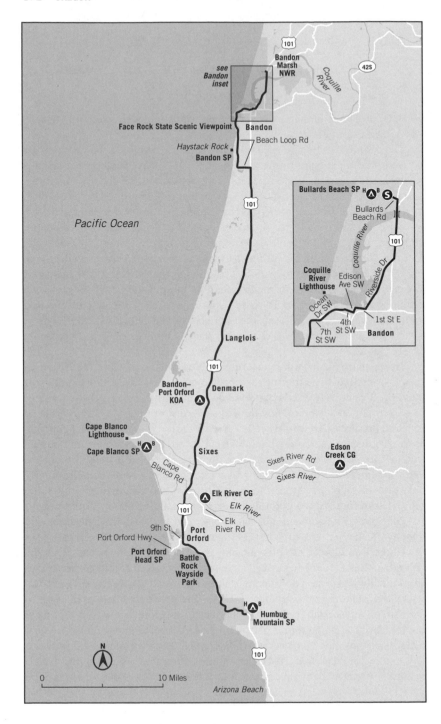

Bandon Marsh NWR

Coquille River

see Bandon inset

Bandon

Face Rock State Scenic Viewpoint

Haystack Rock

Beach Loop Rd

Bandon SP

Pacific Ocean

Bullards Beach SP

Bullards Beach Rd

Coquille River

Coquille River Lighthouse

Edison Ave SW

Riverside Dr

Ocean Dr SW

4th St SW

1st St E

7th St SW

Bandon

Langlois

Bandon– Port Orford KOA

Denmark

Cape Blanco Lighthouse

Cape Blanco SP

Cape Blanco Rd

Sixes

Sixes River Rd

Edson Creek CG

Sixes River

Elk River CG

Elk River

Elk River Rd

9th St

Port Orford Hwy

Port Orford

Port Orford Head SP

Battle Rock Wayside Park

Humbug Mountain SP

N

0   10 Miles

Arizona Beach

on Japan's coast. Giant red lightbulbs the size of bowling balls washed in with Styrofoam sea floats covered in Japanese writing. The most poignant were land markers, wood-and-plastic stakes with property names on them that had been anchored in the ground.

The irony of Washed Ashore is that it's not on, or anywhere near, the shore. It's washed up against the edge of US 101, and the baskets of flotsam and jetsam corralled in nets all around the edges of the property look like today's catch off the fishing boat. Perhaps it is best that you can't see the sea from there, so that all this carefully gathered ocean garbage can never be washed back into the waves.

Soon beyond Art 101 is the West Coast Game Park Safari, an attraction of a different sort that can be smelled before it is seen. It's a wild-animal petting

DROWNING IN AN OCEAN OF PLASTIC

How much plastic are we dumping into our oceans each year? Pull over for a minute when you can see the shore. Then visualize "five plastic grocery bags filled with plastic for every foot of coastline." That would amount to an estimated 8 million metric tons of plastic waste slipping into the sea. Every year.

The depressing visual of bulging plastic bags lining our stunning West Coast beaches came from Jenna Jambeck, an assistant professor of environmental engineering at the University of Georgia who was the lead author of the extensive 2015 study "Plastic Waste Inputs from Land into the Ocean." She told the *New York Times* that, by 2025, the amount would double, to 10 bags per foot of coastline.

Currently, it is estimated that 110 million metric tons of plastic are in the earth's oceans. And the floating islands of garbage are not just unsightly. Much of the plastic waste breaks down into minuscule particles and is ingested by fish, which can cause them to starve and can get into our diets. Some of that plastic is coated with harmful chemicals. What goes around comes around.

In the study, published in *Science* magazine in February 2015, Jambeck and other scientists argued that massive "waste management infrastructure improvements" are needed in many countries around the world in order to stem the incredible plastic pollution.

What can you do? Recycle more of it. In the United States, which is the planet's 20th worst plastic polluter, only about a third of our plastic waste is currently recycled. Also, stop drinking water from disposable plastic bottles. In the United States alone we bought a staggering 49 billion bottles of water in 2015.

Henry the Rockfish, *made entirely of plastic debris fished from the Pacific Ocean, serves as an amazing attraction in Bandon.*

park, where you can feed and view hundreds of uncaged, free-roaming wild-life. Daily, staff introduce visitors to a different "ambassador" animal from their 75 different species of wildlife.

The obvious lunch stop is Langlois, a community established in 1881 at a wide spot in an open valley. At the center sits a renowned market and deli with made-to-order sandwiches and hand-scooped ice cream. Picnic tables on the grounds provide a comfortable respite. Two more tiny towns sit along this stretch, Denmark and Sixes, which can be seen as you pass through the verdant Sixes River valley on the highway.

One more worthy detour is Cape Blanco State Park, 5 miles off the route. It hosts a historic home and lighthouse. If you want to make this cycling day even shorter, it also has a campground with hiker-biker sites. In the park you can visit historic Hughes House, the restored 1898 Victorian farmhouse of Joseph N. Hughes, an Irish immigrant who became a prosperous dairy farmer here.

Even more auspicious is the Cape Blanco Lighthouse. Erected in 1870, the lighthouse stands on Oregon's westernmost point of land, and it is also the most southerly lighthouse on the Oregon Coast. Towering over the head-land 245 feet above the sea, it's the state's oldest continually operating light-house as well, and the first lighthouse in Oregon to be fitted with a first-order Fresnel lens. If that's not enough to send you on the detour to the park, con-sider this final credit: it holds the record for longest service at one lighthouse;

James Langlois worked there for 42 years, and James Hughes, of the locally famous dairy family, served at this light station for 37 years.

Longest used, most westerly and southerly . . . certainly significant hallmarks of settlement. But just down the road is—you guessed it—another historic landmark. Port Orford, the closest town to tonight's campsite, claims the title of oldest town site on the Oregon Coast. Further stacking up the superlatives, it's also the only open-water port on the Oregon Coast. Check out the wetland interpretive walkway off 18th Street, or pedal off the route a dozen blocks west on Ninth Street and Port Orford Highway for dramatic sea-stack views and a free lifeboat station museum at Port Orford Head State Park.

Wheel down the town's main street, a.k.a. US 101, and provision for the night at a convenient grocery before making a dramatic 5-mile climb-and-descent to finish the day at Humbug Mountain State Park, whose campground is woodsy and cool, sitting in the crotch between two towering, tree-covered hills.

MILEAGE LOG

0.0   Depart Bullards Beach State Park, turning left onto Bullards Beach Rd.
0.3   Right onto US 101.
0.7   Cross Coquille River on bridge; use vehicle lane.
1.1   Right onto Riverside Dr.
2.7   Curve right onto 1st St. E. in Bandon.
3.2   Curve left onto Edison Ave. SW and climb hill as 1st St. E. ends.
3.3   Right onto 4th St. SW, which becomes Ocean Dr. SW, then 7th St. SW.
4.0   Curve left onto Beach Loop Rd. as 7th ends.
4.2   Pass Coquille Point on right.
4.8   Pass Face Rock State Scenic Viewpoint.
6.4   Pass Bandon State Park and Haystack Rock.
8.2   Right onto US 101.
10.2 Pass Misty Meadows Jams (restrooms).
11.9 Pass Washed Ashore–Art 101 studio.
12.4 Pass West Coast Game Park Safari.
18.3 Pass Langlois Market and Deli.
21.0 Pass Denmark.
22.3 Pass Bandon–Port Orford KOA campground.
26.2 Pass road to Edson and Sixes campgrounds.
27.1 Pass road to Cape Blanco State Park (lighthouse, camping).
30.4 Enter Port Orford.
31.3 Pass Port Orford Wetland Interpretive Walkway.
31.5 Curve left at Oregon St. to stay on US 101.
32.1 Pass Battle Rock Wayside Park.
37.4 Left into Humbug Mountain State Park.
37.8 Arrive at campground.

HUMBUG MOUNTAIN TO BROOKINGS
Distance: 51.7 miles
Elevation gain: 3300 feet

"Easy does it, Lizzie." Good advice from Louisiana gentleman Darryl to his wife and riding partner, Elizabeth, as they turned onto the shaded highway, which was still wet with dew and devoid of morning sun, being deep in the heart of Humbug Mountain's canyon. Today's cycling begins by slipping around the curves and hunting for the shoulder to reappear so you can exhale and enjoy the climb into the southern Oregon sunshine.

Your last full day in Oregon sports a healthy selection of hills, including one significant climb at Cape Sebastian, a midpoint town well placed for lunch, the highest bridge in the state, plenty of stunning views, a giant basalt whale, and, oh, yes . . . jet boats and dinosaurs.

In fact, before you see much of anything else, there's a *Tyrannosaurus rex*, nearly looming over the highway. Six miles into the ride, dropping back to sea level after the first significant climb, you'll come upon Prehistoric Gardens, a theme park with life-size dinosaur statues peeking through the trees and the aforementioned one gracing the parking lot with a toothy menace. For a fee, see them all on a half-hour trail walk, or just snap a picture under the belly of the accessible giant and hit the gift shop.

At 10 miles, depart the highway for a welcome side road, with little traffic and even less in the way of services. Cedar Valley Road winds and climbs and coasts along the edge of a couple of river valleys. There is an oasis in its dozen miles: Cedar Bend, a public golf course, sits roadside, a great place for a cold drink and restrooms at the clubhouse. Cyclists are welcome (do spend a bit of money if you're going to use the facilities), and the grassy valley view enhances the rest break. There are even rental clubs if you're up for a diversion.

Cattle, ponies, and perhaps a black-tailed deer or wild turkey scampering across the road keep you entertained until the mighty Rogue River comes into sight. From there, Gold Beach and lunch are just a few miles away.

The Rogue is pretty, meandering across its river valley with a few wide sandbars here and there. Surprisingly, the river is quite narrow at spots. A comfortable bridge gets you across into Gold Beach. There are waterside cafés right after the bridge but more services, including a large grocery, on the route through town. Pass the Curry County Courthouse and admire the

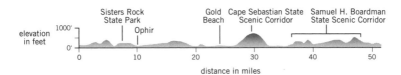

Cyclists need to fend off all sorts of wildlife on the Oregon Coast, including this giant outside the Prehistoric Garden theme park. Release the bike and nobody will get hurt!

area's coat of arms, a triumvirate image of trees, mining, and sheep. A historical museum fills in the gaps, and there's a jet-boat museum out by the bridge.

Eat light, because the day's biggest climb, to Cape Sebastian, comes quickly. A detour in the park sends you a half mile down a side road and another half mile on a walking trail to see the rugged views. Or you can just pedal on by and use the roadside pullout in a few more miles through this expansive park.

The cape was named, so we're told, for Saint Sebastian, and as your heart rate recovers from the climb you might enjoy knowing that this Catholic martyr is the patron saint of athletes. The area was coincidentally named by the Spanish explorer Sebastian Vizcaino in 1603.

Drink in expansive views from the south Cape Sebastian pullout, where it's said you can see 43 miles north, beyond looming Humbug Mountain. South, you can nearly see 50 miles to Crescent City, California, just beyond tonight's stopping point at Brookings, the last stop in Oregon.

Coming down off the cape, look for windsurfers off the Pistol River coastal park, a series of high dunes. Just beyond is a frontage road to the hamlet of Pistol River. The highway turns inland a bit and starts a series of rollers toward Brookings, including a couple more significant climbs. But it's a wide stretch with a good shoulder, and you have one more park to anticipate.

Samuel H. Boardman State Scenic Corridor, a linear piece of coast 12 miles long, delights with viewpoints of sandy beaches, surf, precipitous cliffs, and rugged sea stacks. Boardman, the state's first parks superintendent, was

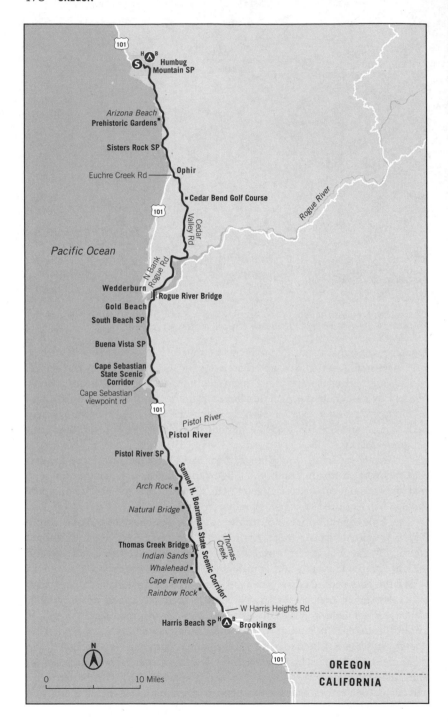

101

H A B
S Humbug
Mountain SP

Arizona Beach
Prehistoric Gardens▪

Sisters Rock SP

Euchre Creek Rd —— **Ophir**

▪ **Cedar Bend Golf Course**

101

Cedar Valley Rd

Pacific Ocean

N Bank Rogue Rd

Wedderburn
▪**Rogue River Bridge**
Gold Beach
South Beach SP

Buena Vista SP

**Cape Sebastian
State Scenic
Corridor**
Cape Sebastian
viewpoint rd

101

Pistol River
Pistol River

Pistol River SP

Samuel H. Boardman State Scenic Corridor

Arch Rock ▪

Natural Bridge ▪

Thomas Creek

Thomas Creek Bridge▪
Indian Sands ▪
Whalehead ▪
Cape Ferrelo
Rainbow Rock▪

— W Harris Heights Rd

Harris Beach SP H A B **Brookings**

Rogue River

N

0   10 Miles

101

OREGON

CALIFORNIA

honored at his retirement in 1950 for his strong commitment to making the coast available to the public. He advocated for the area to become a national park, making deals, acquiring land, and lobbying federal officials. As it panned out, he created the largest state park on the coast.

Today, you can revel in the formations of Arch Rock, House Rock, Whalehead, and Natural Bridge, sentinels of the scenic view. Go a bit down a hiking trail, stand under 300-year-old Sitka spruce trees, and appreciate the beginning of the lush forests of the coastal Shasta mountain range that stretch through much of Northern California.

In the midst of all the Boardman beauty is the Thomas Creek Bridge, which at 345 feet tall is the highest span in Oregon. The modern bridge is perfectly comfortable for cycling, but stop on one side or the other to appreciate the dizzying expanse below.

Rainbow Rock, its grassy offshore massiveness pointing to Brookings, welcomes you to town. Tonight's goal, Harris Beach State Park, is a scant 2 miles farther, with the town's full services—including restaurants, supermarkets, microbreweries, and even motels should you need a night off from the sleeping bag—another half mile beyond the park. Tomorrow: California!

MILEAGE LOG

0.0   Depart Humbug Mountain State Park, turning left onto US 101 S.
6.1   Pass Arizona Beach.
6.2   Pass Prehistoric Gardens.
7.6   Pass Sisters Rock State Park.
10.0 Left onto Euchre Creek Rd. to Ophir.
10.1 Bear right toward golf course.
10.4 Left onto Cedar Valley Rd.
12.4 Pass Cedar Bend Golf Course (restrooms).
18.6 Bear right onto N. Bank Rogue Rd. (unsigned) at stop sign.
19.9 Left onto N. Bank Rogue Rd.
23.3 Enter Wedderburn.
23.5 Left at stop sign to cross Rogue River Bridge and rejoin US 101 S.
24.0 Enter Gold Beach.
25.9 Pass South Beach State Park and Gold Beach Visitors Center.
27.4 Pass Buena Vista State Park.
28.2 Enter north section of Cape Sebastian State Scenic Corridor.
30.9 Pass Cape Sebastian viewpoint road. (Detour 0.5 mile for hike to views.)
32.3 Pass Cape Sebastian overlook.
35.1 Cross Pistol River and pass through Pistol River State Park.
35.7 Pass Frontage Rd. to town of Pistol River.
40.3 Enter Samuel H. Boardman State Scenic Corridor.
41.1 Pass Arch Rock Viewpoint.
42.3 Pass Natural Bridge Viewpoint.

44.0   Cross Thomas Creek Bridge.

44.5   Pass Bruces Bones Creek.

44.8   Pass road to Indian Sands.

46.0   Pass Whalehead Viewpoint.

47.5   Pass House Rock Viewpoint road.

48.3   Pass Cape Ferrelo Viewpoint drive.

48.9   Pass road to Lone Ranch Beach.

50.2   Pass Rainbow Rock Viewpoint at end of Samuel H. Boardman State Scenic Corridor.

50.5   Enter Brookings.

51.4   Right onto W. Harris Heights Rd.

51.7   Arrive at Harris Beach State Park.

Opposite: *Three friends from Georgia and a Canadian cyclist depart the Burlington Campground down the redwood-lined Avenue of the Giants.*

NORTHERN
CALIFORNIA

YOU'RE WELCOMED TO NORTHERN CALIFORNIA with a healthy climb into a unique and fascinating forest, one that you'll experience a few more times on the long haul into San Francisco: the magnificent redwoods.

The northern coast's redwood trees have been preserved in groves throughout the coastal forests from southern Oregon to Big Sur. The greatest concentration of the trees is found in a string of federal and state parks along the route. Bike as slowly as possible through these giants and get off the bike to experience the springy duff blanketing the forest floor. Enjoy their cool, moist, shaded ecosystem; it will provide rejuvenation for the climbs and solace for the soul.

While the route is sparsely populated and towns are farther apart than in Oregon, the seclusion also ensures lower traffic volumes in many sections. Near wine country—a day's drive for Bay Area residents—activity picks up. On the last leg to the Golden Gate, bike trails and suburban riding prevail. When you reach San Francisco, celebrate with a lap around the city that, amazingly, can be done with very little climbing of its famous hills.

BROOKINGS TO ELK PRAIRIE
Distance: 66.4 miles
Elevation gain: 3600 feet

The journey of a thousand miles starts with a single step (on the pedal). That paraphrased adage went through my mind the first time I headed south out of the last towns in Oregon. The first two states in this coastal journey each comprise a manageable three-digit mileage. But point your fenders toward California, and you are ratcheting it up a notch.

Head south out of Harris Beach State Park on the recent trail that extends into Brookings, a quiet lane for the first half mile along busy Chetco Avenue. The bustling town gives you many choices for a hot breakfast before you cross the state line, and you might want to fuel up; this is a long day with a significant amount of hill climbing.

It starts out mellow enough as you cross the Chetco River and pedal to the border out of Harbor, the aptly named last town in Oregon. Skip the highway here and track the coastline on Lower Harbor Road and Ocean View Drive. The cluster of offshore rocks and sea stacks in Chetco Cove is impressive.

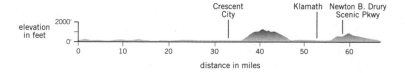

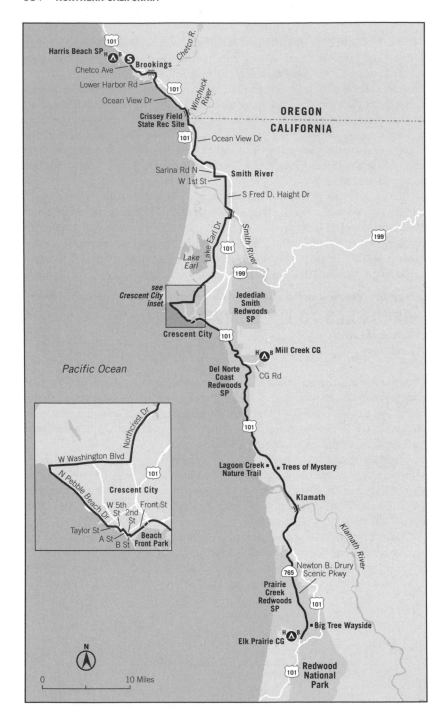

Harris Beach SP

Brookings

Chetco Ave

Lower Harbor Rd

Ocean View Dr

Crissey Field
State Rec Site

Ocean View Dr

Sarina Rd N

W 1st St

Smith River

S Fred D. Haight Dr

Chetco R.

Winchuck
River

OREGON

CALIFORNIA

Lake Earl Dr

Lake
Earl

Smith River

199

199

Jedediah
Smith
Redwoods
SP

see
Crescent City
inset

Crescent City

Mill Creek CG

CG Rd

Del Norte
Coast
Redwoods
SP

Pacific Ocean

Northcrest Dr

W Washington Blvd

N Pebble Beach Dr

Crescent City

W 5th
St 2nd
St

Front St

Taylor St

A St
B St

Beach
Front Park

Lagoon Creek
Nature Trail

Trees of Mystery

Klamath

Klamath River

Newton B. Drury
Scenic Pkwy

765

Prairie
Creek
Redwoods
SP

101

Big Tree Wayside

Elk Prairie CG

Redwood
National
Park

N

0   10 Miles

Pass through the area's working waterfront, then a neighborhood that thins out to farmland for the last few miles to the state line.

Enjoy your Northwest-grown fruits and vegetables before heading into California, because your first stop will be an agricultural inspection station at the California state line. Observe their rules about taking fresh produce into the state to protect their farming operations from imported pests that could be lurking.

Turn back onto the highway briefly at the state line, then cross the highway back onto Ocean View for the first 6 miles in California. Carefully cross back to the west side of the highway at Sarina Road and pedal side roads the next dozen miles into Crescent City. If you want to save a bit of effort and miles, you can skip this section of Ocean View and just continue on perfectly fine on US Highway 101 to Sarina Road.

At the intersection with US 101 in Crescent City you'll find a number of cafés, and it might be good to fuel up before the next section of riding. So far, the day has been flat and uneventful. But after Crescent City, it turns interesting as you climb the Redwood Highway (an apt nickname for US 101 here) through the string of federal and state facilities that make up the Redwood national and state parks strung together along the California coast. They start with Jedediah Smith Redwoods State Park, which you skirt and traverse briefly at Crescent Beach, then you encounter Del Norte Coast Redwoods State Park.

Along with being a steady grind rising more than 1100 feet in 5 miles, US 101 south of Crescent City is a busy stretch of highway, so expect plenty of logging trucks, RVs, and other vehicle traffic to swoosh by as you stick carefully to the intermittent shoulder. Calm your nerves and catch your breath by stopping at safe turnouts and wide shoulders.

"It's a comfortable route, for all the traffic," says Brian Ferguson, a Canadian sweating out the climb alone on a summer 2016 trip. He's biked around North America and says the Pacific Coast route "is a wonderful mix of people of all ages, and it's a comfortable, very safe route." But among the noisy traffic of this climb, perhaps it's his mental state that informs this sunny attitude. As we ride off, he reminds me that "there are just not enough days in the year to enjoy life."

The saving grace in this climb is your knowledge that it is one of the only big climbs of the northern coast (the other being at Leggett, a blissful number of days down the road). Once past this climb and the one that takes you into the redwood forest for tonight's campsite, you will find mellower, wooded rides, and that is certainly something to look forward to.

The inland climb features mostly forest views, including a few redwood stands, with scant services. At nearly 40 miles, pass a turnoff to the Mill Creek Campground (it has a hiker-biker site), which is 2.2 miles up a flat, wooded road. Restrooms can be found at the Lagoon Creek Nature Trail,

A narrow road with slow traffic winds through giant redwood trees.

and all services are at the touristy Trees of Mystery (where you could check out the tree canopy on the Sky Trail gondola). Tiny Klamath offers snacks, restrooms, and the turnoff for the Tour-Thru Tree, where you can bike through the hollowed-out tunnel of a 700-year-old giant redwood for a dollar donation and a brief, steep climb. Plan to provision for the night when leaving Klamath, at the latest. Just beyond town, the modern Klamath River Bridge sports hulking golden bears on its four concrete corners.

Five miles beyond Klamath, in the midst of the day's second long climb, turn off US 101 onto the Newton B. Drury Scenic Parkway, which escorts you comfortably into the heart of the redwood forest. You're 8 miles from tonight's excellent campground, so tarry a while as the road drops you back down and flattens into a curving lane guarded by silent giants: towering trees with deeply grooved bark and foliage that starts a hundred feet above your head.

Among these sentinels, which have guarded this land for many hundreds of years, slow your pedal stroke to nearly a stop. Glide along as slowly as possible. Cast your eyes skyward whenever the light traffic permits it. Open your ears to the profound hush that comes when you are alone on the road. Stop and place your hands on the dark folds of bark. Park your bike in the hollowed-out base of a grand old specimen. Remove your footwear and sink into the soft forest duff. In short, do whatever you can to extend your time with these magnificent trees to fully experience their grandeur.

At the end of today's long trek, less than a mile beyond the Big Tree Wayside, sits Elk Prairie Campground, your spot for the night. A string of hiker-biker sites are secluded from the rest of the campground, backed by trees and fronted by the expanse of Elk Prairie, where a herd of elk will often be seen grazing at sunset or early morning. The park has water, showers, and firewood for purchase, but no other services. Sink into your sleeping bag knowing that you've tackled one of the toughest days on the Northern

California coast and, in the next few days, you will get more chances to commune with those wonderful trees.

MILEAGE LOG

0.0 Depart Harris Beach State Park, turning right onto bike trail.

0.4 Bike trail merges onto Chetco Ave. (US 101).

2.2 Cross Chetco River Bridge in bike lane.

2.4 Right immediately after bridge onto Lower Harbor Rd.

3.5 Sharp right onto Ocean View Dr.

3.8 Right to stay on Ocean View Dr.

7.1 Right onto US 101 as Ocean View ends.

7.4 Cross Winchuck River Bridge in bike lane.

7.5 Pass Crissey Field State Recreation Site.

7.9 Cross state line into California.

8.6 Left onto Ocean View Dr.

14.1 Cross US 101 onto Sarina Rd. N.

14.6 Left onto W. 1st St.

15.7 Right onto S. Fred D. Haight Dr.

15.9 Slight right to stay on S. Fred D. Haight Dr.

18.9 Right onto US 101 S. as S. Fred D. Haight Dr. ends.

19.1 Cross Smith River Bridge; press button to indicate bikes on bridge.

19.4 Right onto Lake Earl Dr.

19.8 Curve left at Bailey Rd. to stay on Lake Earl Dr.

27.1 Continue onto Northcrest Dr. to enter Crescent City.

28.0 Right onto W. Washington Blvd.

30.0 Left onto N. Pebble Beach Dr.

32.1 Right to stay on Pebble Beach at W. 9th St.

32.3 Curve right onto Taylor St.; in 1 block, left onto W. 5th St.

32.5 Right onto A St.

32.6 Left onto 2nd St. as A St. ends.

32.7 Right onto B St.; in 1 block, left onto Front St.

33.3 Right onto bike trail in Beach Front Park at K St. (visitors center, restrooms on right).

33.4 Left onto RV park access road. In 1 block, left onto Sunset Cir.

33.5 Right onto US 101.

35.8 Pass Enderts Beach Rd. and begin climb.

36.6 Enter Del Norte Coast Redwoods State Park.

39.4 Pass Mill Creek Campground Road.

47.8 Pass Lagoon Creek Nature Trail (restrooms).

48.7 Pass Trees of Mystery attraction.

53.0 Enter Klamath.

54.3 Cross Klamath River Bridge.

58.4 Right at Newton B. Drury Scenic Pkwy. (SR 765) exit.

59.3   Stay left on main road to enter Prairie Creek Redwoods State Park.
65.6   Pass Big Tree Wayside.
66.4   Arrive at Elk Prairie Campground.

ELK PRAIRIE TO ARCATA
Distance: 46.3 miles
Elevation gain: 1910 feet

As you ride through the redwoods, you'll see sign after sign dedicating groves to individuals, families, or organizations. These are the forest-loving people who helped save these trees from commercial sale and cultivation, thus building the park and keeping the land in a state as close to wild as possible.

Some are honorary, as in Lady Bird Johnson Grove, which made its own history by triggering a visit from President Richard Nixon in 1969 for its dedication. Topping the list of dignitaries in attendance with Nixon were the named honoree, her husband former president Lyndon B. Johnson, and California governor and future US president Ronald Reagan. The trailhead to her grove is accessed via a 2.6-mile, hilly detour off the highway at Bald Hills Road (probably an unlikely side trip 5 miles into today's trek).

But make it your mantra to thank those named as you cycle by. Certainly, on this fairly short-distance day with no giant climbs, get off the bike occasionally and step back along those paths into the hushed, damp atmosphere of the big trees. Reluctantly depart the park and, after 5 calm miles, enter the burg of Orick.

Once a bustling logging town, Orick is now more known for its burl artists who bring mysterious power and beauty to gnarled segments of abnormal growth crafted from downed trees. Particularly prized are burls with wood that has been attacked by a fungus or insects, thus creating intricate patterns amid the growth rings. Burls can be turned into sculptures, but also into tables, chairs, vessels, even jewelry. The wood is so valuable, park rangers have to patrol against poachers seeking burls from the parks' ancient trees. A few large burlwood artists' galleries sit roadside as you cycle through Orick.

Your next fascinating stop is Stone Lagoon. It's one of the three large lagoons created eons ago by earthquakes splitting the land and creating natural barriers to the sea. A lagoon is by nature brackish water—that is, freshwater that gets mixed regularly with salt water. This happens during big

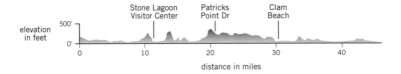

A comfortable rest stop along Trinidad Scenic Drive

midwinter storms. Brackish does not mean lifeless (although odiferous, yes). These large lagoons, which you'll spend many minutes pedaling past on the rolling terrain, are home to 50 bird species, and scores more at migration time. Roosevelt elk often can be seen wading along the shores. At 12 miles, stop at the Stone Lagoon Visitor Center.

At 20 miles you'll be essentially finished with highway riding when you exit US Highway 101 onto Patricks Point Drive. Along this winding, sparsely populated road, you travel past a few inns and cafés. Save your lunch stop for tiny Trinidad, though. Where Patricks Point becomes Trinidad Scenic Drive sit a few cafés and a residential neighborhood leading shortly to a well-maintained state beach park and an overlook on a sleepy harbor.

Trinidad's scenic drive lives up to its name, with the wooded road going to single lane at points, and even an unpaved but navigable section. The conditions keep it a bit wild and the vehicle traffic slow. Stop and savor the sea-stack overlooks.

After a brief return to US 101, join the Hammond Coastal Trail, which carries on nearly into Arcata, with brief on-road stints. A highlight is the Mad River Bridge, on which you rise up above the estuary of the river that runs right next to the sea. Survey the bottomland before spinning down into the farming area north of Arcata and into town.

Arcata, home to Humboldt State University, is picturesque and busy. The route skirts the college, then straightens through the middle of the city, whose town square is ringed by small shops. A natural-food store and a large grocery are on the route—good places to provision, because the night's campground, a former KOA situated too near the loud highway, is just 2 miles south of town.

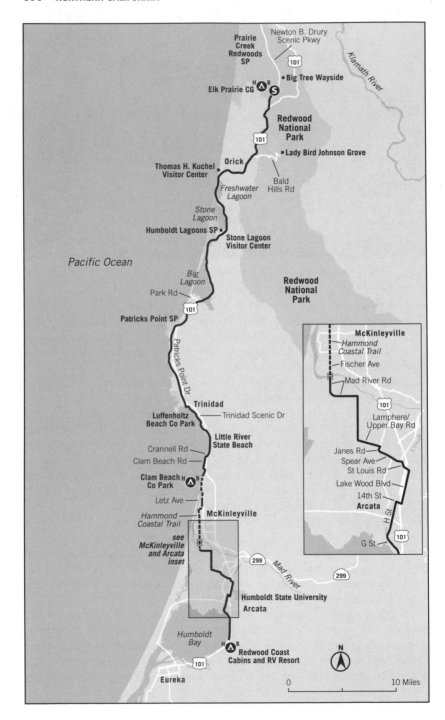

Redwood Coast Cabins and RV Resort has a small hiker-biker area tucked away behind the office and discounts their tent camping rates slightly for cyclists. If riding solo, however, pay full price and get a less-secluded site in the main campground: the Arcata area, the center of California's illegal marijuana farming, seems to attract many transients, and the community grapples with a significant quantity of homeless people. If this element of society makes you uncomfortable with camping, there are plentiful motels in Arcata or Eureka, the larger of the two towns, which is just a couple of miles beyond the campground. No matter where you stay in the Arcata area, pay close attention to your gear.

MILEAGE LOG

0.0   Depart Elk Prairie Campground, turning right onto Newton B. Drury Scenic Pkwy.

1.0   Right onto US 101 toward Eureka.

4.8   Pass Bald Hills Rd. (detour to Lady Bird Johnson Grove).

5.3   Arrive in Orick.

7.9   Pass turnoff to Thomas H. Kuchel Visitor Center for state and national redwood parks.

8.5   Pass north edge of Freshwater Lagoon.

9.9   Pass north edge of Stone Lagoon.

11.8   Pass Stone Lagoon Visitor Center.

12.6   Pass turnoff for Humboldt Lagoons State Park.

14.7   Pass north edge of Big Lagoon.

18.7   Pass Big Lagoon Park Rd.

20.3   Right at exit 734 onto Patricks Point Dr.

21.2   Pass Patricks Point State Park.

26.4   Forward at stoplight onto Trinidad Scenic Dr.

28.5   Pass Luffenholtz Beach County Park.

29.6   Merge left onto US 101 at end of Trinidad.

30.4   Right at exit 725, Crannell Rd.

30.6   Right onto Clam Beach Rd.

31.1   Pass Clam Beach County Park (hiker-biker camping, restrooms).

32.0   Right into parking lot at entrance to US 101. Continue forward on Hammond Coastal Trail adjacent to parking lot.

33.4   Pass parking next to US 101; continue on trail.

33.6   Forward onto Letz Ave. as trail ends.

34.1   Rejoin trail at Douack Rd. as Letz Ave. ends.

34.7   Right onto Murray Rd. as trail ends.

34.9   Forward onto trail at bollards as Murray Rd. curves and becomes Kelly Rd.

35.2   Cross Knox Cove Ave. and continue on trail.

36.0   Forward onto unsigned Fischer Ave. at Hiller Park.

36.1   Forward onto trail at Hiller Rd.

37.2 Cross Mad River Bridge on trail trestle.

37.4 Straight off the trail onto Mad River Rd.

39.8 Left onto Lamphere Rd. as Mad River Rd. ends. In 1 block, Lamphere becomes Upper Bay Rd.

40.5 Right onto Janes Rd., which curves left and becomes Spear Ave.

41.3 Right at roundabout onto St. Louis Rd.

41.4 Left off St. Louis onto unsigned Lake Wood Blvd.; follow Pacific Coast Bike Route sign and cross over US 101.

42.0 Pass Humboldt State University campus.

42.7 Right onto 14th St.; cross over US 101 into central Arcata.

42.9 Left onto H St.

43.1 Pass Arcata's town square.

43.7 Right onto G St. as H St. ends.

44.6 Merge right onto US 101 S. as G St. ends.

46.2 Cross US 101 carefully at Bracut Lumber Co.

46.3 Turn right onto short service road to Redwood Coast Cabins and RV Resort.

ARCATA TO BURLINGTON
Distance: 61.8 miles
Elevation gain: 2610 feet

Today's ride is a healthy distance with cumulative elevation, but it also contains the first part of the best road in Northern California and a few spins through the centers of historic towns.

Begin by heading promptly into Eureka, more historic and attractive than Arcata. Ride the waterfront past a fishing boat–filled marina and then jog east onto Second Street, Old Town's main shopping lane. To the left at this turn is the heavily sculpted Carson Mansion, built by a logging baron in Queen Anne style and reportedly the inspiration for many a haunted house. Across the street is its sibling, the Pink Lady Victorian. Both well-maintained homes deserve a quick look.

The city center offers three dozen brightly painted building murals, as well as brick storefronts and brick-paved intersections. Skip the campground breakfast today and enjoy your morning meal at one of the cafés lining the route.

A unique attraction sits on the north side of Second Street between D and E streets: an homage to a hometown artist. The Romano Gabriel Wooden

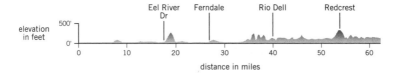

Cyclists may outnumber cars on sections of the Avenue of the Giants, as busy US Highway 101 parallels the road.

Sculpture Garden, visible behind tall glass windows, celebrates the 30-year efforts of folk artist Gabriel, an Italian immigrant who populated his property with whimsical sculptures of flowers, trees, and local people's faces, complete with hairdos, hats, and three-dimensional wooden noses. The works of this delightful outsider contrast with the complex, often moody work of Morris Graves, on display at the Morris Graves Museum of Art, four blocks off the route on F Street. Graves, at the forefront of modernist painting and a leader of Pacific Northwest artists in the late 20th century, lived Humboldt County.

Departing Old Town, the route diverts from a particularly commercial section of US Highway 101 to a residential Eureka neighborhood, rejoining the highway at the city's edge. In a few miles, veer to another lane parallel to the highway and cycle past the College of the Redwoods, the Northern California coast's community college, which also houses the Humboldt Botanical Garden. Cross over the highway again and ride through the farmlands and delta country of the Eel River, crossing the river at 23 miles.

After 4 additional miles of lush, flat farmland, reach the ideal lunch stop: Ferndale. Settled in 1852, it looks like the all-American hometown, with stately spires of churches and outstanding Victorian Gothic architecture. Its brief commercial center offers a deluxe coffee shop and a butcher shop–deli with handmade sandwiches. A destination for area cyclists on a day ride, it hosts fun events like the Lost Coast Beer and Bocce Festival in late September.

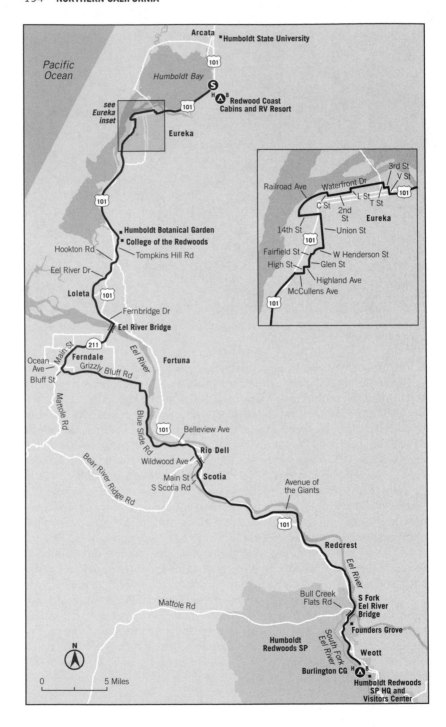

Arcata
■ Humboldt State University

*Pacific
Ocean*

101

Humboldt Bay

S
H ▲ B Redwood Coast
Cabins and RV Resort

101

*see
Eureka
inset*

101

Eureka

101

■ Humboldt Botanical Garden
■ College of the Redwoods

Hookton Rd
Tompkins Hill Rd

Eel River Dr

Loleta 101

Fernbridge Dr
Eel River Bridge

211

Main St
Ferndale Fortuna

Ocean
Ave
Bluff St

Grizzly Bluff Rd

Eel River

Mattole Rd

Blue Slide Rd

101 Belleview Ave

Bear River Ridge Rd

Rio Dell

Wildwood Ave

Main St
S Scotia Rd Scotia

Avenue of
the Giants

101

Redcrest

Eel River

Mattole Rd

Bull Creek
Flats Rd

S Fork
Eel River
Bridge

■ Founders Grove

*South Fork
Eel River*

Humboldt
Redwoods SP

Weott

N

Burlington CG H ▲ B

0   5 Miles

Humboldt Redwoods
SP HQ and
Visitors Center

Eureka inset:

3rd St
V St

Railroad Ave   Waterfront Dr
L St
C St   T St

2nd
St
14th St   Union St   **Eureka**

101

Fairfield St   W Henderson St

High St   Glen St

Highland Ave
McCullens Ave

101

Ferndale also is the departure point for the Lost Coast alternate route via Mattole Road. On the main route, climb Grizzly Bluff Road out of town and note the steeply raked cemeteries, where every plot for former Ferndale residents would seem to have an unobstructed view of the town.

Two more burgs await on your way to the fabled road through the redwoods. Three significant climbs take you to adjacent Rio Dell and Scotia, which sit on a bend in the Eel River and look every bit like the lumber-mill communities they are. A fading green suspension bridge connects the two. Scotia has the giant old mill, a logging museum (open seasonally), a hulking water-storage facility, and a historic hotel. Stop for a cold drink before the last leg of today's journey, 15 miles on the venerated Avenue of the Giants.

A 31-mile stretch of old US 101, this shady two-lane road meanders among the massive redwoods along the Eel River, which is visible at spots. Enter after a climb from Scotia, then pedal through the hushed landscape, enjoying its cool shadiness and the relaxed attitude of many drivers using the road. Those in a hurry seem to stick to the main highway, audible through the trees but mostly out of sight.

"Our best advice is to go slow!" says Alexandra Sawyer, who bicycled with a friend from Seattle all the way to Central America in 2014. "The redwoods are perfect from the seat of a bicycle."

Redcrest, 9 miles from tonight's campground, is the provisioning stop, at 53 miles. The Lost Coast alternate route rejoins the main route via Bull Creek Flats Road at 59 miles. Just beyond that intersection, after a crossing of the Eel River, you'll find the Founders Grove, a worthy stop. Here lies the Dyerville Giant, thought to be the record-setting redwood at 362 feet when it stood. Now spread across the forest, its 17-foot-diameter logs nurse an entire forest ecosystem themselves. A short paved side trail and restrooms make this an easy detour.

Finally, after crossing over US 101 and skirting the edge of tiny Weott, arrive at Burlington Campground, adjacent to the Humboldt Redwoods State Park headquarters and the park's visitors center. Sheltered campsites blanketed in soft redwood duff await weary cyclists. Enjoy an evening under the trees, but know that it's not over yet: the south half of the forest, and another grove farther down the road, await on tomorrow's ride.

MILEAGE LOG

0.0 Depart Redwood Coast Cabins and RV Resort on service road, turning left onto US 101.

4.0 Right onto V St. into Eureka.

4.1 Left onto 3rd St.

4.2 Right onto T St.

4.4 Left onto Waterfront Dr.

4.8 Left onto L St.; in ½ block, right onto 2nd St.

5.1 Right onto C St.; in 1 block, left on Waterfront Dr., which becomes Railroad Ave.

6.6 Left onto 14th St.

6.9 Cross US 101.

7.0 Right onto Union St.

7.9 Right onto W. Henderson St.

8.2 Left onto Fairfield St., which becomes Glen St.

8.6 Right onto Highland Ave. In 1 block, left onto High St.

8.8 Right onto McCullen Ave.

9.2 Left onto US 101.

14.1 Right at exit 698, Tompkins Hill Rd., then left under freeway and right onto Tompkins Hill Rd.

14.7 Pass Humboldt Botanical Garden and College of the Redwoods.

17.1 Right onto Hookton Rd.

17.2 Curve right past northbound US 101 sign and go over freeway. Follow US 101 south sign.

17.6 Straight through stop sign at freeway entrance onto Eel River Dr.

19.8 Enter Loleta.

21.8 Right onto unsigned Fernbridge Dr. (SR 211) as Eel River Dr. ends at highway off-ramp. Follow signs to Ferndale.

22.5 Right at Fernbridge commercial center and Humboldt River Creamery. Cross Eel River Bridge in vehicle lane.

26.1 Enter Ferndale. Road becomes Main St.

27.3 Left onto Bluff St., which becomes Grizzly Bluff Rd. (Right onto Ocean Ave. for Lost Coast alternate route.)

34.1 Forward as Grizzly Bluff becomes Blue Slide Rd., then Belleview Ave.

38.6 Enter Rio Dell.

39.6 Right onto Wildwood Ave. at intersection with US 101.

40.5 Cross Rio Dell Bridge into Scotia.

40.7 Continue forward on Main St., past on-ramp to US 101.

41.2 Curve left to stay on Main St.

42.5 Left, then immediate right at S. Scotia Rd. onto US 101.

44.3 Cross Eel River.

46.4 Right at exit 674, Avenue of the Giants.

46.5 Left under US 101 at end of ramp and forward onto Avenue of the Giants.

49.2 Pass Pepperwood town site.

53.2 Arrive at Redcrest.

57.5 Left at junction with Bull Creek Flats Rd. (Lost Coast alternate route joins main route here), US 101, and South Fork Eel River; follow signs for Avenue of the Giants over South Fork Eel River Bridge.

57.7 Pass Founders Grove.

58.3 Forward as road crosses over US 101.

59.8 Pass Weott.

61.8 Left into Burlington Campground.

ALTERNATE ROUTE: THE LOST COAST
Distance: 70.1 miles
Elevation gain: 8110 feet

Want to test yourself and get away from it all? "The Lost Coast is an incredible little detour for people who are looking for a challenging ride about halfway through," says Carl Chauvin of Toronto, met during a summer 2016 trip. He cites "incredible vistas, desolate coasts, and very few cars" as the high points. "You really get a day kind of wandering along by yourself with not much else."

Your only companion might be the weather. The hilly, wooded area is the wettest on the California coast, getting more than 100 inches of rain a year in some spots. Be prepared for rain and also for the lack of services or even much civilization along this wild route. Make sure you're well supplied with food and water.

The 70-mile route charted here begins at Ferndale and ends at Burlington. So instead of riding through Rio Dell, Scotia, and the first 10 miles of the Avenue of the Giants, you loop west and south on an extremely hilly road that adds almost 40 miles to the route. This might be accomplished in one long day, making the Eureka-to-Burlington ride nearly 100 miles, or you can split it into two days, as there is a comfortable campground at 35 miles after Ferndale. That would make it about a 60-mile day from Eureka, followed by a 35-mile day to reach Burlington. There is an advantage to the two-day strategy: you split the route's two most massive climbs so you tackle one each day.

The Lost Coast route is a single, winding road with not many distractions. An immediate climb out of Ferndale on what's initially a one-lane road gives you a taste for the experience. The road widens, but the climbs do not relent until you reach 1800 feet above sea level, from a start at Ferndale of about 200 feet. At 6 miles the first sense of achievement kicks in, as the road levels and the view opens to vistas of the King Range all the way to the Lost Coast. The route continues to tantalize with such views until dropping into a ravine at the Bear River, which requires another significant climb out on the other side.

Then you are on the Lost Coast itself, which the *Los Angeles Times* called "the wildest coast in California." Cycle with the bluffs and the ocean in view for a time before climbing to Petrolia, one of two towns on the road, at 28

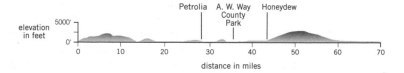

elevation in feet

Sweeping ocean views from Mattole Road

miles. Note: In Petrolia, you'll see a sign advertising camping. This refers to the Punta Gorda Recreation Area, at the coast 4.5 miles west of town.

If Petrolia's name sounds evocative, perhaps it's because this is where the first producing oil well was drilled in California, in 1865. The oil has been long gone, but you can fuel up at the small store here, then climb to depart. As you leave town, a handmade sign urges "don't give up." The road jumps over the Mattole River before passing A. W. Way County Park at 35 miles, which offers the area's campground. It is well appointed and includes showers.

"Road conditions can deteriorate from heavy rains, so confirm conditions locally before choosing this option," advises ACA map 3. They are probably referring to the gravel stretches, some of which are on a steep climb that greets you shortly as you depart the campground. There is a bit of river valley riding to start the day first, however, as you follow the Upper North Fork Mattole River to Honeydew, the area's other burg, which has a small store at 43 miles. From there, you'll climb 2400 feet in about 8 miles.

At nearly 52 miles from Ferndale, after countless switchbacks, the last and largest climb on the route tops out at 2700 feet and you begin a precarious downhill through Humboldt Redwoods State Park. It is tricky because the road is quite potholed and bumpy. The impacts are also hard on a cyclist's hands and wrists. Make sure all gear is securely fastened before you tackle this section, as you don't want to have to retrace uphill to fetch it.

The potholes continue even after the route flattens out when the road becomes Bull Creek Flats Road. The last section finds you snaking between giant redwoods (quickly visit the short Rockefeller Loop for a close-up look) on a quiet, flat stretch that connects to Avenue of the Giants just south of

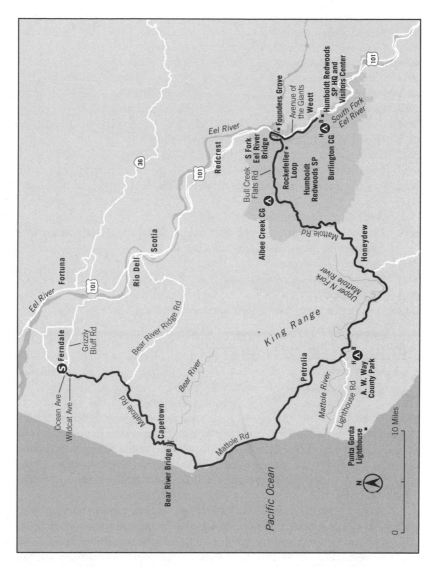

Redcrest. From there it's a few miles to the Burlington Campground, where you can celebrate your achievement of getting lost and then finding the main route again.

MILEAGE LOG

0.0   At Main St. and Bluff St. in Ferndale, right onto Ocean Ave. In 1 block, at big sign to Petrolia, left onto Wildcat Ave., which becomes Mattole Rd.

6.2   Pass Bear River Ridge Rd.

13.9   Pass Capetown.

14.3   Cross Bear River Bridge.

17.8   Road drops to coastline.

24.4   Road departs coast.

28.3   Enter Petrolia.

29.8   Pass Lighthouse Rd.

34.3   Cross Mattole River.

35.5   Arrive at A. W. Way County Park (camping, restrooms).

43.5   Left to stay on Mattole Rd. at Honeydew.

51.7   Enter Humboldt Redwoods State Park.

60.0   Forward as Mattole becomes Bull Creek Flats Rd.

61.0   Pass Albee Creek Campground.

64.5   Pass side road to Rockefeller Loop.

65.9   Right onto Avenue of the Giants after crossing under US 101. Follow signs for Avenue of the Giants over South Fork Eel River Bridge.

66.1   Pass Founders Grove.

66.6   Road curves and crosses over US 101.

68.1   Arrive at Weott.

70.1   Left into Burlington Campground to rejoin main route.

BURLINGTON TO LEGGETT
Distance: 47.4 miles
Elevation gain: 3680 feet

"This is why you would come here," explains Salinas teacher Phillip Deutschle. "This" is the Avenue of the Giants, of course, which comprises the first third, and the best, of today's ride. For 16 more miles you get to blissfully enjoy the pace of a side road flanked by grand trees that mesmerize all who travel through them. Thank the redwoods for your relative comfort on the edge of the road.

"Bicycling through the trees is different than walking through them," says Phillip, on a summer break from teaching physics and astronomy. "Certainly, driving you don't get a feel for it." But he doesn't begrudge the drivers and says the trees have a great effect on them too. "They're a lot more respectful, not pushing you on the bicycle. On a bridge, I just had one wait and let me have the lane."

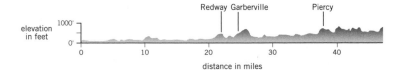

A giant stump from an ancient tree was made into a "shoe house" at the kitschy Confusion Hill attraction.

That's not to say that you won't still encounter challenges. Avenue of the Giants has scant shoulder, and it is a favorite of RV travelers. At points, those land yachts can be too close to be comfortable. But since the road roughly parallels US Highway 101, the faster traffic and certainly all the large commercial vehicles stick to that. My strategy if caught in a gaggle of Winnebagos is to occasionally take shelter in the trees by pulling off at one of the turnouts, stepping off the bike, and hugging a redwood while the traffic streams past.

This south section of the Avenue is, unfortunately, less awe-inspiring than its northern half. The groves are more spread out, the trees are a bit smaller, and there are fewer roadside turnouts. In a couple of spots, the view opens up to the Eel River below and wooded hills beyond.

Less than 4 miles from camp is Myers Flat, not too far to actually delay breakfast until you're here, as the flat start won't have you burning too many calories. A coffee-and-pastry shop sits next to a grocery. Six miles farther along, at Miranda, find a larger market after the day's first climb.

Reluctantly departing the Avenue means hopping onto US 101, where a generous shoulder is a worthy trade-off for loud, fast traffic. You'll spend the next two dozen miles jumping on and off the highway, taking short side-road detours through small towns. It's a relief to merge onto a quieter road, but a bit disconcerting to have to just get back on, over and over. Of course, you could just stay on the highway the entire route, but really, where's the fun in that?

Make another game out of choosing your lunch spot. Redway is first up, but a few more miles down the road is Garberville, which has a nicer luncheon atmosphere. Still farther on is Richardson Grove State Park, where you are back in the beloved redwoods for a bit and a picnic lunch could be had. A fourth option is Grandfather Tree, which is more than halfway through

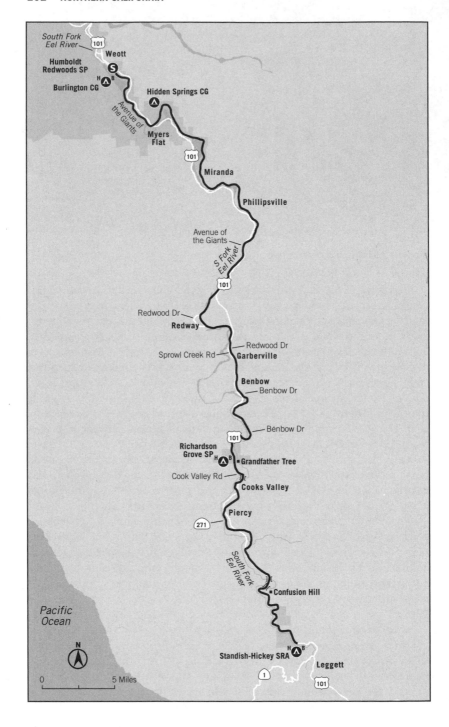

today's route but has a cute touristy vibe, with a café, an espresso stand, gift shops, and curiosities.

The tree is certainly amazing. Grandfather Tree stands 245 feet tall and is 24 feet in diameter, 55 feet in circumference. The giant is estimated to be 1800 years old. Lunching under its canopy, you can't help but consider the changes to the world that have happened during that tree's lifetime, fully a third of human history.

A gift shop, snack bar, and chainsaw carvings huddle in the shade of the ancient fellow and its neighbor, the self-explanatory One Log House. A few miles back is the Legend of Bigfoot attraction, which displays some amazing carvings. Decide for yourself which brings the wow: natural or human-made marvels.

After the lush cover of the redwoods, there is a lot of exposed riding on this leg, especially taxing on a warm afternoon. There is also a steady, inexorable climb through the last half of the ride, punctuated by a couple of steep ascents after the road inevitably drops to the South Fork Eel River in two spots. But the gradually rising elevation is a blessing, because it is preparing your legs for a big challenge tomorrow, the vaunted Leggett road, much discussed by trepidatious cyclists up and down the coast (fueled by the Adventure Cycling Association map's elevation profile that shows it spiking far above everything else). Today's ride gets you halfway up that stalagmite! It's some comfort as you rejoin the highway for the last time at Piercy and wind your way 6 miles along the narrow, snaking road.

One final attraction awaits, just a couple of miles from tonight's camp. Confusion Hill is an old-time family attraction, sort of a wooded carnival, with a miniature train that takes tourists among the grove at Smithe Redwoods State Natural Reserve. There's a giant shoe house carved from a tree stump and, speaking of carving, the believe-it-or-not largest-ever chainsaw-carved totem pole. You'll also find a well-stocked gift shop with restorative ice cream that should get you up the final winding stretch of climbing for the final miles to Standish-Hickey State Recreation Area, tonight's campground. Don't miss it!

Speaking of missing things, the final approach to Standish-Hickey also includes a welcome sight: the Peg House, a well-stocked grocery-deli that sits opposite the campground entrance. It includes outdoor café seating and a unique slogan that lives up to its neighboring attractions: "Never don't stop." Heed that advice as you provision for the night, or start there with a big breakfast burrito on your way to the Leggett climb tomorrow morning. A centrally located hiker-biker camp awaits, and if there's energy and daylight enough, a hike down to the river provides a cooling swim.

MILEAGE LOG

0.0   Depart Burlington Campground, turning left onto Avenue of the Giants.

3.8   Pass Myers Flat.

4.3   Forward under US 101 to continue on Avenue of the Giants.

5.0   Pass Hidden Springs Campground.

10.0   Pass Miranda.

13.9   Pass Phillipsville.

16.6   Forward under US 101, then merge onto it.

19.9   Depart US 101 at exit 642 to Redway.

20.1   Forward onto Redwood Dr. at exit.

21.6   Enter Redway.

24.4   Cross over US 101, then enter Garberville.

24.6   Right onto Sprowl Creek Rd.; follow signs for US 101.

24.7   Left onto US 101 after crossing over it.

27.2   Depart US 101 at exit 636; go left under freeway.

27.4   Left onto Benbow Dr.

31.4   Left at stop sign onto US 101 as Benbow ends.

32.5   Pass Richardson Grove State Park (camping).

33.5   Pass Grandfather Tree attraction.

34.2   Right onto Cook Valley Rd. (SR 271).

34.5   Cross bridge over Eel River.

37.6   Keep left at intersection with County Rd. at Piercy; pass under US 101 to stay on SR 271.

37.8   Cross off-ramp after going under US 101, then curve right to stay on SR 271.

40.1   Cross over US 101, then turn left onto it.

41.6   Freeway ends, becomes two-lane road.

41.7   Cross bridge over South Fork Eel River in bike lane.

42.1   Cross second bridge, also in bike lane.

42.4   Pass Confusion Hill attraction.

47.4   Arrive at Standish-Hickey State Recreation Area.

LEGGETT TO FORT BRAGG
Distance: 41.8 miles
Elevation gain: 3500 feet

Okay, it's a fairly relentless climb. Once you depart US Highway 101 at just over 1.5 miles from the campground, be ready for a steady uphill pedal for the next 5 miles. But think of the Leggett climb this way: it's like the best gym workout you've ever had. Or consider this: once you've done it, you have tackled the largest climb on the entire California coast tour. And a third thought: it's not as difficult as your imagination makes it out to be.

My first trek up this winding road lined with craggy rock walls, I rode with Chris, who took a decidedly relaxed approach to bicycle touring. The California native personified the state's laid-back attitude. He was riding a

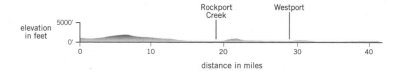

comfortable hybrid bike, barely set up for touring. His trip combined back-packing and cycling, so his bulky gear was crammed into back-wheel pan-niers and a backpack strapped to his rack. He was riding with flat pedals, wearing tennis shoes, regular shorts, and no bike gloves. His helmet wavered on his head like a bobblehead on a car dashboard. We had met on the route the previous day and decided to ride today's climb together. We talked about the hill, reviewed the map, obsessed on it a little too much. I upped my water intake and resolved to fuel up with a good breakfast before taking off. I don't know how Chris slept, but I tossed and turned in my sleeping bag.

By midmorning, well into the climb, we both were sweating but were much calmed down. We had mentally built the climb into a mountain that we'd need oxygen and Sherpas to scale. Truth: it is a steady grade, at times pitching steep, but at some points flattening out so a cyclist can easily stop, lean the bike on a guardrail, take a rest, and begin pedaling again without stress. In other words, it is not Everest. It is not even a mountain pass, which can be a relentless, grueling grade stretched over many more miles.

Along with the short, steep sections, the greatest challenge on this climb and the opposite descent is the vehicle traffic. The road is scarcely two car-widths wide, so meeting a large vehicle or having one pass you can be

PROTECTING THE PLOVERS

Ten Mile Dunes Nature Preserve on the north edge of MacKerricher State Park is special. It contains Inglenook Fen, which nurtures a diminutive but valued bird.

A fen has characteristics of a bog and a marsh, being a wet environment that prevents flooding and provides wildlife habitat. The dunes of Inglenook, the only known remaining fen on the California coast, are the winter home to many breeding pairs of the western snowy plover, a threatened sparrow-size shorebird.

At many parks along the coast, you will see signage indicating protected snowy plover nesting grounds, and with good reason: there are only an estimated 2100 adult breeding plovers in the world. Walk on the beach rather than through the dunes to give these rare little birds a fighting chance. Learn more: www.westernsnowyplover.org.

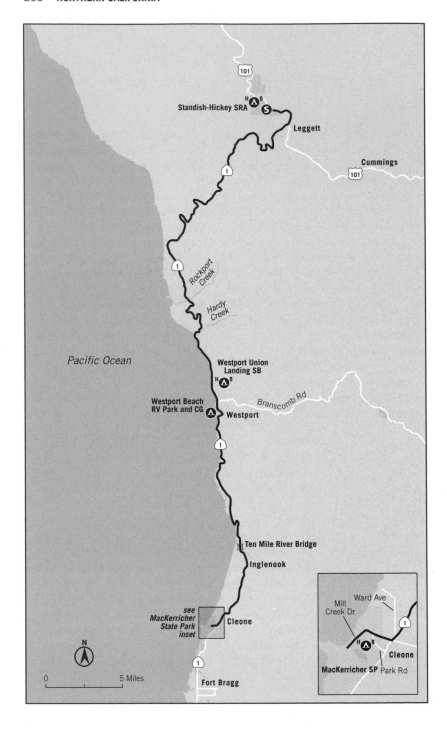

Pacific Ocean

Standish-Hickey SRA

Leggett

Cummings

Rockport Creek

Hardy Creek

Westport Union Landing SB

Westport Beach RV Park and CG

Westport

Ten Mile River Bridge

Inglenook

Branscomb Rd

see MacKerricher State Park inset

Cleone

N

0   5 Miles

Fort Bragg

Mill Creek Dr

Ward Ave

MacKerricher SP Park Rd

Cleone

Flowering pampas grass provides a wispy foreground in late summer along California's central coast.

unnerving. You likely will encounter an oncoming logging truck or RV, but there is enough space for those vehicles to stay in their own lane on an outside curve. A few cars will come and go. By starting early in the day, we avoided much of the traffic and saw only a handful of vehicles each way. And those vehicles, due to the winding nature of the road, were mostly moving at slow speeds, 25 to 35 miles per hour.

This is not to say that you shouldn't prepare for this climb and all the other significant climbs and distances ridden on the Pacific Coast route. A bit of obsession stiffens the resolve and urges a cyclist beyond normal routine to take practical measures such as properly hydrating and eating in advance of tackling a difficult challenge. So prepare, worry a little, but know that Leggett is surmountable.

And for the screaming downhill on the other side, salt air stinging your nose as your eyes drink in the glittering ocean, make sure you have prepared your bike with adequate brake pads. Worn out or maladjusted brakes are the most significant danger on this stretch.

Once you are along the coast on California State Route 1, here called the Shoreline Highway, enjoy a nice lunch at Westport's grocery-deli. A bit more climbing and some rollers take you through dusty foothills with coastal glimpses. The edge of MacKerricher State Park begins just beyond the excellent new bridge over Ten Mile River, a bird-filled estuary. More birding awaits at Cleone Lake, in the park adjacent to the campground. The park also offers whale watching in spring, seals perched on the rocks, and exploration of teeming tide pools.

As you approach the park entrance, a bike route sign offering a "scenic alternate" would take you down to the Old Haul Road in the park that runs parallel to the sea edge. But a few more pedal strokes deliver you to the official park entrance. The rest of the Haul Road, a 3-mile ride into the town of Fort Bragg, is on tomorrow's route. And after this relatively short but challenging ride, you may want to continue into town for provisions before settling down in camp or visiting the beach for a well-deserved Pacific Coast sunset.

MILEAGE LOG

0.0   Depart Standish-Hickey State Recreation Area campground, turning right onto US 101 S.

1.6   Right onto SR 1 at Leggett.

7.0   Reach peak of climb at 1900 feet elevation.

15.9   Highway turns south and flattens.

19.3   Pass Rockport Creek; climb begins.

21.5   Reach peak of climb at 775 feet.

23.3   Pass beach parking area at Hardy Creek.

25.8   Pass Westport Union Landing State Beach (restrooms, camping).

27.5   Pass Branscomb Rd.

28.2   Pass Westport Beach RV Park and Campground.

29.1   Pass Westport grocery.

36.7   Cross Ten Mile River.

36.8   Pass MacKerricher State Park north section, on right.

38.2   Pass Inglenook.

40.8   Enter Cleone.

41.1   Pass Ward Ave.

41.5   Pass Mill Creek Dr. (scenic alternate route to campground).

41.8   Right onto MacKerricher State Park Rd. to campground.

FORT BRAGG TO GUALALA
Distance: 64.9 miles
Elevation gain: 4670 feet

Today is a day of rollers. California State Route 1 provides close to two dozen rolling climbs, along with a few major ascents, after dropping down to sea level to cross one of the many rivers or streams that empty into the Pacific. And with a significant distance to cover today, short stops are best in the handful of cute small towns encountered along the way.

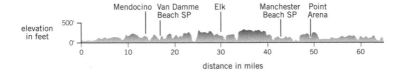

FROM DELHI TO THE REDWOODS

You see a lot of small groups cycling the Pacific Coast, but if you're on the Northern California route in June, an unusual sight might top the hill: kid after kid after kid pedaling in a long line, dark-skinned and eyes sparkling from the

adventure. That would be the Inme group, and they are from India.

Each summer, the experiential learning organization Inme (short for "infinite me") takes a varied group of kids up to age 18 on adventure experiences, of which the Great American Bicycle Ride is one of the most adventurous.

"It's been exhilarating," says high schooler Abhip (right in photo), from Noira, a city close to Delhi. The summer 2016 trip—the only Inme expedition outside of India—was his first to the United States, but his fourth camp with Inme. "I was getting prepared from the other camps for this camp," he says.

His challenges: uphill climbs, daily distances up to 50 miles, and ending each day camping under whatever conditions. In camp, the kids set up their own tents and have group chores. "However, when you look at where the challenge is placed, with the ocean right beside you and all the wonderful people to meet, it just keeps motivating you," he says. "It doesn't feel like a challenge anymore, it's more like fun."

The Seattle-to–San Francisco route, accomplished in June, can offer sketchy weather conditions. "We've ridden in the rain," he says, warming to his topic like a comedian. "We've slept in the rain. We've pitched tents in the rain, we've cooked in the rain. We've done everything in the rain."

As we talked under a bright sun, it was evident that the rain didn't dampen enthusiasm. "I've been to many mountain ranges," he says, "but if I look there it's all mountains, and if I look there it's the ocean. And then such a clear sky! All these three things coming together when you're biking, it's just something else."

The kids carefully stowed the remains of their snacks in a box on the support pickup's tailgate as their six adult instructors urged them back to their bikes. Abhip shook my hand and offered one piece of advice: "Keep going. There are moments where you feel like stopping. If you keep going in a rhythm, you'll have all these people to motivate you and the scenic beauty to motivate you. Just keep going." Learn more: www.inme.in.

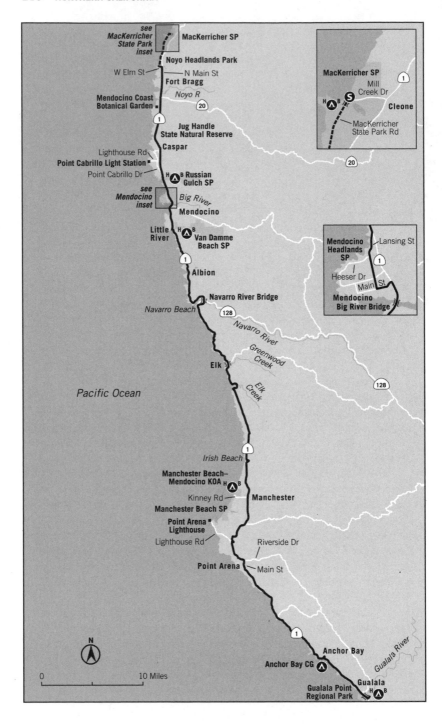

Ninety-nine percent of today's ride is on SR 1, but start with a quiet pedal from the campground into Fort Bragg. The old road, which is open only to pedestrians and bikes, is sandy and potholed in spots, but a welcome alternative.

The road from the campground to town won't be affected, but north of the camping area, the road is being removed along with invasive plants to restore the dunes along the Ten Mile River within MacKerricher State Park. The purpose is to preserve the only coastal fen left in California and one of the few relatively pristine sets of dunes on its coast. The marshy area, frequently flooded, provides a unique wildlife habitat, home to some of the endangered snowy plovers (see sidebar). You will see many signs along the coast alerting visitors to snowy plover protected areas and nesting grounds.

Mendocino wins the popularity contest among today's small towns. But first you'll pass a notable coastal site. The Point Cabrillo Light Station, a working lighthouse, is picturesque with its white stone buildings and red roofs. But trekking 2 miles each way off the route to see it is a task mostly for true lighthouse nerds. However, if you happen by in March, make the effort. Its bluffs provide a superior vantage point to spy gray whales as they migrate north from Baja California lagoons to their summer feeding grounds in Arctic waters.

At 15 miles into the ride, Mendocino is too early for a lunch stop. Veer off the ACA route to bike through town, a detour that adds neither mileage nor elevation. Before the village center, a quarter-mile side trip takes you to an incredible overlook at Mendocino Headlands State Park. The town is filled with well-kept Victorian homes. A few blocks of Main Street shops overlook the headlands. An expansive gourmet coffee shop beckons just prior to the Main Street turn.

The road south continues to offer views of sea stacks and archways below the tabletop bluffs. As you pass the Navarro River watershed, admire twin shark-fin rock formations rising from a classic bay, then cycle along the river a bit to a bridge crossing at SR 128 to remain on the SR 1 route. Elk, a tiny burg exactly halfway down today's route, offers an ideal lunch spot: a grocery-deli sits roadside across from a petite park with benches, shade, and a view of massive Wharf Rock rising from Greenwood Cove.

A switchback-laden climb follows after a comfortable new bridge, carrying you up to a flat inland ride into Manchester, on a dry prairie with hills to the east. Manchester Beach State Park occupies large ocean frontage nearly to the town of Point Arena. Although Manchester's campground was closed in recent years with no announced plans to reopen, if you want to end the day here, a well-appointed KOA sits in the park across the road from the campground entrance. It offers reasonable rates to cyclists.

The landscape moves from arid to green approaching Point Arena, a notable farming area. The town of Point Arena offers a cute commercial strip

Sea stacks along State Route 1

and a worthy place to stop for afternoon refreshments before making the final push to the campground, 15 more miles that include a couple more significant climbs.

On the way to Gualala, pass through Anchor Bay at the top of a curving climb just above a private campground nestled at the base of the small bay. A well-stocked grocery sits roadside, but supplies are also available in the town of Gualala, 4 miles ahead. Beyond that town, and of course at the top of the hill, is the entrance to Gualala Point Regional Park, whose campground is home for the night. The campground road loops down to the waters of Gualala Bay, waiting for sweaty cyclists who've just completed a challenging day to jump in.

MILEAGE LOG

0.0 Depart MacKerricher State Park campground loop, turning left onto MacKerricher State Park Rd., then left again onto Mill Creek Dr.

0.3 Bear left onto Old Haul Rd.

0.4 Bear right at T in road under overpass, then immediately left onto trail at the bollards.

2.8 Cross Pudding Creek on bridge, then rejoin trail in parking lot.

3.3 Left onto W. Elm St. at intersection with Noyo Headlands Park.

3.5 Right onto SR 1, signed as N. Main St. in Fort Bragg.

5.2 Cross Noyo River Bridge.

5.7 Pass intersection with SR 20.

6.2 Forward at roundabout at Old Coast Hwy. to continue on SR 1.

6.5 Pass Mendocino Coast Botanical Garden.

8.7 Pass Jug Handle State Natural Reserve.

9.6 Pass Caspar.

11.9 Pass Brest Rd. (detour west to Point Cabrillo Light Station, east to Russian Gulch State Park and hiker-biker camping).

12.9 Right onto Lansing St. to enter Mendocino.

13.3 Pass Heeser Dr. (detour to Mendocino Headlands State Park).

13.7 Arrive at Mendocino town center.

13.9 Curve left onto Main St. as Lansing St. ends.

14.2 Right onto SR 1.

14.5 Cross Big River Bridge.

16.6 Cross Little River.

16.7 Pass Van Damme Beach State Park (camping).

20.6 Enter Albion.

24.4 Left onto Navarro River Bridge at intersection with SR 128. Stay on SR 1.

29.9 Enter Elk.

33.2 Cross Greenwood Creek.

39.5 Pass Irish Beach.

42.7 Pass Kinney Rd. (detour in 0.5 mile to Manchester Beach State Park, Manchester Beach–Mendocino KOA).

43.4 Pass Manchester.

47.0 Pass Point Arena lighthouse road.

48.6 Enter Point Arena.

48.8 Curve left onto Main St. at Riverside Dr. to stay on SR 1.

59.3 Pass Anchor Bay Campground.

59.5 Enter Anchor Bay.

62.3 Enter Gualala.

63.9 Cross Gualala River Bridge.

64.3 Left into Gualala Point Regional Park.

64.9 Enter campground.

GUALALA TO BODEGA BAY
Distance: 46.3 miles
Elevation gain: 3420 feet

You might not think of California as having a Russian influence, but evidence of early Russian settlements can be found on this leg of the route. You'll skim over Russian Gulch Creek, traverse a bridge at the mouth of the Russian River, and pass by a historic Russian colony.

But first, if you greet the morning at the day-use section of Gualala Point Regional Park, stop to appreciate the Russian-inspired posts set into the grounds overlooking Gualala Point. These are *serges*, ceremonial hitching

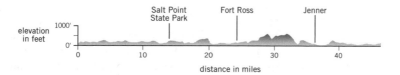

The Sea Ranch Chapel

posts created by master carvers from Siberia's Sakha Republic, whose ancestors came to this part of California with the Fort Ross settlement. Erected in 2014, the towering carvings aim to cast a blessing on their people to survive the elements; may that spirit extend to you as you visit them.

When planning for today's ride, ensure you're well supplied with food and drink, because you're greeted by long stretches of open road with few services. The first stop, one without amenities, is Sea Ranch Chapel, visible on the edge of a slight valley less than 3 miles from your start. Evoking shapes of waves or flames, the unusual chapel was a crowning creation of San Diego artist and architectural designer James Hubbell. It uses native redwood and local stone. The nondenominational chapel, just a quarter mile from the road, is well worth a brief visit.

You're riding through the expansive development of Sea Ranch, begun by architects wanting a luxurious planned community of secluded homes on the coast. Aside from views of the closest estates and the ever-present ocean, the area holds little for the cycling tourist, although a nice restaurant at its well-appointed lodge at 8 miles might be visited for coffee and a small store is roadside at 10 miles.

While the first 20 miles of today's ride present only a moderate elevation challenge at Salt Point State Park, getting to Fort Ross requires effort. Not only is it a significant climb, but it sits on an exposed, rocky stretch of road high above the sea with a sustained grade. It can be baking hot and windy, or cold and clammy with fog (requiring extreme care). The road has no shoulder, and cattle guards are set into the pavement for a section of open range. The former Russian colony now known as Fort Ross might entail a more extensive visit midpoint on today's ride. Named after an alternative spelling of the country, "Rossiia," the enclave sits high on a grassland shelf overlooking a sheltered cove below craggy bluffs hundreds of feet high.

Founded by the Russian-American Company in 1812, this was originally a pelt-trading outpost, but the expansive site, which includes coastal prairie as well as forested hills, was also used to grow wheat that was shipped to Russians living in Alaska. It represents the southernmost point of Russian settlement in North America. In its 30-year heyday up to 1841, the compound hosted a multicultural community of Russians, Siberians, Alaskans, Hawaiians, Native Americans, and people of mixed European descent.

Much of the initial encampment is gone, but the remaining original building was the home of the company's last onsite manager, and other buildings of the era have been re-created. The distinctive double towers of the chapel and weathered-wood tops of other buildings are visible from the road, and a Russian cemetery, with Orthodox crosses that include three horizontal crossbeams (one placed diagonally), is accessible roadside.

A second climb comes after the fort, but the road there mercifully includes a shoulder. After two hours of serious climbing, enjoy the sweeping vistas down into Russian Gulch from the fort property's southern border, before the road delightfully aims you back toward the coast.

"Every so often there's a little special moment," recalls Tom Hickish, from London. As we rested our bikes and lunched in the shadow of one of the many coastal lighthouses, he described one of his favorites. "When Highway 1 drops down into Jenner and you do all that twisting and there are no barriers. And you top this hill, and you see this beautiful little town, Jenner . . . that was a special day."

A series of rolling hills delivers you into the sea-level seaside burg of Jenner, then to the Russian River at State Route 116. Here, you could detour up the river valley for a wonderful wine country visit (see Side Trip: Russian River Wine Country). The main route crosses the river, then there's one last climb in Sonoma Coast State Park before a flat, 5-mile spin into Bodega Dunes Campground. The well-supplied village of Bodega Bay is a half mile on.

MILEAGE LOG

0.0   Depart Gualala Point Regional Park campground, turning right onto access road.

0.6   Left onto SR 1.

2.7   Pass Sea Ranch Chapel.

7.7   Pass Sea Ranch Lodge.

10.1 Pass Stewarts Point.

14.0 Enter Salt Point State Park.

15.4 Pass Fisk Mill Cove.

17.3 Pass Stump Beach Cove access.

18.1 Pass Salt Point campgrounds.

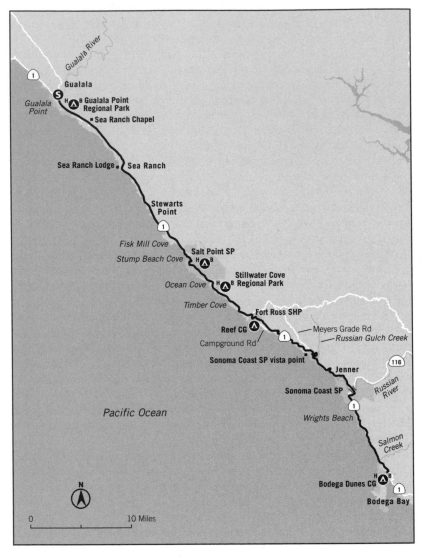

20.3 Pass Ocean Cove grocery-café.

21.4 Pass Stillwater Cove Regional Park (camping).

22.9 Pass Timber Cove.

23.8 Enter Fort Ross State Historic Park.

26.6 Pass Reef Campground.

31.4 Pass Meyers Grade Rd.

31.4 Pass Vista Rd. to Sonoma Coast State Park vista point.

33.6 Cross Russian Gulch Creek.

35.8 Enter Jenner.

36.8 Pass Jenner town center.

37.9 Right at intersection with SR 116 to Guerneville (detour left for Russian River Wine Country side trip); continue on SR 1 to Bodega Bay.

38.1 Cross Russian River Bridge.

38.9 Pass Goat Rock Rd. to Sonoma Coast State Park.

41.2 Pass Wrights Beach.

45.5 Cross Salmon Creek.

46.3 Arrive at Bodega Dunes Campground.

SIDE TRIP: RUSSIAN RIVER WINE COUNTRY
Distance: 45.7 miles roundtrip from Guerneville
Elevation gain: 1620 feet

If you'd like to see a little of the Northern California wine country, a one-day detour from the main coastal route makes it pretty easy. Here's what you do:

1. Depart from the coast route at Jenner on the Gualala–Bodega Bay segment. Ride to Guerneville instead of Bodega Bay. This creates a 50-mile day instead of a 46-mile day, but 200 feet less in elevation gain.

2. Do the prescribed side-trip loop ride the next day to Healdsburg and back to Guerneville, a mellow 46-mile spin.

3. After the Healdsburg loop, continue on to Bodega Bay, which makes that ride a 66-mile day with 2685 feet of elevation gain. This is a less attractive choice if you want to linger and enjoy the wine country.

(As a more relaxing alternative, you could ride from Guerneville to Lagunitas the next day. This replaces the main route's Bodega Bay–Lagunitas segment. This would be a 51-mile ride with 2482 feet elevation gain rather than 42 miles with 2258 feet elevation gain. It skips a slight bit of the coast but includes the best part of that day's ride, along Tomales Bay. This route is not charted with turn-by-turn directions.)

The Russian River area is worth a look. Not as famous as its cousins to the southeast—Napa and Sonoma valleys—this northwestern Sonoma County area actually encompasses three wine-growing appellations: Russian River Valley, Dry Creek Valley, and Alexander Valley. This route goes through the first two and offers a suggestion for extending your trip by taking another day in Alexander Valley.

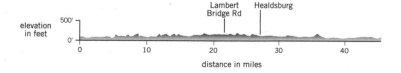

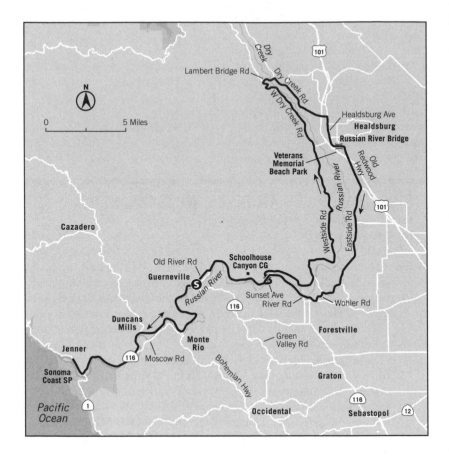

The Russian is the major river running through these valleys, roughly paralleling US Highway 101 until it veers west at Healdsburg. There are plentiful small creeks coming into the valleys from the Mayacamas Mountains to the east. But it can be a warm, dry place with cool nights and even coastal fog. Grapes love it.

The road inland from Jenner, State Route 116, runs along the river. It's 11.5 miles to Guerneville with very little elevation gain. The major challenge is the lack of shoulder, but the winding road keeps traffic speeds down. Ease the stress by crossing the river at Duncan Mills at 3.6 miles and using Moscow Road, which parallels the river, up to Monte Rio. Cross back over the river at 7 miles and rejoin SR 116.

Using Guerneville as a home base has its benefits. The town is well stocked with stores and cafés for supplies and refreshments. A number of private campgrounds dot the area, mostly along the river. While they don't offer hiker-biker rates, the tent rates are still modest. Many of them have river access, so you can swim or float in an inner tube at the end of a long cycling day. There are expensive inns and lodges as well, should you want to splurge. Johnsons Beach, River Bend, and Schoolhouse Canyon are three popular Guerneville-area campgrounds that would very likely need advance booking.

Heading northeast along the river, your first winery encounter is Korbel, just 3 miles from town. Their sparkling wine is legendary, and their tasting room contains a well-appointed deli. Here you are riding on River Road, which can be a fast, busy highway. (The first section, SR 116 from Jenner nearly to Guerneville, has sporadic shoulders, but here and farther inland the route's shoulders are consistent and generous.)

Depart the highway at 5 miles, though, and you're on lesser-used Westside Road to Healdsburg. Local cyclists are abundant. The river turns here and runs parallel to Westside, so views include verdant valleys as well as rows of grapevines marching up the hills.

At 17 miles you are parallel to central Healdsburg, but continue north into the Dry Creek Valley for more expansive river views, a plethora of wineries, and a stop at the revered Dry Creek General Store. At the route's northern terminus at 23 miles, the store is a welcome coffee or lunch stop, sporting a gourmet deli and plentiful outdoor seating. Rack your bike with the locals' sleek road bikes and at least enjoy an espresso.

In 5 more miles, arrive at central Healdsburg, where it's time to park the bike and walk the streets. Wine-tasting rooms and tony shops line the shady town square. Lunch choices are abundant, or pack a picnic and stop at Veterans Memorial Beach Park, just beyond the Russian River Bridge on the way out of town.

(Note: To enjoy an extra day in the area, extend your trip by cycling into the Alexander Valley east of Healdsburg. The Alexander Valley RV Park and Campground on Alexander Valley Road near Jimtown offers tent camping, as does the Liberty Glen Campground at Lake Sonoma, which is a number of miles northwest of the Dry Creek Valley, closer to Geyserville.)

Return to Guerneville via Eastside Road, where the wineries are fewer and the land tends more to farming. Abundant small lakes and ponds make this area greener. Pick up busy River Road again for the last 9 miles. Wash the dust off in the river, enjoy a quiet campground evening, and set off in the morning on a 20-mile segment to rejoin the coastal route.

(To finish the side trip in the morning, head west 5 miles on River Road to the intersection with Bohemian Highway at Monte Rio. Turn south here and skirt the forested hills 10 miles to Freestone, where a 5-mile section into the open range at Valley Ford puts you back on the main coastal route to Tomales and beyond.)

Vineyards off Dry Creek Road

MILEAGE LOG

0.0   From SR 116 and River Rd. in Guerneville, head ½ block north, then turn east on Old River Rd.

1.1   Left onto River Rd. as Old River Rd. ends.

2.8   Pass Korbel Winery.

4.9   Right onto Sunset Ave.

5.1   Cross River Rd. onto Westside Rd. Caution: fast traffic.

8.2   Pass Wohler Rd.

16.8 Left onto W. Dry Creek Rd.

21.8 Right onto Lambert Bridge Rd.

22.5 Right onto Dry Creek Rd.

25.1 Continue forward on Dry Creek under US 101.

26.1 Right onto Healdsburg Ave.

27.2 Arrive at Healdsburg town square.

27.7 Bear left to stay on Healdsburg Ave. at US 101 on-ramps.

28.1 Cross Russian River Bridge.

28.3   Pass Veterans Memorial Beach Park.

29.1   Continue forward under US 101; road becomes Old Redwood Hwy.

30.6   Right onto Eastside Rd.

37.0   Left onto Wohler Rd.

37.7   Right onto River Rd.

44.7   Right onto Old River Rd.

45.7   Arrive back at Guerneville town center.

BODEGA BAY TO LAGUNITAS
Distance: 42.1 miles
Elevation gain: 2260 feet

Bays, birds, and the last park before San Francisco: that's what is in store on today's straightforward ride from the Sonoma coast to the edges of inland suburbia in Marin County. There are plentiful diversions on this short, moderate cycling day.

One mile from the campground sits the town of Bodega Bay, an easy spot for breakfast or coffee after decamping from the dunes. There's a nice run along the quiet, protected bay for a couple of miles before the route turns inland at Doran Regional Park. The first climb takes you to the town of Bodega (yes, the other one), where a half-mile detour deposits you in the center of the small town known mostly for its connection to a great film.

At 7 miles into today's ride, you could be ready for a bit of small-town kitsch, so why not make it Hitch-kitsch and check out the Bodega General Store? It lays claim to the greatest amount of paraphernalia from *The Birds*, Alfred Hitchcock's classic thriller that was filmed in the area. Across from the store is the Potter School, which also got its star turn in the movie, and up the street is the St. Theresa of Avila Catholic Church, which has not one but two claims to fame. It was also a *Birds* location but had previously been the subject of an Ansel Adams photograph, circa 1953.

The inland route that goes by Bodega continues through rolling hills on a fine, shouldered road to Valley Ford at 10 miles (the Russian River Wine Country side trip could reconnect with the main route here) and Tomales at 16. This is prime farming area, so look for local products in each town's small groceries. Tomales also offers a sandwich shop popular with cyclists, with Adirondack chairs on the wide sidewalk offering a perfect spot for scarfing

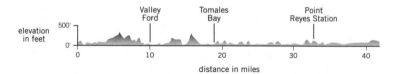

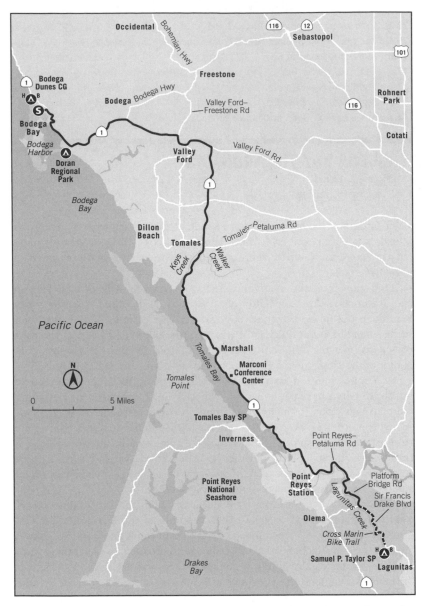

down lunch. A picturesque river-canyon road winds south out of Tomales along Keys Creek and carries you back to the ocean, via one impressive climb.

The creek, and you, descend precipitously to Tomales Bay, which stretches 15 miles south toward Point Reyes. The mile-wide bay evokes an inviting calm, due to the extensive Drakes Estero State Marine Conservation

Area, a verdant peninsula that separates the mainland from the Pacific and connects at its south end to the Point Reyes National Seashore. The road hugs the hills along the shore, overshadowed by eucalyptus and pine trees. Enjoy the contrast of the brown rolling hills and the glittering blue bay.

As a break from the rollers, stop along the way and sample the famous Tomales Bay oysters. At one of the oyster company's retail locations, you get a sense for the city clientele who escape here when you see valet parking offered by the shop and luxury cars lining the road.

An additional gourmet stop is de rigueur along this route, but requires a very short side trip. At 33 miles the route heads inland again, toward Petaluma. At the turn onto Point Reyes–Petaluma Road, detour into the tiny town of Point Reyes Station, again just a half mile off the route.

Cowgirl Creamery is the gastronomical star in this six blocks of inviting shops, which also includes an excellent bookstore and a bike shop. This was Cowgirl's original creamery, with milk from the herds of Jersey cows you see in the hills today. But the creamery has long since expanded as they became beloved across the Bay Area. They still make one cheese there, Red Hawk, and you should taste it and possibly splurge on a wedge for tonight's camp. Grab more provisions at the well-stocked grocery in town, as the last 10 miles of today's ride is mostly rural.

Marin County is rightfully proud of its bike trail network, signed and numbered routes that use a combination of roads and trails. After navigating a winding arroyo road toward Petaluma signed as Bike Route 85, you'll join Bike Route 75 just after the bridge at Tocaloma. Grandly named the Cross

Smiling cyclists depart the campground for another day on the road.

Marin Bike Trail but extending only as far as you ride it today, the shady, paved rail trail ushers you quietly the last 3 miles into Samuel P. Taylor State Park. The trail parallels Lagunitas Creek and, on its east side, Sir Francis Drake Boulevard. The busy park is well maintained and offers a number of day hikes if you're ready for a day off the bike. And at the hiker-biker corral, you'll enjoy the babbling creek, as the campground adjoins it.

MILEAGE LOG

0.0   Depart Bodega Dunes Campground, turning right onto SR 1 S.
1.0   Arrive at Bodega Bay.
6.5   Pass Bodega Hwy. (detour to Bodega).
9.9   Arrive at Valley Ford (Russian River Wine Country side trip rejoins main route here).
11.7   Right to stay on SR 1 at Valley Ford Rd.
16.5   Arrive at Tomales.
16.6   Continue straight at intersection with Tomales-Petaluma Rd. to continue on SR 1.
19.8   Arrive at Tomales Bay.
24.0   Pass Marshall.
25.7   Pass Marconi Conference Center.
32.9   Left onto Point Reyes–Petaluma Rd. at Point Reyes Station.
36.2   Right onto Platform Bridge Rd. after the bridge.
38.6   Right onto Cross Marin Bike Trail before intersection with Sir Francis Drake Blvd., then bear left on trail.
40.2   Enter Samuel P. Taylor State Park on trail.
41.7   Enter lower campground area.
41.9   Bear left at day-use area; continue to campground registration.
42.1   Arrive at campground entrance.

LAGUNITAS TO SAN FRANCISCO
Distance: 30.7 miles
Elevation gain: 1800 feet

If you're biking to San Francisco, to paraphrase an old folk song, wear flowers in your hair. I'd been riding with a gregarious young Frenchman, a letter carrier from a small mountain town, and he kept singing that song's refrain. After a couple of times, I had to ask why he was giving me that ear worm. Turns out it was his sister's wedding song, even though the couple was not married there. Now he was heading for the Golden Gate Bridge and

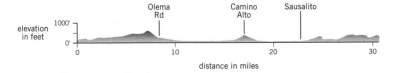

determined to sing it for them in a video—complete with the flowers in his hair—when he cycled across.

The prospect of San Francisco will make you a bit giddy like that. I loved the idea and agreed to be his videographer. We tooled down this last leg from Samuel P. Taylor State Park, mostly on suburban residential or commercial streets, humming the '60s hippie tune and fully expecting to "meet some gentle people there" when we arrived.

But first, some navigation. This leg is not a long ride into the city, but the miles are necessarily slower when many turns through city streets must be navigated, complete with traffic and stoplights. And then there's the Bridge. You'll want to stop at each end to gape and gawk, and biking across is generally slow as you thread your way among throngs of tourists, some of them unsteady or slow on cruiser rental bikes. Finally, when you reach the city, I hope you'll stop and spend a day or so. Arriving midafternoon will give you time to navigate the city tour to a hostel or other lodging.

But before traversing the International Orange–colored Golden Gate Bridge (why did the builders not choose gold? Because the reddish hue

CONNECTIONS: SFO AND AMTRAK

If your trip ends in San Francisco and you're flying or taking the train home, here are the best ways to get to your connections.

San Francisco International Airport (SFO): The easiest way to reach SFO is by taking Bay Area Rapid Transit (BART) via the Millbrae line; fare at the time of publication was about $9 from the farthest station in San Francisco. Arriving at the airport, walk your bike onto the AirTrain system and take it to the Airport Travel Agency in the International Terminal near boarding area G. There you can buy a bike box and use conveniently located tools to disassemble your bike for boxing.

To bike to SFO, about a 20-mile ride from Golden Gate Park, take the first leg of the main route in Chapter 5, Central California, from San Francisco to Half Moon Bay, and from Skyline Boulevard, turn east onto John Daly Boulevard. Turn right (south) on Hillside Boulevard, which becomes Sister Cities Boulevard, then right onto Airport Boulevard, which parallels US Highway 101 to the airport. At the intersection with San Bruno Avenue, turn right onto North McDonnell Road, which leads to SFO's International Terminal.

Amtrak does not service San Francisco; its closest station is in Oakland, at Jack London Square. BART is again an efficient option, its Lake Merritt station about 10 blocks from the train station. The best way, however, is the San Francisco Bay Ferry, which departs from four San Francisco piers to dock at Jack London Square; fare was about $7 at the time of publication. A bike lane is being developed on the new Oakland Bay Bridge, so bicycling to Oakland will be an option in the future.

The Golden Gate, one of the world's most photographed bridges

blended so well with the surrounding hills), enjoy a last bit of Northern California countryside and some Marin-style scenes.

The first few miles take you through the San Geronimo Valley, where the towns are small and the trees plentiful. Spin through Lagunitas, Forest Knolls, San Geronimo, and Woodacre. Appreciate the manicured fairways and greens of the municipal golf course straddling the road. It has something unique: some of its water features are streams that salmon still traverse to spawn, and as such, they are protected waterways, so no diving for a ball gone astray. The valley's unincorporated small towns each seem to have one grocery and perhaps one place to stay. The most inviting location is a combination of both: the Valley Inn and its Two Bird Café combine a small organic restaurant with four rooms above for a luxurious getaway.

Climb out of the valley at the Loma Alta Open Space Preserve and then drop down into suburbia, here known as Fairfax. From there to the city you'll be on side streets with plentiful cafés, bike shops, and other services. The towns blend one into the next, and before you know it, you're getting peekaboo views of the City on winding Camino Alto and then dropping down to the Mill Valley–Sausalito Path, where you'll pedal along the saltwater wetlands of Richardson Bay. The route returns to the street at Sausalito's vibrant, visitor-filled downtown, then climbs an exposed road to the Golden Gate Bridge.

Note: This book departs from the ACA maps' bridge approach for a more direct route onto the bridge. No matter how you get onto the bridge, cyclists are required to use one side or the other of the bridge's two bike-ped paths, depending on time of day and weekday or weekend. The East Side Path across the bridge is open 5:00 AM–3:30 PM weekdays and 9:00 PM–5:00 AM every night (6:00 PM closure in winter), which means if you cross at other times, you'll follow a short alternate route onto the West Side Path, 3:30–9:00 PM weekdays and 5:00 AM–9:00 PM weekends (6:00 PM in winter).

While the ACA's map section 3 ends at the San Francisco side of the bridge, this book's route takes you a bit into the city, to the eastern edge of Golden

Gate Park. It's a centrally located point where this book's San Francisco city tour begins and ends, and it's an easy spot from which to strike out to lodging in many directions.

Whether you have flowers in your hair or intend to leave your heart here, arriving in this glittering jewel of California cities represents a great milestone on the Pacific Coast bike tour. Congratulations and welcome!

Note: You may wonder why you didn't travel the last section into San Francisco along State Route 1 through the Point Reyes National Seashore and Mount Tamalpais State Park. That route adds 10 miles and quite a bit of elevation compared with the mapped route, and there are scant facilities. Much of the road is narrow, winding, and dangerous, and a section experiences landslides, which would require retracing the route to an extremely hilly multimile detour.

MILEAGE LOG

0.0 Depart Samuel P. Taylor State Park, turning right onto Sir Francis Drake Blvd.

2.8 Enter Lagunitas.

3.2 Enter Forest Knolls.

4.8 Cross San Geronimo Valley Dr.

5.9 Cross Railroad Ave. into Woodacre.

8.2 Enter Fairfax.

8.6 Right onto Olema Rd.; follow bike route sign.

9.5 Right onto trail (Marin Bike Route 20) at intersection with Sir Francis Drake Blvd.

9.6 Right onto Broadway Blvd. as trail ends.

9.9 Pass Claus Dr. (detour to Marin Museum of Bicycling).

10.0 Forward as Broadway becomes Center Blvd. at Pacheco Ave.

10.3 Jog right onto Landsdale Ave. at Pastori Ave. intersection stop sign; follow bike route signs.

10.8 Forward as Lansdale curves slightly right and becomes San Anselmo Ave.

11.2 Left to continue on San Anselmo at intersection with Hazel Ave.

12.0 Right to continue on San Anselmo at Center Blvd.

12.1 Right onto Bolinas Ave.; in 1 short block, left onto Shady Ln.

12.7 Left onto Lagunitas Rd.

12.8 Right onto Ross Common, which becomes Poplar Ave., then Kent Ave.

13.8 Slight right onto College Ave. after crossing Woodland Rd., unsigned at corner stop sign.

13.9 Forward as College becomes Magnolia Ave.

15.4 Slight left at intersection with Madrone Ave. to stay on Magnolia through Larkspur.

15.9 Forward at stoplight at Redwood Ave. onto Corte Madera Ave., which becomes Camino Alto through Mill Valley.

18.3 Left onto E. Blithedale Ave. at light. Caution: traffic; easy to miss at end of downhill.

18.4 Right onto San Francisco Bay Trail before next stoplight.

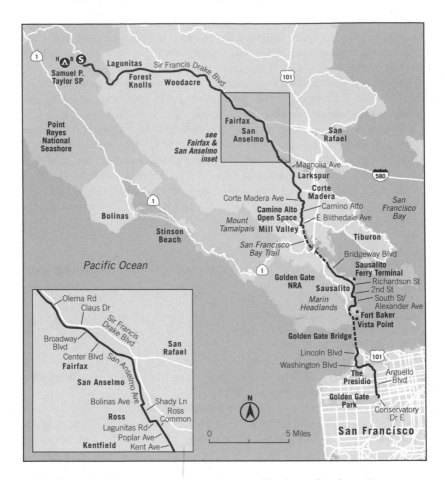

18.7   Forward at bike roundabout to continue on Bike Route 5 to Sausalito.

20.0   Forward as trail travels under US 101.

20.1   Forward across Pohono St. to continue on trail.

21.3   Right at Harbor Dr. to cross onto bike lane on Bridgeway Blvd. southbound.

22.7   Pass Anchor St. (entrance to Sausalito Ferry Terminal for ferry to San Francisco waterfront).

23.2   Forward onto Richardson St. as road curves right; in 1 block, left onto 2nd St.

23.5   Road curves left at top of climb and becomes South St., then Alexander Ave.

23.7   Pass East Rd. (detour to Fort Baker, Bay Area Discovery Museum).

24.6   For East Side Path across Golden Gate Bridge, left at intersection with US 101 off-ramp onto short connector trail to East Side Path at Vista Point (5:00 AM–3:30 PM weekdays, 9:00 PM–5:00 AM every night). At other times, take alternate crossing (see below).

24.8 Arrive at Vista Point visitors center at north end of Golden Gate Bridge.

25.0 Forward onto East Side Path and cross Golden Gate Bridge.

26.7 Left to exit Golden Gate Bridge onto trail at Golden Gate Bridge Welcome Center at south end of bridge.

26.8 Right at welcome center parking to travel under US 101 toll plaza. In 1 block, left onto Cranston Rd.

26.9 Right onto Merchant Rd. into the Presidio.

27.0 Right onto Lincoln Blvd.

27.4 Left onto Washington Blvd.

27.9 Curve right to stay on Washington at intersection with Compton Rd., then left to stay on Washington at intersection with Battery Caulfield Rd.

28.3 Cross over Veterans Blvd. (SR 1).

28.9 Right onto Arguello Blvd. as Washington ends.

29.2 Forward on Arguello across W. Pacific Ave. to depart the Presidio.

30.3 Forward across Fulton St. into Golden Gate Park.

30.4 Left onto Conservatory Dr. E. in ½ block, signed NO ENTRY EXCEPT FOR BICYCLES.

30.7 Arrive at John F. Kennedy Dr.

ALTERNATE CROSSING OF GOLDEN GATE BRIDGE

24.6 For alternate bridge crossing when East Side Path is closed to cycling (3:30 PM–9:00 PM weekdays, 5:00 AM–9:00 PM weekends; 6:00 PM closure in winter), from intersection of Alexander Ave. and US 101 off-ramp, continue straight on Alexander Ave. through tunnel under US 101.

24.8 Right onto Conzelman Rd., then immediate left to stay on Conzelman Rd. toward trailhead parking.

24.9 Forward onto West Side Path to cross Golden Gate Bridge.

26.7 Right to exit Golden Gate Bridge onto trail, then immediate right to loop under bridge on trail.

26.8 Forward to join East Side Path at Golden Gate Bridge Welcome Center.

26.9 Right at welcome center parking to travel under US 101 toll plaza. In 1 block, left onto Cranston Rd.

27.0 Right onto Merchant Rd.

27.1 Right onto Lincoln Blvd.

27.5 Left onto Washington Blvd.

28.0 Curve right to stay on Washington at intersection with Compton Rd., then left to stay on Washington at intersection with Battery Caulfield Rd.

28.4 Cross over Veterans Blvd. (SR 1).

29.0 Right onto Arguello Blvd. as Washington ends.

29.3 Forward on Arguello across W. Pacific Ave. as park ends.

30.4 Forward across Fulton St. into Golden Gate Park.

30.5 Left onto Conservatory Dr. E. in ½ block, signed NO ENTRY EXCEPT FOR BICYCLES.

30.8 Arrive at John F. Kennedy Dr.

CITY TOUR: SAN FRANCISCO
Distance: 23.2 miles
Elevation gain: 1200 feet

Is it insane to think that long-haul cyclists can schlep their worldly belongings around famously vertical San Francisco? A city with a made-for-tourism official count of 49 hills, where many of the neighborhoods have "hill" or "heights" or even "mount" in their names? Well, even if its most famous street, Lombard, has a 27 percent grade on its zigzaggy block and you'd be better suited to climbing it attached to a cable car tow, you *can* enjoy San Francisco by bike. Thousands of locals zip around every day for work and play, and many are shaped more like hippies than Tour de France racers.

Check it out! You can't just skirt the city's western edge and content yourself with a ride through its grand Golden Gate Park before heading for Half Moon Bay. That would be criminal. Stray from the ACA maps and stay a bit. Let me show you around.

This day tour is designed to familiarize, not to be comprehensive. It steers a relatively level path, looping around many of those famous hills. Along the way I gesture toward detours that would send you to more sites and into more challenging terrain.

Begin at Golden Gate Park, the end point for your ride into the city and the starting point for the main route's continuation south to Half Moon Bay in the next chapter. Here, on the east edge of one of the nation's largest urban parks, lies the Panhandle, a narrow strip of parkland beribboned with a bicycle path. Proceed east to the Wiggle, a serpentine path that guides a flat route through the edge of Haight-Ashbury.

Notice the bike route signs by number, aiming you this way and that. At the end of the Wiggle, an expansive bike mural defines a short bike trail connecting to Market Street. The Wiggle is mostly charted by Bike Route 30, which connects with Bike Route 45 at Valencia Street, a worthy cycling lane through the Mission District.

It wouldn't be right to just spin by this area's namesake, so take a brief detour to visit the Mission Dolores. The mission was 240 years old in 2016, making the squat tan church the oldest building in San Francisco; the area was colonized in 1776 with the mission and a military encampment at the Presidio. Escape into the cool darkness beyond its 4-foot-thick walls. You

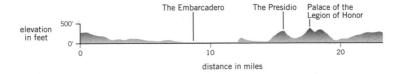

The trail through China Basin Park overlooks AT&T Park, home to the San Francisco Giants baseball team.

might recognize it as a location for the Alfred Hitchcock movie *Vertigo*, for which you'll see plenty of homage in the mission gift shop.

On to Valencia's bike route, bolstered by a "Green Wave," a transportation trick with the traffic lights. On Green Wave streets, the lights are timed to keep traffic moving at bike speeds, in this case 13 miles per hour. At this comfortable pace, enjoy a street of artists and bohemian shopping with plenty of refreshment stops.

One favorite is 826 Valencia's pirate store, a fund-raising shop that helps power that nonprofit's youth tutoring efforts. Kids take writing workshops behind the shop's stacks of pirate supplies. Belying its address, the shop is between 19th and 20th streets. On a related track, Mission Pie is worth a few-block detour east of Valencia at 25th Street. It slides out slices of savory and sweet pies along with coffee and also supports youth who want to bring themselves up in the world. (Down the main route a bit, on the way to Santa Cruz, you'll pass Pie Ranch, which supplies many of the farmed ingredients for the pie café and also trains youth in farming and entrepreneurship.)

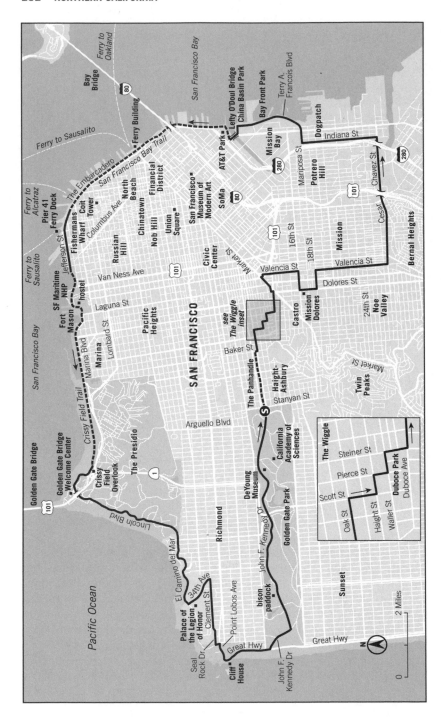

Ferry to Oakland

Bay Bridge

San Francisco Bay

80

Lefty O'Doul Bridge
China Basin Park

Bay Front Park

Terry A. Francois Blvd

Ferry to Sausalito

Ferry Building

The Embarcadero

San Francisco Bay Trail

Mission Bay

Dogpatch

Indiana St

280

Ferry to Alcatraz

Pier 41
Ferry Dock

Jefferson St

Coit Tower

North Beach

Columbus Ave

Financial District

AT&T Park

280

Mariposa St

Potrero Hill

101

Chavez St

280

Ferry to Sausalito

Fishermans Wharf

Russian Hill

Chinatown

Nob Hill

San Francisco Museum of Modern Art

SoMa

80

Cesar

Mission

Bernal Heights

San Francisco Bay

SF Maritime NHP

Hostel

Fort Mason

Van Ness Ave

Union Square

Civic Center

Market St

16th St

18th St

Valencia St

Laguna St

Pacific Heights

101

Valencia St

Dolores St

24th St

Noe Valley

Lombard St

Marina

Marina Blvd

SAN FRANCISCO

see The Wiggle inset

Castro

Mission Dolores

Crissy Field Trail

Baker St

Market St

Golden Gate Bridge

The Presidio

Golden Gate Bridge Welcome Center

Crissy Field Overlook

1

The Panhandle

Haight-Ashbury

Stanyan St

Twin Peaks

Arguello Blvd

S

California Academy of Sciences

The Wiggle

Steiner St

Golden Gate Bridge

101

Lincoln Blvd

Richmond

DeYoung Museum

John F. Kennedy Dr

Golden Gate Park

Pierce St

Scott St

Duboce Park

Duboce Ave

El Camino del Mar

34th Ave

Point Lobos Ave

Oak St

Haight St

Waller St

Palace of the Legion of Honor

Clement St

Sunset

Pacific Ocean

Seal Rock Dr

Cliff House

Great Hwy

Great Hwy

John F. Kennedy Dr

bison paddock

N

2 Miles

0

As Valencia's funky business district peters out, turn toward the city's industrial southeast. Duck under Interstate 280's massive girders and circle round Potrero Hill through the gentrifying Dogpatch neighborhood. This brings you to the famous Embarcadero, the city's long, tourist-filled waterfront. Bike by the recently built AT&T Park, home to baseball's San Francisco Giants, at China Basin Park, then pedal the street bike lane or broad sidewalk north along the water. The Ferry Building, from which boats travel to Sausalito, Oakland, and other destinations, is a worthy lunch stop with its vibrant market and café scene. If you took a detour a few blocks up Howard Street on Bike Route 30, you'd find the swanky new San Francisco Museum of Modern Art, on Third before Mission. This SoMa neighborhood also houses many other museums.

North of Market, surrounding nearby Union Square, sits a gaggle of live-theater venues. The iconic Transamerica Pyramid building anchors the Financial District a few blocks northeast. A block west of that is Portsmouth Square, the historic spot where Spanish settlers congregated in a town named Yerba Buena, renamed San Francisco after the United States acquired the area from Spain in 1846, just three years before the area population would explode after the discovery of gold in the nearby Sierras. Today the square is the heart of the city's storied Chinatown. Access those sites by pedaling a half mile up Washington Street, crossed just north of the Ferry Building.

Continuing north along the Embarcadero, pass the ferry to Alcatraz Island and dive into the heart of serious tourism at Fishermans Wharf. Inland, the North Beach neighborhood conjures Italy, with the columnar Coit Tower looming above. Beyond the throngs of visitors on foot, a fishing fleet begun a century ago largely by Italian immigrants is still berthed at the wharves, and many of the fishing operations are run by their descendants. Dungeness crab is the prized catch, steamed in broth that is soaked up by crusty sourdough bread.

Join a parade of rental bikes past the Maritime Museum and Aquatic Park and cycle up to Fort Mason, which sits on a bluff above the bay. Pedal smugly by other tourists, walking their bikes at the first hint of an incline. Just within the fort's grounds at Battery Road sits one of the city's three hostels, and perhaps the most boisterous, given its location. The other locations, all run by Hostelling International, are in the theater district near Union Square and nearby in City Center. All require advance reservations.

Fort Mason is connected to the Presidio via Crissy Field, a former military airfield along the water that now hosts a pleasure-boat marina, tidal marshlands, and recreational areas. It's a climb from the waterfront to the Presidio's roads that you pedaled coming off the Golden Gate Bridge. On this trip, hug the western edge along the park and exit above Baker Beach into the luxurious Sea Cliff neighborhood.

The route flows into Lincoln Park, which houses the Palace of the Legion of Honor, the second of the city's three great museums. You might not be able to visit all three on a day's bike tour, but if you didn't detour to SFMOMA, perhaps stop at this grand French-inspired palace to view its extensive European art collection. You'll get one more museum possibility ahead in Golden Gate Park.

Pedal through the golf course that occupies most of the park and out toward Lands End, which houses the famous Cliff House restaurant, as well as a visitors center and café, all overlooking crashing ocean waves and often socked in with fog.

Nearly done with your city loop, coast downhill to the first entrance to Golden Gate Park, entering between the landmark Dutch windmills. Now you will pedal the entire 3-mile length of the park, past the grazing bison (yes, as in American buffalo), past anglers fishing in casting pools, and past the DeYoung Museum, the third location in the city for fine arts. Its striking building complex (rebuilt after extensive earthquake damage early in this century), along with the neighboring California Academy of Sciences and Japanese Tea Garden, is a worthy stop, even if you're not entering to see its American art collection. The lush grounds and architecture are fantastic.

End the tour at the corner of John F. Kennedy Drive and Stanyan Street, which defines the park's east border. If you need a little chain oil, pedal three blocks south to Frederick Street, where you'll find the city's oldest bike shop, American Cyclery.

MILEAGE LOG

0.0   Depart Golden Gate Park heading east on John F. Kennedy Dr.

0.1   Forward at Stanyan St. onto bike trail down center of the Panhandle.

0.9   Right onto Baker St.; in 1 block, left onto Oak St.

1.2   Right onto Scott St.—the Wiggle.

1.5   Left onto Haight St.; in 1 block, right on Pierce St.

1.6   Left onto Waller St.

1.7   Right onto Steiner St.

1.8   Left onto Duboce Ave.

2.0   Bear right to continue on Duboce to cross rail tracks as road becomes 1-block multiuse path.

2.1   Cross Buchanan St., then left onto Market St. in bike lane.

2.3   Cross Octavia Blvd., then immediate right onto trail.

2.4   Right onto Valencia St.

3.0   Right onto 16th St.

3.2   Left onto Dolores St.

3.3   Arrive at Mission Dolores.

3.3   Left onto 18th St. (detour right to Castro District).

3.6   Right onto Valencia St. in Mission District.

4.6   Left onto Cesar Chavez St.

5.3   Forward onto sidewalk at on-ramp to US 101; follow bike signs under freeway. Beyond last overpass, bear left to return to Cesar Chavez St.

5.5   Forward to continue on Cesar Chavez St.

6.1   Cross under I-280, staying in bike lane.

6.2   Left onto Indiana St. through Potrero Hill District.

7.2   Right onto Mariposa St.

7.4   Bear left onto Terry A. Francois Blvd. along waterfront.

8.3   Bear left at China Basin Park.

8.4   Right onto 3rd St.; cross Lefty O'Doul Bridge.

8.5   Right onto sidewalk San Francisco Bay Trail at AT&T Park.

9.4   Pass under I-80 onto the Embarcadero.

9.7   Pass Howard St. (detour left to San Francisco Museum of Modern Art).

9.9   Pass Ferry Building (ferries to Oakland, Sausalito, etc.; detour left to Financial District, Chinatown).

11.2   Arrive at Fishermans Wharf.

11.4   Left onto the Embarcadero as San Francisco Bay Trail ends at North Beach neighborhood, then immediate right onto Jefferson St.

11.9   Forward into Square Park at Hyde St., where bike path resumes through San Francisco Maritime National Historical Park.

12.2   Right at end of park onto Van Ness Ave.

12.3   Left as street ends at Aquatic Park Pier onto Fort Mason Trail.

12.4   Pass Battery St. (detour to Fishermans Wharf Hostel).

12.4   Bear right on park trails to exit Fort Mason.

12.7   Bear right at Laguna St., then curve left onto trail next to Marina Blvd.

13.6   Enter Crissy Field Trail as Marina Blvd. becomes Old Mason St.

14.7   Left onto Crissy Field Ave., then immediately right; follow signs to overlook.

14.9   Right onto Lincoln Blvd. at Crissy Field Overlook.

15.2   Pass under US 101 off-ramps from Golden Gate Bridge.

15.7   Continue on Lincoln past Washington Blvd. on left (main route into San Francisco after crossing Golden Gate Bridge).

16.6   Continue forward as Lincoln becomes El Camino del Mar after leaving the Presidio.

17.6   Left onto 34th Ave. through Lincoln Park, past Palace of the Legion of Honor.

18.2   Right onto Clement St. to exit park.

18.8   Bear left as Clement becomes Seal Rock Dr.

19.0   Left onto El Camino del Mar. In ½ block, right onto Point Lobos Ave.

19.3   Pass Cliff House.

19.5   Forward as Point Lobos Ave. becomes Great Hwy.

19.9   Left onto John F. Kennedy Dr. after first of two Dutch windmills at entrance to Golden Gate Park.

20.4   Left to stay on JFK Dr.

20.9 Pass bison paddock on left.

22.6 Pass DeYoung Museum on right.

23.1 Pass Conservatory Dr. E. on left (main route into San Francisco after crossing Golden Gate Bridge).

23.2 Arrive at Kezar Dr. to end tour at the western end of the Panhandle.

Opposite: *The Bixby Creek Bridge*

CENTRAL
CALIFORNIA

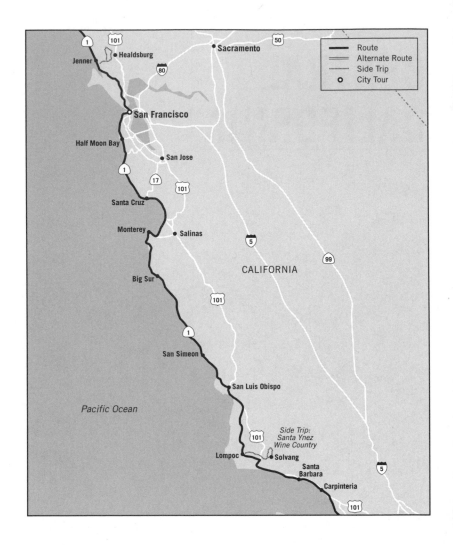

THE SAN FRANCISCO BAY AREA'S urban effects linger as you continue south. The city and its suburbs sprawl southeast around the bay, while a rugged stretch of Highway 1 provides a rural buffer from high-tech Silicon Valley and the populous South Bay communities just inland over a range of coastal hills.

Tracing the arc of Monterey Bay from Santa Cruz to Monterey takes you from sea life to the central coast's voluminous agriculture. Flat fields are offset farther along by a wild Big Sur coast that's craggy and remote. The winding highway clings to jagged hills rising from a rocky shore.

Palm trees appear and the weather warms as you enter the middle of the state. The land begins to flatten. Stretches of dry coastal prairie signal a thirsty environment. Vast fields are cultivated, migrant laborers tackle the work, and the cyclist's senses are filled with farm odors and row crops receding to the horizon.

Amid a giant ranch, the excesses of money and fame are on display in the hodgepodge, uniquely American Hearst Castle. Skirting the edge of another winemaking region—and detouring inland to visit it if you'd like—drop down again to the sea to end this chapter at blooming Santa Barbara, which fills its coastal valley.

SAN FRANCISCO TO HALF MOON BAY
Distance: 28.8 miles
Elevation gain: 1680 feet

Hope for a rare windless day when you (reluctantly) depart San Francisco. (Don't fret, today's short ride allows you to linger in the city till midday.) You'll hope for calm not because you curse headwinds that slow your pace or fear side gusts that can be treacherous on bridges but, rather, because you cherish a clean, well-oiled chain: wind coming into the city means sand blown into your derailleurs.

Although San Francisco is known more for its hills than its beaches, the city was once nearly half sand. The western portion was labeled the Great Sand Bank on an 1853 map of the peninsula that would become the city, and billowing, drifting dunes reached 100 feet high. Planners bemoaned the landscape as unbuildable, and when horticulturalists designated the area for Golden Gate Park, they were ridiculed for proposing to turn it green. But in less than 10 years of planting, adding soil, and irrigating, the giant park was established and citizens flocked to its promenades and trails. The dunes lurk beneath.

As you pedal through the park, imagine the landscape without grassy lawns, giant shade trees, and layers of fragrant shrubs and colorful flowers. The park is even home to the city's botanical garden. And ponder the amount of water it took, and still takes, to feed this thirsty terrain. That, too, triggered an ingenious idea: the two large windmills on the western corners of the

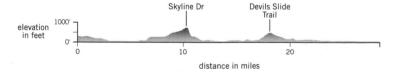

South of San Francisco the riding becomes rural pretty quickly. To increase safety for all traffic, cyclists should attempt to ride well to the right of the white line (on the shoulder), especially on blind curves like this one.

park drove pumps that brought freshwater up from deep wells drilled for park irrigation.

Turn south on the Great Highway, as State Route 35 is known here, and you may wish for a chain guard, because the next few miles out of town parallel beaches where the ever-drifting sand can still be seen washing bus-ily over the breakwater and the road. You might even see giant machinery resculpting it to continue to tame nature for the populace. A trail runs next to the road, but the street-side bike lane is a bit less sandy and traffic is not too heavy to preclude pedaling the road.

The highway curves past the San Francisco Zoo, then by large Lake Merced, east of which sits San Francisco State University. Then it passes the only area in the city where the former duned landscape can still be viewed: Fort Funston. No, it's not a military-themed amusement park, but a former US Army fort that protected the city with five gun batteries in the era of the first two world wars.

Today, though, some fun is definitely brought to the old fort, now part of the Golden Gate National Recreation Area. For one thing, it's the city's largest off-leash dog park. More thrillingly, its ocean-side cliffs are literally a jumping-off point for hang gliders, who take advantage of the ever-present winds. In their day, the military took to the sky above the fort too: they had large balloons stationed at each end that would hoist soldiers aloft to track ship movements and serve as spotters for artillery targets and hits. The wind vexed them, while today it delights experienced hang-gliding enthusiasts.

Climb away from the coast into Daly City, and you may be singing the refrain to Malvina Reynolds's "Little Boxes" song about cookie-cutter suburbs with houses that are different colors but all look the same. It was inspired by this very view. At Thornton State Beach in Daly City, you will see another way to enjoy the dunes as you pass riding stables and bridle trails.

Make a major climb up through the little boxes lining Skyline Drive, then drop back down along the beach. At a brief departure from the ACA route at 12 miles, a tiny park hugs the coastal bluffs on Esplanade Avenue, with benches that invite a break from the bike seat to watch the abundant sea life of whales, seals, and birds. The route also spins through a short commercial area with a grocery and cafés and a busy beach, then back out to the highway briefly before another welcome side trail through Mori Point, a headland promontory at Rockaway Beach. The short trail runs between marshland and hills, with trailside gardens and benches.

Beyond Rockaway Beach, the trail continues up a series of switchbacks next to the highway, but it's easier to just climb that hill on the road shoulder and then switch to the trail at a curb-cut atop the hill. Pacifica State Beach is next, followed by a climb through the Devils Slide area. The name sends a bit of a shiver, doesn't it? Not to worry, because it's been tamed. The Devils Slide area of SR 1 was notorious for its regular landslides. Unstable rock formations caused slides onto the road here multiple times over the decades. At one point in the 1990s, the road was closed for two years. It took hours in a car to detour around the mess, and of course the coastal bike route was thrown into disarray.

A fractious, decades-long debate raged over how to secure the only road through this somewhat remote coastal area of San Mateo County. Planners wanted a freeway bypass over verdant Montara Mountain, but plentiful environmentalists wanted no such thing. Finally, the tunnel solution was enacted by a statewide initiative and vote. The double tunnel opened in 2013, and besides solving the slide problem, it created a new bike trail. The 1.3 miles of old road are now the Devils Slide Trail for cyclists and hikers. There's a bit more elevation gain than if you shoot through the tunnel (which has beautiful wide shoulders, by the way), but the scenic views of Egg Rock and the wild cliffs are worth the extra effort. At 17.7 miles, as the tunnels come into view, turn off on the side road to Pedro Point to access the old road. It has viewpoints and restrooms. And if a slide has closed it, simply turn around and resort to the tunnel solution.

Leave the coast at Moss Beach and bike through farmland, with the Half Moon Bay Airport between you and the ocean. Pick up another waterfront trail at Pillar Point Harbor. Cycle past the harbor's parking and find the trail, which continues with good signage and a couple of short road connectors to tonight's destination. Pass the beach resorts and tony estates at Miramar. The bay is edged with a thin strip of white sand, and the black dots of surfers bobbing in sparkling water are visible as you pass Half Moon Bay State Beach day-use areas before arriving at the park's campground.

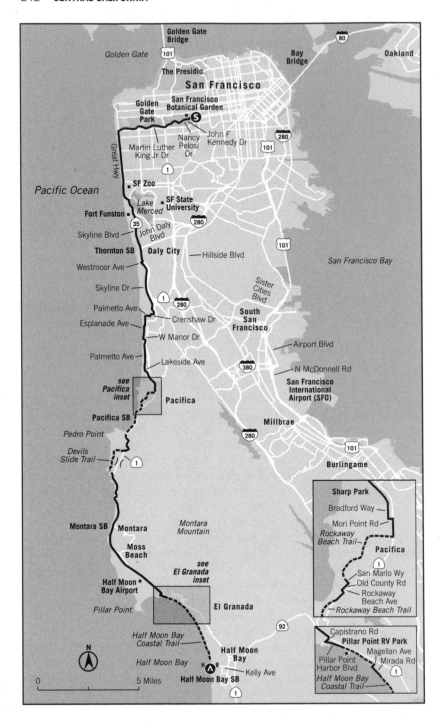

Before ending the ride at Half Moon Bay's campground, ride into town to provision for the night's dinner or have an evening out. Depart the park on Kelly Avenue just beyond the gate. In a half mile inland, connect with SR 1 and turn left to find Half Moon Bay's plentiful groceries and cafés. A natural-food store, coffee roastery, and a few blocks of local shops lining a quaint downtown street are delightful parts of the area's commerce. Later, drift off in your sleeping bag to the gentle hooting of the bay's foghorn, rhythmically matching the lapping waves.

Note: If you got an early start or want a bit more pedaling today, you can continue on past Half Moon Bay to Pigeon Point Light Station, another 20 miles, to enjoy a night in a hostel bed at the lighthouse (reservations recommended), perched on a rocky point. This option would make today's ride 50 miles and tomorrow's ride, into Santa Cruz, about 37 miles.

MILEAGE LOG

0.0   Depart Golden Gate Park from Stanyan St., heading west on John F. Kennedy Dr.

0.1   Left on unsigned Nancy Pelosi Dr. (signed for Bike Route 65).

0.2   Left to stay on Nancy Pelosi Dr. at Bowling Green Dr.

0.4   Forward at stop sign onto Martin Luther King Jr. Dr.

0.8   Right at stop sign to stay on MLK Dr.

1.1   Pass San Francisco Botanical Garden. Continue forward, following Bike Route 34 and TO OCEAN BEACHES signs.

3.4   Pass by Dutch windmill to exit park.

3.5   Right onto Lincoln Wy.; in ½ block, left onto Great Hwy. (SR 35).

6.1   Curve right onto Skyline Blvd. as beach road ends just south of San Francisco Zoo.

6.8   Pass entrance to Fort Funston.

8.0   Pass Thornton State Beach at Daly City.

9.1   Right onto Westmoor Ave. (unsigned), then immediate left onto Skyline Dr.

10.9   Left onto Crenshaw Dr. In 1 block, right onto Palmetto Ave.

11.6   Right onto Esplanade Ave. at bike route sign. In 1 block, curve left to stay on Esplanade. Note: Departure from ACA route.

12.0   Left onto W. Manor Dr.

12.1   Right onto Palmetto Ave. (return to ACA route).

13.4   Curve left on Palmetto, which becomes Clarendon Rd. In ½ block, right onto Lakeside Ave.

13.6   Right onto Francisco Blvd., which becomes Bradford Wy. through Sharp Park.

14.4   Curve left as Bradford becomes Mori Point Rd.

14.5   Right onto SR 1.

14.8   Right at Reina del Mar Ave. onto trail to Rockaway Beach.

15.5   Left onto San Marlo Wy. as trail ends at a parking lot.

15.6   Right onto Old County Rd.

15.7   Left onto Rockaway Beach Ave., then immediate right onto SR 1.

15.9   Merge right onto trail at top of hill.

16.9   Right onto SR 1 as trail ends at Pacifica State Beach parking.

17.7   Right onto Devils Slide Trail at approach to tunnel's north portal.

19.2   Right onto SR 1 as trail ends at tunnel's south portal.

21.1   Pass Montara State Beach.

23.7   Pass Half Moon Bay Airport.

24.8   Right onto Capistrano Rd. at Pillar Point Harbor. In ½ block, left onto Pillar Point Harbor Blvd.

25.2   Forward onto trail as road ends.

25.5   Pass Pillar Point RV Park in El Granada.

26.2   Right onto Magellan Ave. as trail ends. Magellan curves left and becomes Mirada Rd.

26.5   Forward over bike-ped bridge onto Half Moon Bay Coastal Trail as Mirada ends.

26.7   Pass Half Moon Bay State Beach, Roosevelt Beach.

27.8   Pass Half Moon Bay State Beach, Venice Beach.

28.1   Pass Half Moon Bay State Beach, Dunes Beach.

28.6   Pass hiker-biker campground sites.

28.8   Arrive at Half Moon Bay State Beach entrance gate to register.

HALF MOON BAY TO SANTA CRUZ
Distance: 57.3 miles
Elevation gain: 3030 feet

The coast south of San Francisco is wild and remote, surprisingly so given its proximity to the dense urbanity and sprawl of suburbanity around San Francisco Bay. But between the population centers and the coast is a long ridge of craggy hills, many of which are set aside as open space preserves or parks, including two that protect the giant redwoods. So departing from Half Moon Bay, expect miles of relatively quiet, rolling coastal riding, with stunning scenery to enjoy.

Most of today's route uses the intermittent shoulder of the Cabrillo Highway, as State Route 1 is called here. You'll pass the day with long stretches of farmland and grasslands, interspersed with brief but significant visits to the coast.

SR 92 comes down from San Mateo to meet SR 1 at Half Moon Bay, and the next crossroad heading inland is SR 84, 10 miles south. Just before it, find today's biggest climb, as the road veers inland from the coast for a bit. SR 84 leads through the Silicon Valley area to Redwood City, but just 0.75

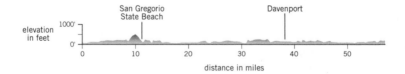

mile up that highway, also known as La Honda Road, is tiny San Gregorio, whose general store sits at the intersection with Stage Road. La Honda is another 7 miles along.

The route passes a series of beaches, quite popular with surfers, but perhaps the tourism highlight of the area is the Pigeon Point Light Station, a state historical park passed at 21 miles. The 115-foot-tall lighthouse, perched on a point with water on three sides, has been in use since 1872, with a modern beacon having replaced its hefty Fresnel lens. Although it's closed due to damage, the grounds are open for visiting, and there's a nearby beach from which to watch the surf break on the craggy reefs beneath the lighthouse.

A cyclist from London, England, checks out the Pigeon Point Lighthouse.

If you continued cycling past Half Moon Bay and want to end your day here, you are in for a treat. The lighthouse hosts a hostel, operated by Hostelling International, which has unique accommodations. Four houses built in the late 1950s perch on the edge of the bluff, and each can house about 14 people, most in dorm-style rooms with a few individual bedrooms. The houses have kitchens and comfortable living rooms, and outdoors are gardens with chairs around fire pits. Movies are shown nightly in the adjacent Fog Signal building. As you might expect, reservations are highly recommended for a stay at Pigeon Point.

But the high point of the stay would be the cliff-hanging hot tub, rentable by the half hour each evening. Its deck offers the best views of the lighthouse, rocks, harbor seals, and, of course, the sunset. If you're there in spring, watch for the spouting sprays from migrating gray whales.

Pigeon Point is visible from the hillside campground of the Santa Cruz North–Costanoa KOA, 3 miles south of the lighthouse and a half mile up Rossi Road. Extensive facilities here include a large lodge with a bar and grill, dry saunas, and spa treatments.

Another of nature's incredible shows is on deck south from the light station at Año Nuevo State Park, passed at 28 miles. This coastal park, which

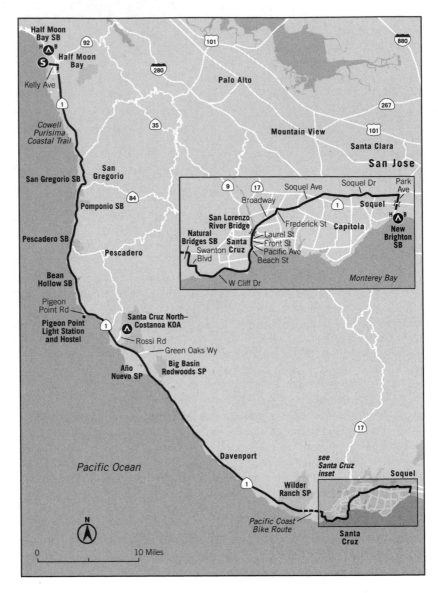

you must get a pass to visit, is home to the migrating elephant seals, those furry brown sea mammals with fleshy protruding noses; these giant creatures can weigh 800 to 2000-plus pounds. They haul ashore to breed in the winter and return throughout spring and summer in smaller numbers to molt and rest from their journeys. For most of the year, passes are issued at the park entrance on a first-come basis, but in breeding season, visitors must join a guided 2.5-hour walk. In all seasons, the long trail to the bluffs is the only way to view these amazing animals.

At the intersection with Green Oaks Way, pass (and hopefully stop at) Pie Ranch. If you visited Mission Pie in San Francisco, you probably ate produce from this affiliated ranch, which trains youth in farming and small-business endeavors. A farm stand is open seasonally with produce, cold drinks, and, of course, pies whole or by the slice. Displays tell of the ranch's educational work, and a large, shady patio rounds out a relaxing stop.

As you enter Santa Cruz County, the road begins once more to hug the coast. Brown hills rise to the east. The town of Davenport offers a good little oasis. Clustered roadside are a café, bakery, grocery, and tasting room for Bonny Doon Vineyard.

Departing from the Adventure Cycling Association mapped route in Santa Cruz, tour the city of Santa Cruz's surfing-mad coastline. Along West Cliff Drive you'll pass a surfing museum and a heroic sculpture of a surfer. A broad, sandy beach showcases much surfing talent. With a local surf club that's been operational since 1936, the sport has a good hold on this sun-baked city. The busy Santa Cruz Wharf is visible beyond the beach.

Navigate around the edge of the touristy wharf and through the center of Santa Cruz, whose bustling downtown sits on the San Lorenzo River. As you cross the river, rejoin the ACA bike route to continue through suburban development to Soquel. Turn toward the water and head for New Brighton State Beach for tonight's campground, with hiker-biker sites on the bluff above a broad, curved beach that beckons.

MILEAGE LOG

0.0   Depart Half Moon Bay State Beach heading south on Half Moon Bay Coastal Trail.

0.2   Left onto Kelly Ave.

0.8   Right onto bike trail parallel to SR 1.

2.0   Forward onto SR 1 shoulder as bike lane ends.

5.6   Pass Cowell Purisima Coastal Trail (restrooms).

11.4   Pass intersection with SR 84 to Redwood City (detour to San Gregorio).

11.5   Pass San Gregorio State Beach (restrooms, water).

13.1   Pass Pomponio State Beach.

15.7   Pass Pescadero State Beach (restrooms).

16.9   Pass Bean Hollow State Beach.

21.6   Pass Pigeon Point Rd., where you can detour out to the lighthouse and a scenic hostel.

25.3   Pass Rossi Rd. (detour to Santa Cruz North–Costanoa KOA).

27.6   Pass Green Oaks Wy. (detour to Pie Ranch).

28.1   Pass Año Nuevo State Park entrance road.

30.8   Pass Big Basin Redwoods State Park.

38.4   Pass Davenport town center.

44.6 Pass Wilder Ranch State Park first entrance.

45.9 Right and then immediate left onto Pacific Coast Bike Route, parallel to highway.

46.3 Enter Santa Cruz.

46.8 Cross Shaffer Rd.

47.1 Right onto Natural Bridges Rd.

47.4 Left onto Delaware Ave. at Natural Bridges State Beach. Follow Coastal Bike Route sign.

47.5 Right onto Swanton Blvd.

47.9 Left onto W. Cliff Dr. or adjacent sidewalk trail.

49.7 Pass Santa Cruz Surfing Museum in Lighthouse Field State Beach.

50.5 Slight right onto Beach St.

50.6 Forward onto Pacific Ave. at roundabout (third exit).

50.7 Right onto Front St.

50.8 Slight right at 3rd St. to stay on Front.

50.9 Slight right at Pacific to stay on Front.

51.1 Right onto Laurel St.

51.2 Bear left onto Broadway when crossing San Lorenzo River.

51.3 Curve right to stay on Broadway at Riverside Ave.

52.2 Forward to continue on Broadway as road splits.

52.4 Left onto Frederick St.

52.7 Right onto Soquel Ave.

53.2 Slight left to stay on Soquel at Capitola Rd.

53.9 Cross over SR 1; continue on Soquel Dr. through Soquel.

56.8 Right onto Park Ave.

57.1 Cross under SR 1.

57.3 Left onto McGregor Dr. into New Brighton State Beach campground.

SANTA CRUZ TO MONTEREY
Distance: 42.2 miles
Elevation gain: 1680 feet

Today you traverse the shoreline of Monterey Bay. Sounds idyllic, but it's not all a sand-between-your-toes experience. On a bike, it's more like a hop from town to town, with intensely farmed land between. Still, there are opportunities to visit the beach and welcome diversions on a relatively easy cycling day. Also, an excellent recreational trail keeps cycling tourists off the main roads for much of the route.

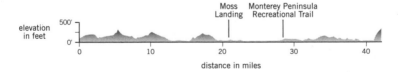

The Monterey Peninsula Recreational Trail cuts through a dry scrubland with the glittering bay visible nearby.

Begin by turning away from the sea and toward the foothill neighborhoods of Soquel and neighboring Aptos along the bike lane of winding Soquel Drive. If you skipped a camp breakfast, the shops at Aptos Village offer sustenance, and a bike shop, at 3 miles.

Cross over busy State Route 1 and then angle back toward the beach, nearly touching it at Manresa State Beach. Manresa's Uplands Beach unit offers camping, but no hiker-biker facilities. Farther along, the Monterey region's KOA is right on the trail with the usual amenities of pool, hot tub, and Wi-Fi, but it offers an additional twist: outdoor movies. Two miles farther, the campground at Sunset State Beach, accessed at 11 miles, does have hiker-biker sites.

Nearing Watsonville, the route opens into farming country in the Pajaro Valley. To conserve water, fields are covered in white plastic mulch, with holes punched for crops like strawberries, kale, and brussels sprouts. At harvest season, the sweet odor of ripe berries drifts through the air.

A brief return to SR 1 sends you over a modern bridge with a generous shoulder. This leads into Moss Landing, and you pass over the verdant Elkhorn Slough before exiting the highway. Beyond the small coastal town, home to Salinas River State Beach and the research institute for the Monterey Bay Aquarium, the route again turns inland and picks up the regional Monterey Peninsula Recreational Trail, farther on known as the Monterey Bay Coastal Trail. It parallels farm roads across a dusty valley, with prairie dogs (a burrowing rodent) popping out of their holes in the desert landscape.

After skirting a shopping center on side roads, pick up the trail again and ride it right onto the city of Monterey's bustling waterfront. There should be time for exploration of this busy town and provisioning at the shops before climbing the last mile to the hilltop Veterans Memorial Park, which offers a

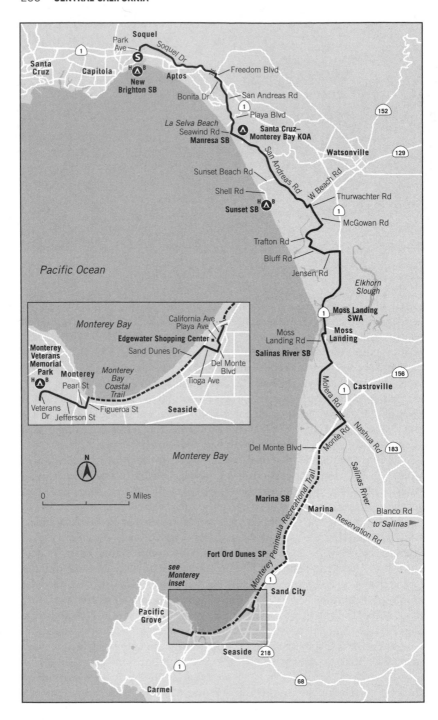

Soquel
Park Ave
Soquel Dr
Santa Cruz
Capitola
Aptos
New Brighton SB
Bonita Dr
Freedom Blvd
San Andreas Rd
Playa Blvd
La Selva Beach
Seawind Rd
Manresa SB
Santa Cruz–Monterey Bay KOA
Watsonville
Sunset Beach Rd
Shell Rd
Sunset SB
Thurwachter Rd
McGowan Rd
Trafton Rd
Bluff Rd
Jensen Rd
Elkhorn Slough
Pacific Ocean
Moss Landing SWA
Moss Landing Rd
Moss Landing
Salinas River SB
Monterey Bay
California Ave
Playa Ave
Edgewater Shopping Center
Sand Dunes Dr
Del Monte Blvd
Tioga Ave
Monterey Veterans Memorial Park
Monterey
Monterey Bay Coastal Trail
Pearl St
Seaside
Veterans Dr
Jefferson St
Figueroa St
Castroville
Monte Rd
Nashua Rd
Molera Rd
Salinas River
Monterey Bay
Del Monte Blvd
Blanco Rd
to Salinas
Reservation Rd
N
0   5 Miles
Marina SB
Marina
Fort Ord Dunes SP
Monterey Peninsula Recreational Trail
see Monterey inset
Sand City
Pacific Grove
Seaside
Carmel

large hiker-biker corral. The park, in a quiet neighborhood with no services, can be busy and the sandy camping corral tight with traveling cyclists and local hikers.

MILEAGE LOG

0.0 Depart New Brighton State Beach, turning left onto McGregor Dr.

0.1 Right onto Park Ave.

0.6 Right onto Soquel Dr.

1.1 Pass Cabrillo College.

2.8 Enter Aptos Village.

3.9 Right to stay on Soquel Dr. at Huntington Dr.

4.8 Right onto Freedom Blvd. and cross over SR 1. Caution: off-ramp traffic.

5.1 Left onto Bonita Dr. at the T.

6.2 Right onto San Andreas Rd. as Bonita ends.

7.4 Pass Playa Blvd. (detour to La Selva Beach).

8.1 Pass Seawind Rd. (detour to Manresa State Beach).

9.0 Pass Santa Cruz–Monterey Bay KOA.

11.2 Pass Sunset Beach Rd. (detour to Sunset State Beach, camping).

13.2 Left onto W. Beach Rd. at bike route sign.

13.3 Right onto Thurwachter Rd., which becomes McGowan Rd.

14.4 Right onto Trafton Rd.

16.0 Left onto Bluff Rd. as Trafton ends at a T.

16.8 Left onto Jensen Rd.

17.5 Right onto SR 1.

19.2 Pass Moss Landing State Wildlife Area.

21.0 Cross Elkhorn Slough.

21.6 Right onto Moss Landing Rd.

21.8 Enter Moss Landing; pass turnoff for Salinas River State Beach.

22.4 Left onto Potrero Rd., then immediate right onto SR 1.

23.2 Right onto Molera Rd.

26.1 Cross over SR 1.

26.6 Right on Monte Rd. (detour straight onto Nashua Rd. for Salinas).

27.7 Cross over Salinas River.

28.4 Left onto Del Monte Blvd.

28.5 Slight right onto Monterey Peninsula Recreational Trail at intersection with Lapis Rd.

30.2 Enter Marina.

31.1 Cross Reservation Rd. (detour to Marina State Beach). Forward on trail under SR 1.

33.2 Cross Stilwell Hall (detour to Fort Ord Dunes State Park).

36.3 Forward on trail under SR 1 as it U-turns.

36.4 Left onto California Ave. and forward under SR 1. Caution: on-ramp traffic.

36.6 Pass Edgewater Shopping Center.

36.8 Left onto Playa Ave.
36.9 Right onto Del Monte Blvd.
37.1 Right onto Tioga Ave.; cross over SR 1 into Sand City.
37.4 Left onto Monterey Bay Coastal Trail at Sand Dunes Dr. into Seaside.
38.1 Cross Canyon del Rey Blvd., then Sand Dunes Dr. to stay on trail.
38.3 Enter Monterey State Beach.
40.4 Arrive at Monterey Municipal Beach.
40.6 Left at Municipal Wharf 2 to cross Del Monte Ave. onto Figueroa St.
40.8 Right onto Pearl St. into Monterey.
41.1 Bear right onto Jefferson St. at Y with Polk St.
41.7 Forward as Jefferson becomes Veterans Dr.
42.2 Arrive at Monterey Veterans Memorial Park.

MONTEREY TO BIG SUR
Distance: 44.3 miles
Elevation gain: 2760 feet

Many visitors wax poetic about the Big Sur region, and with good reason. It's wild and beautiful, so lightly populated that you'll forget how close you are to the densely packed Bay Area. On today's route, the distance is modest but the scenery is grand. And with few services along the way, it's more travelogue than exploration. But there are a few worthy stops before you get to the rugged coast.

Unfortunately, heavy rains in the winter of 2016–2017 caused destruction of the Pfeiffer Canyon Bridge (on the Big Sur to Pacific Valley segment) and a massive mudslide at Mud Creek (on the Pacific Valley to San Simeon segment). At the time of this book's publication, neither segment could be ridden. Officials expected the bridge to be replaced by late 2017 but the highway to be closed due to the mudslide well into 2018.

During the road closure, cyclists must make an extensive detour from Monterey to Cambria or San Luis Obispo (on the San Simeon to Pismo Beach segment). The Adventure Cycling Association released a three-day cycling route inland to detour around the area (see "Map Updates and Corrections" on www.adventurecycling.org), which returns to the coast south of Cambria near San Simeon State Park. Or, cyclists could take Amtrak from Salinas to San Luis Obispo and rejoin the route there. If desired, a side trip north from Morro Bay

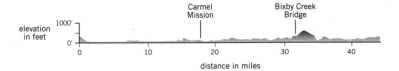

VISIT SALINAS, STEINBECK'S BIRTHPLACE

John Steinbeck made Monterey's Cannery Row famous, but the Nobel Prize–winning author grew up in nearby Salinas. The dusty farm town has recently experienced a renaissance and is worth a visit. Have lunch in the restored Steinbeck family home and tour the National Steinbeck Center two blocks away. Enjoy the modest town center with plentiful art deco architecture. Pick up a copy of *Travels with Charley*, which is sure to become your favorite touring book, as it is mine.

For a 20-mile detour to Salinas, head straight onto Nashua Road instead of turning onto Monte Road at 26.6 miles (see Santa Cruz to Monterey mileage log). Turn left on Blanco Road and 8 miles later you're in Salinas. Turn left on Davis Road, right on Ambrose Drive, and left on University to Central Avenue. A right on Central takes you past Steinbeck's birthplace and to the center of town. Turn right on Main Street, where the National Steinbeck Center sits on the left. Continue on Main Street for cafes and shopping, and exit town with a right turn back onto Blanco at 11.5 miles. Continue on Blanco to a right turn at 17.5 miles to Reservation Road, which intersects with the Santa Cruz to Monterey route at its 31.1-mile point.

could be made to tour Hearst Castle outside San Simeon. Cyclists are advised to explore the Monterey section of this route and then tackle the detour.

The ride begins on Monterey's waterfront trail, which soon delivers you to Cannery Row. Made famous by the great American novelist John Steinbeck, the huge former sardine canneries that were central to his 1945 novel are now reimagined as a center of commerce and tourism. It's such a far cry from his bleak novel of the Great Depression that it's tough to make the connection, and the streets bear little resemblance to Steinbeck's colorful, rough-and-tumble setting. However, the renovated area holds its own delights, such as a quiet bike trail paralleling the shopping street, and the world-class Monterey Bay Aquarium, a major attraction at the south end of the strip.

After the aquarium comes the famed 17 Mile Drive. The road winds sedately with mansions on the dry side and unobstructed views of the rocky coastline in a continual ribbon of parkland on the wet side. Look for the famous Lone Cypress, a solitary California cypress tree perched on a rocky promontory.

Ignore the "bike route turns" sign at Spyglass Hill to continue on 17 Mile Drive, turning off it only when you reach the intersection with the road to Carmel-by-the-Sea. Here sits another worthy historic stop: the San Carlos Borromeo de Carmelo Mission.

The Carmel Mission, begun in 1770 and the second of the state's 21 missions, houses extensive museums, one of which is dedicated to Junipero Serra, the Spanish founder of California's missions. Father Serra lived here, and his rooms are restored. Visitors can see his library, which was California's

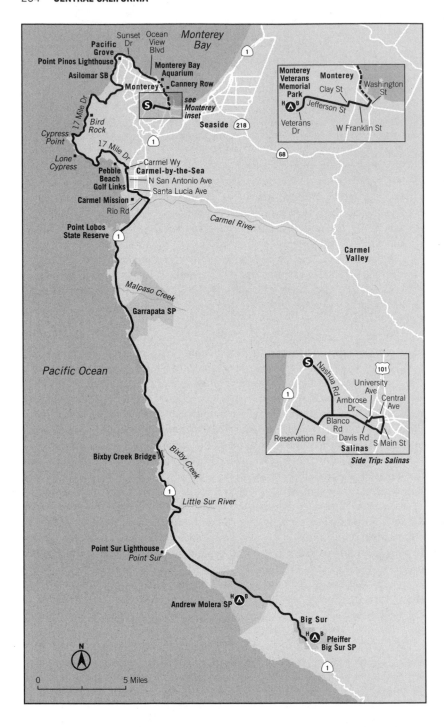

Monterey Bay

Sunset Dr
Ocean View Blvd
Pacific Grove
Point Pinos Lighthouse
Asilomar SB
Monterey Bay Aquarium
Monterey
Cannery Row

1

17 Mile Dr

Bird Rock

Cypress Point

17 Mile Dr

Lone Cypress

Pebble Beach Golf Links

Carmel Wy
Carmel-by-the-Sea
N San Antonio Ave
Santa Lucia Ave

Carmel Mission
Rio Rd

Point Lobos State Reserve

1

see Monterey inset

S

Seaside   218

1

68

Monterey Veterans Memorial Park
Monterey
Clay St
Washington St

Jefferson St

Veterans Dr

W Franklin St

Carmel River

Carmel Valley

Malpaso Creek

Garrapata SP

Pacific Ocean

Bixby Creek Bridge

Bixby Creek

S   Nashua Rd

1

University Ave

Ambrose Dr

Central Ave

Blanco Rd

Reservation Rd   Davis Rd

S Main St

Salinas

101

Side Trip: Salinas

1

Little Sur River

Point Sur Lighthouse
Point Sur

Andrew Molera SP

Big Sur

Pfeiffer Big Sur SP

1

N

0   5 Miles

Surveying the Bixby Creek Bridge from a pullout a couple of miles south

first. He also died here, and the mission contains a shrine to Serra, who was granted sainthood in 2015.

Tackling the rugged coastline south of Carmel means enduring an intermittent lack of road shoulder as well as a couple of historic (read: narrow) bridges. But new bridges, including the generous Bixby Creek Bridge, make room for bikes, and parts of the road include adequate shoulders. Navigating these rolling hills does require attention to traffic and, especially if the weather is foggy, steel nerves.

Drag your gaze from a winding climb to gauge the blueness of coastal waters, fading from sparkling azure at the shoreline to dusky navy on the horizon.

Pass the Point Sur Lighthouse, which sits dramatically atop a 300-foot rock jutting into the ocean. The road and climb to the lighthouse are accessible only by group tour, where you can learn of the many shipwrecks that lie beneath the waves, including an unusual one that came from the sky. The USS *Maron*, a Navy dirigible, sank in 1450 feet of water in February 1935. The craft, nearly 800 feet long (three times the length of a Boeing 747), was made of an aluminum frame and cotton skin. It carried four scout planes, which it could launch and recover with a trapeze mechanism, and traveled at 80 miles per hour.

Perhaps the late-day sun will turn the windswept coastal hills red as you approach the wooded campground at Pfeiffer Big Sur State Park. The scattered resorts that make up the small town prior to the park offer provisioning options, and Big Sur Lodge, adjacent to the campground, has a café and grocery store.

MILEAGE LOG

0.0   Depart Monterey Veterans Memorial Park, turning left onto Veterans Dr.

0.5   Forward onto Jefferson St. at Y with Johnson St.

0.7   Left onto Clay St.

0.8   Right onto W. Franklin St.

1.4   Left onto Washington St.

1.5   Cross Del Monte Ave., then left onto Monterey Bay Coastal Trail at Fishermans Wharf.

2.6   Pass Steinbeck Plaza at Cannery Row.

2.8   Pass Monterey Bay Aquarium.

3.8   Right onto Ocean View Blvd. as trail ends at 17th St.

3.9   Road curves left at Lovers Point Park.

5.0   Pass Pacific Grove Marine Gardens Park.

5.1   Pass John Denver memorial; road becomes Sunset Dr.

5.5   Pass Point Pinos Lighthouse.

6.5   Pass Asilomar State Beach.

7.4   Right onto 17 Mile Dr.; use bike route detour on right at gate.

8.5   Bear right to stay on 17 Mile Dr.

10.6   Pass Bird Rock vista point.

11.1   Pass Spyglass Hill Rd.

12.1   Bear right at Y with Portola Rd. to stay on 17 Mile Dr.

12.3   Bear left at Y with Sunset Point to stay on 17 Mile Dr.

13.1   Pass Lone Cypress tree.

13.7   Straight at Cabrillo Rd. intersection onto Cypress Dr.

13.9   Straight at Stevenson Dr. intersection onto 17 Mile Dr.

14.1   Pass Pebble Beach Golf Links.

14.4   Bear right to stay on 17 Mile Dr. at Peter Hay Golf Course.

14.5   Bear right at Alvarado Ln. to stay on 17 Mile Dr.

16.0   Right onto Carmel Wy., becomes N. San Antonio Ave. in Carmel-by-the-Sea.

16.4   Right to stay on San Antonio at 4th Ave.

17.2   Left onto Santa Lucia Ave.

17.7   Right onto Rio Rd.

17.8   Pass Carmel Mission Basilica.

18.4   Right onto SR 1.

18.7   Cross Carmel River.

20.6   Pass Point Lobos State Reserve.

23.2   Cross Malpaso Creek.

25.2   Pass Garrapata State Park.

28.0   Pass Garrapata State Park beach.

31.6   Cross Bixby Creek Bridge.

35.0   Cross Little Sur River.

37.0   Pass Point Sur Lighthouse.

40.0   Pass Andrew Molera State Park.

42.3   Enter Big Sur.

44.3   Left into campground at Pfeiffer Big Sur State Park.

BIG SUR TO PACIFIC VALLEY
Distance: 33.3 miles
Elevation gain: 3230 feet

Sometimes it makes sense to pass swiftly through the wildest, most remote areas, returning to civilization quickly. But occasionally, take time to revel in isolation and seclusion. On this section of the central California coast, you can take either approach. Today's ride is short but with plenty of climbing. Even so, stopping for the day at the appointed campground offers an afternoon at the nearby white-sand beach. Or you can combine this route and the next for a longer day in the saddle that eats up a lot more of this uneventful coastal area. It depends mostly on your mood.

Get ready for a climb right out of the campground, followed by a rolling, winding route far above the crashing waves. Intermittent stone walls edge the road, their notched, mortared castle-tops framing the surf. Rocky or scrub-covered hillsides rise from the road, sometimes trapping fog. A narrow shoulder adds to the challenge, especially on weekends, when coastal traffic from day-trippers increases. As they enjoy the view, such drivers are often not paying attention to cyclists.

Few services exist along this section. A restaurant called Nepenthe and its Phoenix art gallery cling to an outcropping, designed by a talented student of Frank Lloyd Wright. Another café and gallery are found a few miles on, and the tony, new age Esalen Institute secludes itself below the road. An unusual site is the Henry Miller Memorial Library, a bookstore and arts center just beyond Nepenthe that honors the late writer, who was a Big Sur resident.

But are there towns? Well, there's one, and it's little more than an extended resort facility. Tiny Lucia, 10 miles before tonight's campground, has an overpriced general store and restaurant along with its phalanx of motel rooms. Its café patio looms high over the surf, justifying its higher-priced but tasty fare and making it a welcome lunch stop.

You pass by three parks with campgrounds along the way, but only one, Kirk Creek Campground, offers hiker-biker sites, and that location does not have potable water. Julia Pfeiffer Burns State Park has only a few campsites and water but no showers, while Limekiln State Park offers full services; however, both are small and popular with no hiker-biker sites, so advance reservations are recommended.

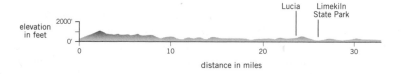

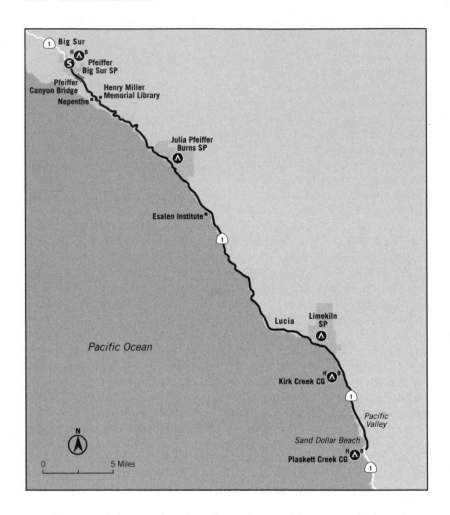

This part of the coastline has always been wild. In pioneer days, lime-stone was mined (the reason behind the name Limekiln) and shipped back to San Francisco to be used in mortar for bricklaying. Tanbark was harvested for making tannic acid used to tan leather; lumberjacks stalked the valuable redwoods, the fog-loving giants that find their southern terminus here. A brief gold rush in the 1880s brought speculators. All the commodities were hauled away by ship from the rugged coastline.

With fewer people, wildlife is abundant. Sea otters swim among the kelp that flosses the shore, while gray whales can be spotted spouting off in the distance. Birds are plentiful; in the woods, there are many species of wildlife, including predators like mountain lions. So there's a bit of danger in nature here. Dozens of creeks splash into the ocean, where riptides and sneaker waves are common. Poison oak is prevalent, triggering warnings for hikers at every trailhead.

No services are available near tonight's campground, so provisioning ahead is required, either the day before or in tiny Lucia. The alternative is to cycle 2 miles past the campground to Gorda, which has a small grocery.

At Plaskett Creek Campground, this segment's suggested terminus, an open central lawn houses cycling campers. There are no showers. What makes Plaskett Creek a desirable stop is the beach. Just north of the campground is a trail to Sand Dollar Beach, an arcing expanse of white sand popular with surfers. Explore the tide pools, comb the beach for treasures, or simply dig in your toes and listen to the pounding waves. If you're going to spend an afternoon off the bike, this is a great place to do it.

MILEAGE LOG

0.0   Depart Pfeiffer Big Sur State Park campground, turning left onto SR 1 S.
1.1   Cross Pfeiffer Canyon Bridge
3.0   Pass Nepenthe.
3.3   Pass Henry Miller Memorial Library.
6.1   Pass Coast Gallery and Coast Café.
11.1 Pass Julia Pfeiffer Burns State Park (camping).
14.3 Pass Esalen Institute.
23.8 Pass Lucia.
26.0 Pass Limekiln State Park (camping).
28.0 Pass Kirk Creek Campground (hiker-biker camping, no water).
31.0 Pass through Pacific Valley.
33.1 Pass Sand Dollar Beach.
33.3 Left into Plaskett Creek Campground.

The route crosses through arid, open Pacific Valley.

PACIFIC VALLEY TO SAN SIMEON
Distance: 34.8 miles
Elevation gain: 2720 feet

"Miss Morgan, we are tired of camping out in the open at the ranch in San Simeon and I would like to build a little something." So began William Randolph Hearst's odyssey, as he engaged the renowned San Francisco architect Julia Morgan to build a castle in the middle of a quarter million acres of ranch land he owned by the tiny coastal burg of San Simeon.

From his inquiry to Morgan in 1919 until the project ended in 1945, they erected Casa Grande, the iconic twin-spired castle, and three smaller (yet still grand) *casas* in a complex that included two impressive swimming pools, extensive gardens, and the largest private zoo in the world. It grew to 165 rooms (58 of them bedrooms) in 80,000 square feet of living space, with 127 acres of gardens, terraces, pools, and walkways.

The complex, housing his legendary art collection, became known and in some cases derided for its vast array of architectural styles borrowed from around the world. The eclectic mishmash often resulted from Hearst's purchasing architectural features from historic buildings, dismantling them, and then reassembling them wholesale into his California hillside behemoth.

Hearst called the giant ranch La Cuesta Encantada (Spanish for "Enchanted Hill") and it is a worthy tourism destination, if you're riding this route post-repair of the 2017 road damage that caused a major detour. If you are following the detour around this segment, you can still visit the castle and other area attractions, but you'll have to ride north from Morro Bay, where the detour returns to the coast.

But before you visit the media magnate's ranch on the hill, you'll find some climbing along the last of Big Sur's undulating coastline. The route drops closer to the water after Gorda, the small town south of Plaskett Creek. Now that you're within hearing distance of the waves, the sea seems even grander. Chaparral-covered hillsides open to river valleys as you leave Los Padres National Forest.

Ragged Point Inn, a well-appointed, casual resort with a mini-mart, short-order café, and restaurant, offers an ocean-side break for lunch and restrooms, and also marks the end of the day's major climbs. The road widens, flattens, and becomes a bit monotonous. You might need to dodge

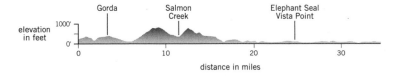

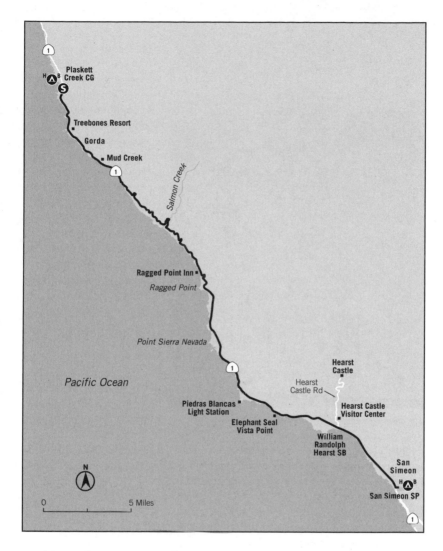

tumbleweeds. The warm, windy open range starkly departs from the tree-lined, foggy, winding coast route you've been experiencing. Green fades to brown, and for a time the sea becomes a distant sliver of blue beyond coastal prairie fenced with barbed wire.

Return to the coast at Piedras Blancas. Cycle by the area light station, a lighthouse without a cap, its flat-topped white tower visible in the distance. Just beyond is the premier viewing spot for elephant seals, as well as sea otters, harbor seals, and sea lions. The attraction is well advertised, and bus-loads of tourists join you on the wide wooden walkways to gape at the giant

The route is pretty well-signed.

mounds of sea mammal lounging on the rocks and shore. They roar and stink, occasionally building up enough energy to plop themselves back into the waves, where they surely must feel much more graceful.

You're riding through Hearst country, and the ranch sells wine and beef as well as tickets to the castle, visible high on a distant hill above the seal rookery. Before hitting tonight's campground, bike through San Simeon, a village with plenty of chain motels with their own cafés, pools, and spas. There are two small groceries but otherwise very little shopping. San Simeon State Park is delightful, with nature trails, bird-filled wetlands, a secluded hiker-biker area within hearing distance of the surf, and trails under State Route 1 that are an easy walk to the beach from the campground.

MILEAGE LOG

0.0 Depart Plaskett Creek Campground, turning left onto SR 1 S.

2.6 Pass Treebones Resort.

3.4 Pass Gorda.

11.4 Pass Salmon Creek.

15.2 Pass Ragged Point Inn (restrooms).

24.1 Pass Piedras Blancas Light Station.

25.7 Pass Elephant Seal Vista Point.

29.7 Pass Hearst Castle Rd. (detour to tour the grounds).

30.2 Pass William Randolph Hearst State Beach.

33.2 Enter San Simeon village.

34.8 Left into San Simeon State Park.

SAN SIMEON TO PISMO BEACH
Distance: 53 miles
Elevation gain: 1990 feet

Your coastal seclusion is coming to an end, as the route enters more heavily populated areas on the way to the big sun-drenched megalopolis of Los Angeles. Today's ride starts quiet, enjoyably departing State Route 1 for a couple of sections, first at the village of Cayucos, and sends you through a few small coastal towns. It then turns inland for a spin through San Luis Obispo, an enthusiastic cycling city, before returning you parallel to the highway into the Five Cities, a string of connected beach communities. The hills are numerous but small, with plenty of flat riding between.

Out of the campground, depart the highway route for a second cup of coffee at Cambria, just 2.5 miles into the ride. Turn left at Windsor Boulevard, then quickly right onto Main Street, which parallels the highway. Find the local java roastery for a fresh cup, and enjoy the vaguely medieval-mixed-with-Old-West architecture as you pedal through town.

It's easy to examine the Fresnel lens from the Piedras Blancas Light Station: the 10-foot-tall lens sits at eye level in a small building on Main. It was removed from the lighthouse, which sits on an outcropping north of San Simeon, after an earthquake in 1948 caused the building to be deemed unstable. Today it is a Cambria attraction next to the Pinedorado, a gussied-up Western-style fairgrounds that hosts a big do over Labor Day. Return to the highway just beyond these attractions via Cambria Drive.

Next the highway delivers you to Morro Bay, worth a detour for a look at its unusual bay and rock formation. Exit onto Main Street, then turn toward the touristy waterfront on Harbor and consider Morro Rock, which looms over the water. This 581-foot volcanic plug separates the harbor from the sea and is connected to the mainland with a causeway. The hulking mound defines the town, shielding the water to a calm glassiness, shading the shore late in the day, and glowing at sunrise. Its imposing outline makes for a dramatic sunset scene.

If you're exploring the town, depart south on Main Street and ride through Morro Bay State Park, where there's hiker-biker camping, a quiet marina, a natural history museum, and a public golf course. Rejoin the route with a right onto South Bay Boulevard. If you skirt the town on the highway, turn right onto South Bay, which edges the neighboring town of Los Osos. Turn onto Los Osos Valley Road and enjoy a quiet two-lane road through wetlands and farm country. You

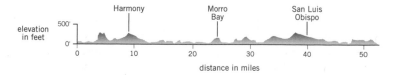

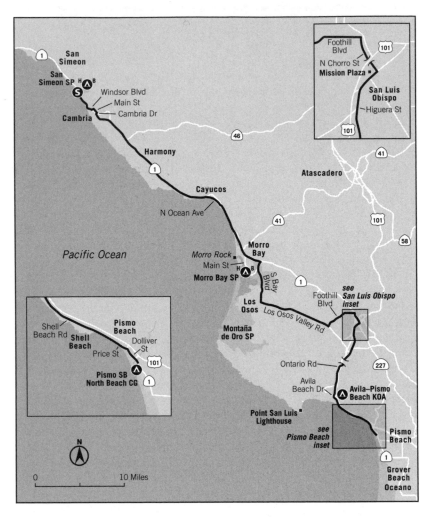

might be tempted to detour to Montaña de Oro State Park, 2 miles off the route. This extensive park features quiet trails and roads and a stunning seashore.

Join local cyclists on the well-pedaled route through dry ranch land into the city of San Luis Obispo. A couple of turns takes you to the tree-lined city center, a bustling area befitting a college town (SLO is home to California Polytechnic State University). One block off the route sits the old mission, and a few blocks farther is the art museum. Mission Plaza, fronting San Luis Obispo Creek, connects the two and hosts festivals and events. Here is the perfect opportunity to "SLO" down, take a break, and have some lunch.

US Highway 101 joins with SR 1 at SLO, but fortunately there are comfortable side roads that allow cyclists to stay off of it, paralleling the highway into

A volcanic plug, hulking Morro Rock calms the waters of Morro Bay.

Shell Beach, the first of the Five Cities. At the entrance to Shell Beach is the side road to Avila Beach, beyond which sits the Point San Luis Lighthouse. Pass the area KOA facility and a small hot-springs resort near this intersection. The route winds along the water past the cute Dinosaur Caves Park and on to Pismo Beach, and then skips two of the five cities, Grover Beach and Arroyo Grande, which are inland on US 101.

Tonight's destination is the North Beach Campground at Pismo State Beach, though it has a higher campground fee than the next option. The extensive, family-friendly site borders a popular sandy stretch of Pismo State Beach. Another mile south is the Coastal Dunes RV Park and Campground, adjacent to Pismo Dunes; the small, rather unappealing campground, though it offers hiker-biker sites, sits on a narrow, chain-link-enclosed strip between the highway and railroad tracks, with the hiker-biker sites remote and exposed at one end. Across the highway, the Pismo Dunes' undulating hills of sand stretch far and wide along the water, an area popular with the all-terrain vehicle tourists, so expect some noise if visiting the dunes.

Just beyond the North Beach Campground is a delightful roadside stop: the Monarch Butterfly Grove. In season (October through February), the large orange monarchs stop here en masse as they migrate along the coast. They rest in the park's eucalyptus trees, crowding onto branches and hanging onto each other so densely that the trees look blanketed with folded orange-and-black wings. The quarter-mile jaunt from the campground is a nice leg stretcher after a day on the bike.

MILEAGE LOG

0.0 Depart San Simeon State Park, turning left onto SR 1 S.
2.0 Enter Cambria.

2.2 Pass Windsor Blvd. (detour to Cambria town center).

2.7 Pass Cambria Dr. (south end of town center).

6.8 Pass SR 46 intersection.

8.6 Pass Harmony, population 18.

16.2 Right on N. Ocean Ave. to go through Cayucos.

16.5 Bear left to stay on N. Ocean at Lucerne St.

17.9 Forward onto SR 1 on-ramp as S. Ocean ends.

23.1 Pass Main St. exit to Morro Bay (detour to Morro Rock, Morro Bay State Park, camping).

24.8 Right onto S. Bay Blvd.

25.7 Pass Main St. intersection.

27.5 Enter Los Osos.

29.0 Left onto Los Osos Valley Rd. (detour left in short mile to Montaña de Oro State Park).

35.9 Left onto Foothill Blvd. Caution: fast traffic.

37.8 Enter San Luis Obispo.

38.7 Right onto N. Chorro St.

39.4 Forward on Chorro to cross under US 101.

39.7 Pass Mission Plaza on right.

39.8 Right on Higuera St.

40.8 Merge left at intersection with Madonna Rd. to stay on Higuera.

43.8 Forward on Higuera at on-ramp to northbound US 101. Caution: turning traffic.

44.3 Forward on Higuera under US 101 at southbound on-ramp.

44.4 Right onto Ontario Rd., then immediate left to stay on Ontario.

46.5 Continue straight on Ontario Rd. at intersection with San Luis Bay Dr.

47.4 Pass Avila–Pismo Beach KOA.

47.5 Left onto Avila Beach Dr.

47.8 Right onto Shell Beach Rd. (detour left to Point San Luis Lighthouse).

48.1 Enter Pismo Beach.

50.5 Pass Dinosaur Caves Park. Shell Beach becomes Price St.

51.8 Bear right onto Dolliver St. at off-ramp from US 101. Follow SR 1 sign into Grover Beach.

52.6 Cross Pismo Creek.

53.0 Right into Pismo State Beach North Beach Campground.

PISMO BEACH TO GAVIOTA
Distance: 64.7 miles
Elevation gain: 3360 feet

No coast. No fog. No tourist towns. Today you'll discover a new part of California: dusty, hot, inland, irrigated farmland. But as you return to the coast and approach the garden-laden coastal city of Santa Barbara at the end of

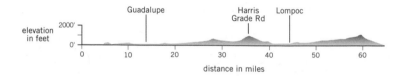

Leaving Pismo Beach, pass by the Monarch Butterfly Grove and stop in

this chapter, you'll be leaving it all behind. So enjoy this departure from the stereotypical coastal experience.

Leaving Pismo Beach, pass by the Monarch Butterfly Grove and stop in for a quick view of the grand insects if you're there in season. Then pedal past the Oceano Dunes area, also worth a brief detour to look over the ocean of sand, just to channel your inner Lawrence of Arabia.

Once it departs from the Five Cities, State Route 1 steers you into farm fields. This book's route departs a bit from the ACA maps, which send you on a farm-road loop through the valley east of town. Instead, take the signed alternate bike route on South Halcyon Road, which includes a steep, quarter-mile climb at the end.

Heading south, busy US Highway 101 is visible east across the flat valley, with denuded hills behind it. Pedal through tiny Guadalupe, which sports a Mexican-inspired grocery that caters to the local population of migrant workers. Then head back into the dusty fields of the Santa Maria Valley, where those workers toil.

The town of Orcutt is a welcome detour at 25 miles and a good lunch choice. East off the route just a half mile, it sports a six-block town center with plentiful cafés. Its attitude is hometown USA. SR 135 joins here, and SR 1 splits off to the west a couple miles south of town. Continue on SR 135 to a right turn onto Harris Grade Road, and be ready for a climb. (Yes, a road with "grade" in the name probably includes elevation gain.) On a hot day, this can be grueling, as much of its steady climb is exposed along a rocky hillside.

Views from atop the climb cheer you on, with the destination of Lompoc visible across the flat land below. Drop down on a series of switchbacks onto the northern edge of the city, where you pick up a bike lane into town. Jog over to streets a bit quieter than the commercial traffic of SR 1 to make your way through town. None of the three parks with hiker-biker campgrounds on this strip of coast leading into Santa Barbara have nearby stores for provisions, so stock up at Lompoc.

Lompoc offers an interesting tourist attraction, if you're not burned out on old religious missions. The La Purisima Mission here is an excellent example of a complete complex: long, low adobe buildings spread out around central plazas. Connected rooms housed the many functions of mission life: weaving, tanning, cooking, and, of course, worshiping. You can imagine many people living in the sprawling, solid complex. The extensive water-storage system, essential in this near-desert environment, is impressive. The mission

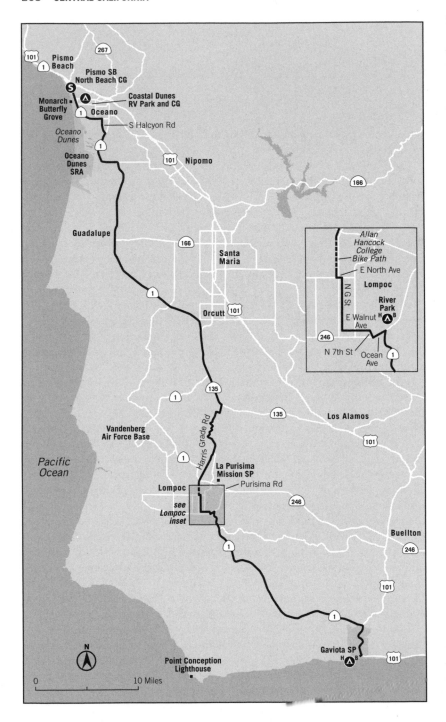

The La Purisima Mission outside Lompoc offers one of the more complete views of life in the pioneer religious communities.

sits on the northeast end of town, accessible via Purisima Road north of town or off SR 246, which continues east of town.

In Lompoc, at about 45 miles, you also have an option of taking a diversion and a choice to eat up some more miles. The side trip heads east, into the Santa Ynez wine country across the valley. You could camp at River Park in Lompoc tonight, then take a day to ride the 45-mile route that leads you through the Danish-themed town of Solvang and into the wine country. (See the Santa Ynez Wine Country side trip.) That diversion ends by delivering you to Gaviota State Park, where this day's main route ends.

To continue on today's route without a side trip, turn south to stay on SR 1 just before reaching the riverside campground. Pedal for a few miles through a cut in the hills before beginning a long climb up into the coastal range that offers good vistas. At nearly 60 miles, begin your descent on a 7.5 percent grade and, at 62 miles, join the busier US 101 for a few last downhill miles to Gaviota State Park.

Gaviota is the first of the three parks with hiker-biker campgrounds, and it is farthest from the highway, while the next camp, Refugio State Beach (another 9 miles), offers the most comfortable hiker-biker sites, which sit virtually on the beach under a large tree canopy with nearby restrooms. The third, El Capitán (3 miles past Refugio), is situated above the beach with vistas toward Santa Barbara. The paved Aniso Trail along the bluffs connects Refugio and El Capitán. All campgrounds are aurally interrupted by trains that regularly pass on the tracks between the highway and the camps. Especially annoying is the 2:00 AM freight. Not even the mighty Pacific can drown that out.

MILEAGE LOG

0.0　Depart Pismo State Beach North Beach Campground, turning right onto SR 1 southbound.

0.2　Pass Monarch Butterfly Grove.

1.8　Pass Pier Ave. (detour 0.5 mile to Oceano Dunes).

2.8　Bear left at Front St. to stay on SR 1 through Oceano.

4.0　Right onto S. Halcyon Rd.

5.3　Right onto SR 1.

14.4　Enter Guadalupe.

25.4　Pass W. Clark Ave. (exit for Orcutt).

26.3　Forward as SR 135 joins SR 1 south of Orcutt.

29.8　Forward to continue on SR 135 as SR 1 splits to the west.

32.5　Right onto Harris Grade Rd.

40.4　Cross Purisima Rd. and enter Lompoc.

40.9　Bear right onto Allan Hancock College Bike Path.

41.5　Forward onto bike lane on SR 1 as bike path ends.

42.1　Left onto E. North Ave.; in 1 block, right on N. G St.

43.1　Left onto E. Walnut Ave.

44.0　Right onto N. 7th St. as Walnut ends.

44.1　Left onto Ocean Ave. (SR 1).

44.5　Right onto SR 1 (detour straight on Ocean Ave. to River Park campground).

59.4　Reach top of long climb.

62.2　Right onto US 101.

64.7　Right into Gaviota State Park.

SIDE TRIP: SANTA YNEZ WINE COUNTRY
Distance: 44.5 miles
Elevation gain: 2330 feet

Send your trip sideways for a day by taking a detour into the Santa Ynez wine country, just north of Santa Barbara. There are three reasons the day will go "sideways": (1) You'll head east instead of south; (2) the hills of this wine country are perpendicular to the hills of most quality winemaking regions, which run north-south; and (3) this is the area where they filmed the 2004 movie *Sideways*, so named because of reason number 2.

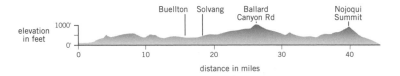

Copenhagen? Nej! (no), it's Solvang, a Danish-themed town at the base of the Santa Ynez wine country.

To do this sideways extension, take a shorter day out of Oceano and end your ride at Lompoc, a 45-mile day. Then ride this route, ending it at Gaviota State Park, the original destination from Oceano, another 45-mile day. Then you'll be back on track for the following day's route. Alternatively, you could ride the extra 15 miles from Lompoc to Buellton, which is where the wine country tour really begins, to allow more time on the wine country tour. Best

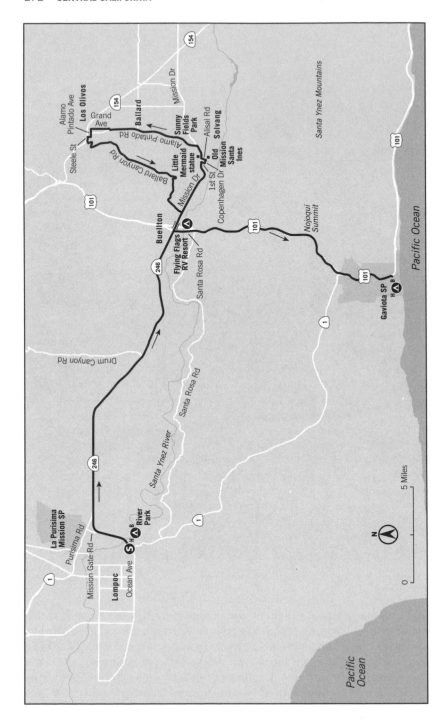

times of year to take this side trip are spring and fall, as it can get blazingly hot in the dry valley during summer. In spring, find wildflowers blanketing the hills and a March event, the Solvang Century, which brings thousands of cyclists to the area.

Accommodations for your overnight can be found in the many Lompoc motels or at the modest River Park, which has a basic hiker-biker corral. A cluster of average-cost motels can be found in Buellton, along with Flying Flags RV Resort, which offers tent camping in a KOA-like experience, but not at hiker-biker rates. For an overnight in the more populous, touristy Solvang, you'll find many more motels, but with higher rates, and no camping options.

The ride from Lompoc to Buellton is on State Route 246, a flat, busy farm road, with one winery along an allée of tall trees just out of Buellton. (The snaky, longer Santa Rosa Road runs parallel to SR 246 a mile south of Lompoc.) At SR 246's intersection with US Highway 101, find a cluster of cafés, including Pea Soup Anderson's, famous for its . . . you guessed it: Reuben sandwich. No. Pea soup. The Hitching Post is also a Buellton favorite, a barbecue joint whose bar hosted some scenes in *Sideways*.

Four miles farther east on SR 246 is Solvang, a town famous for its Danish theme, expressed in its architecture, food, museums, and parks. A replica of Copenhagen's famous *Little Mermaid* statue relaxes in a fountain on its main street, next to a bike shop and across from Hans Christian Andersen Museum. Coffee shops and bakeries urge you to dine like a Dane, or at least to eat like a tourist in Denmark would.

The most interesting local site existed long before the Scandinavian influence, though. The Franciscan Mission Santa Ines, overlooking the river valley on the east edge of town, was established in 1804. Extensive restoration and care of highlights such as the mission reservoir, created from a dam and an aqueduct, have kept this active church as a valued historic artifact.

Depart Solvang north into the valley that houses the villages of Ballard and Los Olivos. Along the way, farm stands and wineries beckon. Sunny Fields Park would make a fine picnic stop. You'll be cycling along the Dan Henry Bike Route here. If you're a club cyclist, that name should ring a bell.

The route's namesake, an enthusiastic cyclist and pioneer in the sport, retired in the area after a career as a commercial pilot. He died in 2012, four days before his 99th birthday. Henry designed a directional route-marking system to keep cyclists on the preferred routes of event rides. His system was adopted by the League of American Bicyclists and is widely used by many cycling clubs. The marks, often spray-painted onto the pavement near key intersections, are commonly called "Dan Henrys."

Los Olivos has an Old West way of being cute. The town was founded as a stagecoach rest stop, and it's a meet-up corral for local cyclists. Casual cafés and fine dining coexist, along with tasting rooms, art galleries, upscale shopping, and a well-stocked general store. For more area exploration and some hill climbing, you could detour north to Figueroa Mountain or Foxen Canyon roads, but this side trip's route turns around here and heads back to Buellton via winding, picturesque Ballard Canyon Road. You'll pass ranches with cattle and even bison, along with a couple more wineries, over a rolling 7 miles.

Return to Buellton and then head south on US 101 toward Gaviota. You must exit Buellton via Santa Rosa Road and merge onto the highway south of town, as bicyclists are prohibited on the highway section through town. The remaining route is a long climb to Nojoqui Summit, and that's no joke, although it is also not a steep or punishing climb. From there, spin downhill into the state park, situated at the point where US 101 turns sideways toward Santa Barbara.

MILEAGE LOG

0.0   Depart River Park campground, turning left onto SR 246 eastbound.

1.4   Pass Mission Gate Rd.

2.2   Pass Purisima Rd.

14.7   Enter Buellton.

15.9   Cross over US 101.

16.5   Continue straight on SR 246 at intersection with Ballard Canyon Rd.

18.2   Enter Solvang, where SR 246 becomes Mission Dr.

19.1   Pass Solvang Park (tourist information center).

19.2   Right onto 1st St.

19.3   Left onto Copenhagen Dr. In 1 block, left onto Alisal Rd.

19.5   Right onto Mission Dr. In 1 block, pass entrance to Old Mission Santa Ines.

19.8   Left onto Alamo Pintado Rd.

20.5   Pass Sunny Fields Park.

22.6   Pass Baseline Ave. in Ballard.

23.8   Bear right at Santa Barbara Ave. to stay on Alamo Pintado Rd.

23.9   Left onto Grand Ave.

24.6   Arrive at Los Olivos town center.

24.7   Left onto Alamo Pintado Ave.

25.1   Bear right onto Steele St. as Alamo Pintado ends.

25.3   Bear left onto Ballard Canyon Rd. as Steele ends.

30.5   Right to stay on Ballard Canyon Rd. at Chalk Hill Rd. intersection.

32.5   Right onto SR 246 as Ballard Canyon Rd. ends.

33.1   Cross over US 101.

33.4   Left onto Avenue of the Flags, which becomes Santa Rosa Rd.

34.1   Left, then immediate right onto US 101 S. on-ramp.

39.6   Arrive at Nojoqui Summit.

42.0   Pass intersection with SR 1.

44.5   Right into Gaviota State Park.

GAVIOTA TO CARPINTERIA
Distance: 46.1 miles
Elevation gain: 1520 feet

Start today with a beautiful ride along the sunshiny coastline north of Santa Barbara. Beautiful, that is, if you like divided-highway traffic, with the sun shining in the reflection off the passing cars. Truth is, the first dozen miles into palm-tree-and-garden-filled Santa Barbara is loud and busy. At least the big highway's shoulder is generous, and a nice breeze off the water washes away the exhaust fumes.

For your first stop from the campground, take a quick break at the Arroyo Hondo Bridge at its vista point. You can see the original 1918 bridge here, a picturesque concrete span that has been retained to show the size and scope of the original US Highway 101. Be thankful you are on the highway's wider version 2.0.

Interpretive signage tells about the Channel Islands, visible off the coast here when the fog lifts—turns out they used to be one superisland due to a drop in the sea level during the Ice Ages. Linger over the sign panels and you will be surprised, and I bet delighted, to learn about how the bicycle craze of the 1880s affected area residents. Cyclists would ride the newly tracked train to Ventura and bicycle back home or vice versa. And, so the sign says, the nation's oldest continuous operating bicycle shop as of 2015 was Hazard Cyclery in Santa Barbara.

Pass the exits to Refugio State Beach and El Capitán State Beach, and bask in the knowledge that you could enter and take a break at either of these beaches free of charge. Cyclists can always visit day-use areas at state beaches for free, as fees are collected only from those driving and parking their motorized transportation. If you want a break from the highway, turn off at Refugio and find the start of the Aniso Trail at the south edge of the campground. This paved 2.5-mile ribbon through the dry brush connects Refugio and El Capitán. You'll soar like an *aniso* (the Chumash word for "seagull") along the bluffs above the shore.

After one long climb, exit the highway onto Hollister Avenue into Goleta, the town hosting the University of California–Santa Barbara. A paved trail takes you to and through the UCSB campus, past its students' fleets of bikes crammed into sprawling racks, jogging between playfields and then classroom

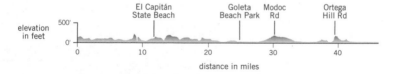

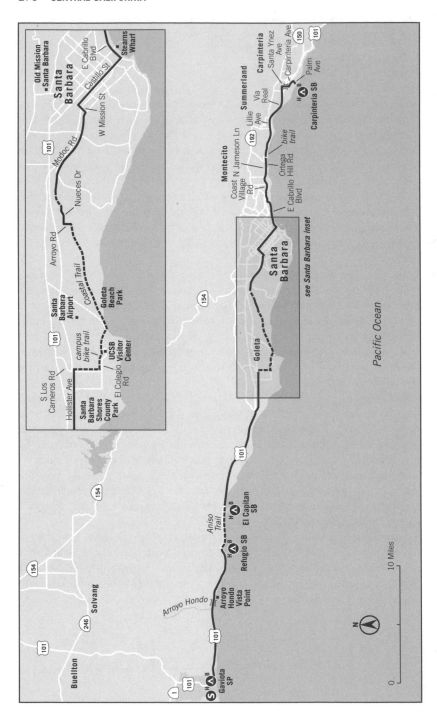

buildings on its way back to the waterfront. Keep your eyes peeled for "Coast Route" directional signage, especially at the bike roundabouts. After a turn at Goleta Beach Park, the trail heads inland and follows Atascadero Creek through wetlands between you and the ocean.

In Santa Barbara, enjoy the consistent bike lanes as you travel through this busy city. It's worth a stop to enjoy the picturesque Old Mission Santa Barbara by taking a detour after you cross under US 101, taking East Mission Street north a half mile. Get back on the main route by cycling through the vibrant, human-scale downtown with its upscale shops, along State Street. (Or take the quieter Anacapa Street and pass stately municipal buildings and the city's historical museum.)

A wide sidewalk trail leads along the shore in central Santa Barbara.

Santa Barbara's waterfront shows off its penchant for gardens, with blooms everywhere. A climate that changes little throughout the year makes for a lengthy growing season, and the marine breeze moderates the climate, which can be very hot in the hills around the city. On Stearns Wharf, find cafés and entertainment, and in the extensive waterfront park you may stumble across one of the plentiful festivals.

East of the city, ride along the edges of coastal communities that line US 101, including welcoming Summerland. Cross over the highway and head into Carpinteria, where you'll find the busy, open campground at Carpinteria State Beach. A large shopping center at the turn onto Palm Avenue is best for provisioning, but restaurants sit street-side throughout the area.

MILEAGE LOG

0.0 Depart Gaviota State Park, turning right onto US 101 S.

4.9 Pass Arroyo Hondo Vista Point.

9.2 Pass exit to Refugio State Beach (camping; start of Aniso Trail).

12.0 Pass exit to El Capitán State Beach (camping; end of Aniso Trail).

19.1 Take exit 110 onto Hollister Ave. into Goleta.

19.5 Right onto Hollister at end of off-ramp, then left in ½ block.

22.2 Right at S. Los Carneros Rd. onto paved campus bike trail on east side of road.

22.4 Cross Mesa Rd.

22.7 Bike trail curves left and runs parallel to El Colegio Rd.

23.1 Forward at roundabout at Stadium Rd. to continue on trail.

23.4 Forward as trail crosses Ocean Rd.

23.5 Forward through trail roundabout to continue on trail, with UCSB Visitor Center on right.

23.7 Forward as trail curves right, then left at chemistry building; follow signs for Coastal Trail.

23.9 Forward as trail curves between engineering and physics buildings; follow signs for Coastal Trail.

24.4 Forward at trail roundabout by environmental science building.

24.1 Cross Lagoon Rd. and continue on trail as it exits campus next to Ward Memorial Blvd. (SR 217).

24.6 Bear right at intersection with S. Fairview Ave. bike route to stay on Coastal Trail.

24.8 Left onto Sandspit Rd. as trail ends in Goleta Beach Park. Immediate left to cross bridge over Tecolotito Creek, then right to get back onto trail.

26.3 Cross S. Patterson Ave. and continue on trail.

27.7 Forward as trail crosses Atascadero Creek.

28.0 Cross Puente Dr. and continue on trail.

28.2 Bear left with bike trail to cross Atascadero Creek Bridge. Forward onto Arroyo Rd. as trail ends.

28.4 Right onto Nueces Dr.; follow signs for Coastal Trail.

28.7 Forward onto "no outlet" street (connector trail at end).

28.9 Rejoin Nueces Dr.

28.9 Cross Nogal Dr. to continue on trail.

29.2 Right onto Modoc Rd.

30.1 Cross Las Palmas Dr.

31.3 Cross Las Positas Rd. (SR 225) and continue forward on Modoc.

32.1 Left onto W. Mission St.; follow Pacific Coast Bike Route signs.

32.2 Cross under US 101. Caution: freeway ramps.

32.3 Right onto Castillo St. (detour left to Old Mission Santa Barbara).

33.8 Bear left at intersection with US 101 on-ramp at W. Haley St.; continue on Castillo under it.

34.0 Cross W. Montecito St.

34.1 Left onto W. Cabrillo Blvd. at Santa Barbara waterfront.

34.7 Cross State St. (intersection with Stearns Wharf). Continue forward as road becomes E. Cabrillo Blvd.

36.7 Cross Los Patos Wy.

36.8 Cross under US 101.

36.9 Bear right onto Hot Springs Rd.

37.0 Bear right at roundabout onto Coast Village Rd.

Historic, picturesque Old Mission Santa Barbara

37.8 Left at stop sign at intersection with Olive Mill Rd. and freeway on-ramp, then immediately right on N. Jameson Ln.

39.4 Right onto Ortega Hill Rd., then immediate right onto bike trail.

39.6 Right onto Ortega Hill Rd. as bike trail ends.

40.2 Forward as Ortega Hill becomes Lillie Ave. in Summerland town center.

40.9 Forward as road becomes Via Real.

44.7 Right onto Santa Ynez Ave. to cross over US 101.
44.9 Left onto Carpinteria Ave.
45.7 Right onto Palm Ave.
46.1 Arrive at Carpinteria State Beach.

Opposite: *Southern California offers flat riding, palm trees, and plenty of beachfront development.*

SOUTHERN CALIFORNIA

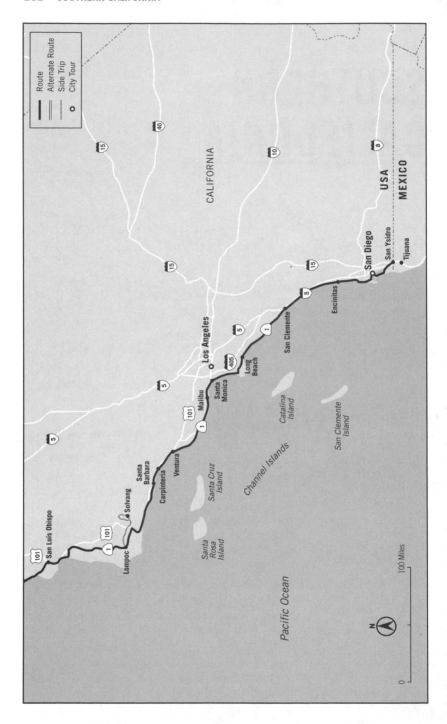

LEAVE THE HILLS AND FORESTS behind because sunny days and sparkling seashores await. Californians' love of the ocean becomes evident, as state beaches replace state parks, and the sea is dotted with the bobbing dark figures of surfers paddling out to catch a wave.

After skirting the natural barrier of the Santa Monica Mountains that reaches nearly to the shore, enter the West Coast's largest city, a sprawling metropolis experienced only slightly if you stay on the coast. As you hop from suburb to suburb, you find each coastal city hosting a municipal pier bustling with attractions.

Bike trails lead you from beach to beach, and side routes carving wiggly shoreline lanes offer escape from highway riding. There are more urban and suburban stretches than rural scenes. Day after day delivers predictably perfect weather, which culminates in approachable San Diego, a fitting place to relax and celebrate the achievement of a long trek.

CARPINTERIA TO POINT MUGU
Distance: 43.2 miles
Elevation gain: 720 feet

Shrouded in the omnipresent fog beyond the tent flap this morning are the Channel Islands, a defining feature of the Santa Barbara coast. The northern five of the chain's eight islands are a national park. They lurk off the coast all the way from here to Los Angeles and are accessible for a hike or even primitive camping via boat transportation from Ventura (logistically difficult for bicycle travelers, as you can't take the bike). The southernmost island, Catalina, offers a delightful day trip from Long Beach, but that's a couple of days farther along the route.

Aim your handlebars south and summit the day's only climb along the Carpinteria bluffs just a couple of miles from camp. After that mellow ascent, settle into the flat beach-to-beach cycling of Southern California. Palm trees, spiky yucca plants, and desert-dry hills provide the distinctive backdrop to this lower third of the Golden State's coast.

A brief stint on US Highway 101, here called the Ventura Freeway, provides stunning views of the water but also makes you glad for the recently opened Ralph Fertig Memorial Bike Path, attached to the edge of the big highway and hanging over the curving bay south of Rincon Point. The grade-separated

Set in the woods, the hiker-biker campground at Sycamore Canyon has the typical accommodations of a picnic table and fire ring.

path greatly increases safety along this compressed highway section where the rugged hills slope sharply to the coastline.

The route takes you on and off the highway, then under it and onto State Route 1, your old friend the Pacific Coast Highway. Approaching Emma Wood State Beach on the northern edge of Ventura, pick up the Omer Rains bike path, which eventually takes you under the highway and into the city of Ventura. Watch for an easy-to-miss right turn at the end of the Ventura Beach RV Resort after a bridge over the Ventura River.

The trail takes you through Seaside Wilderness Park to the town's waterfront. Gulls wheel aloft over moored sailboats as you pedal through Surfers Point Park parallel to Shoreline Drive. To visit the shopping district, exit the trail left as the road curves away from the park. It becomes Figueroa Avenue and delivers you to Main Street in a quarter mile, at San Buenaventura Mission. You can pedal south on Main through a half-dozen blocks of casual shopping and cafés, then return to the waterfront route with a right on California Street. The trail is just beyond the Beach House, a grand restaurant perched on a pier.

After passing the town's marina, cross the Santa Clara River and bear right onto the bike lane along East Harbor Boulevard. Pass a historic lighthouse and wharf, with the sparkling new development brightening up this canal-filled neighborhood. Pedal through Oxnard and into Port Hueneme, home of a large US Navy operation, which you must navigate around. Pass the Seabee Museum, then back to the coast at Port Hueneme Beach Park, which includes a seasonal café concession. Small grocery stores along the route through town offer other options to provision for a lunch stop: a picnic at the park.

South of Oxnard, the smell of artichokes may announce your return to farmland, stretching for a few miles along Hueneme Road. (If you don't know what artichokes smell like now, you will very soon.) An interesting roadside stop is US Navy Missile Park, which showcases a dozen of the military missiles, complete with plaques that tell of their era of service and destructive power. Just beyond is the main gate for Naval Base Ventura County at Point Mugu. Return to SR 1 for the last leg of today's ride, along the edge of the Santa Monica Mountains National Recreation Area. Sycamore Canyon Campground in Point Mugu State Park, with its hiker-biker spot tucked away in the woods, sits across the road from a popular day-use beach.

MILEAGE LOG

0.0   Depart Carpinteria State Beach campground heading straight on Palm Ave.

0.4   Right onto Carpinteria Ave.

2.5   Left onto unsigned Rincon Rd., then immediate right onto US 101 on-ramp.

3.0   Right at exit 83, near Rincon Beach; follow Pacific Coast Bike Route sign.

3.2   Forward across road at end of off-ramp onto two-way Ralph Fertig Memorial Bike Path along US 101.

5.9   Forward as bike trail ends at US 101 off-ramp, then resumes after intersection.

6.8   Forward as trail ends; continue on Mobil Pier Rd. Left in 1 block as road ends.

6.9   Right onto Pacific Coast Hwy. (SR 1).

7.6   Route goes under US 101.

8.1   Pass Hobson County Park.

9.9   Pass Faria Beach Park.

13.5   Bear right onto bike lane when passing Emma Wood State Beach.

15.2   Bear left onto Park Access Rd. and continue forward under US 101.

15.4   Curve right with trail at W. Main St. Cross Ventura River Bridge.

15.9   Right when approaching SR 33 to continue on Omer Rains Trail (detour straight, across SR 33 on Main St., to Ventura shopping district).

16.0   Cross under US 101.

16.3   Forward on trail through Seaside Wilderness Park; follow as it curves left into Surfers Point Park.

16.7   Forward onto Ventura Promenade in Seaside Park.

17.0   Pass Figueroa Ave. at end of parking (detour to downtown Ventura).

17.3   Pass Ventura Pier, then curve left to stay on trail at end of parking.

18.3   Forward onto Pierpont Blvd. in bike lane as trail ends.

19.0   Left onto Peninsula St.

19.3   Right onto Seahorse Ave.

19.5   Left onto Oyster St.; in 1 block, right onto Seaview Ave.

19.9   Left onto Beachmont St.

20.0   Right onto E. Harbor Blvd.

20.9   Pass Ventura Harbor Village (detour to ferry to Channel Islands National Park).

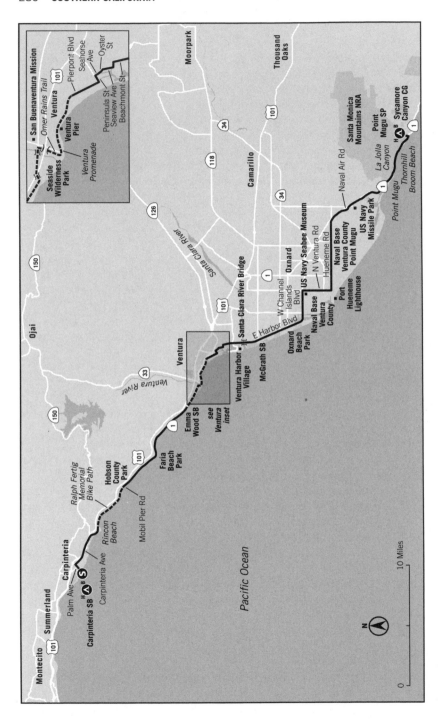

21.3 Bear right onto bike path adjacent to E. Harbor Blvd. over Santa Clara River Bridge.

21.6 Forward on E. Harbor Blvd. after bridge.

21.9 Pass McGrath State Beach.

25.2 Pass Oxnard Beach Park.

25.8 Curve left onto W. Channel Islands Blvd.

27.8 Right onto N. Ventura Rd.

28.2 Pass US Navy Seabee Museum.

29.7 Left onto Hueneme Rd.

34.5 Right onto Naval Air Rd. at on-ramp to SR 1.

35.7 Pass US Navy Missile Park. Continue forward on Naval Air Rd.

36.3 Pass main gate for Naval Base Ventura County Point Mugu.

37.3 Left as road Ts at base entrance, then right onto SR 1.

39.0 Enter Santa Monica Mountains National Recreation Area.

40.1 Pass Point Mugu and Point Mugu Rock.

41.6 Pass La Jolla Canyon and Thornhill Broom Beach.

43.2 Left into Sycamore Canyon Campground. Caution: fast traffic.

POINT MUGU TO SANTA MONICA
Distance: 32 miles
Elevation gain: 1310 feet

The dry hills to the east wear a heavy morning shadow as you bike south out of Point Mugu, in stark contrast to the waves glittering to the west. Today's ride is a mesmerizing stretch past the Santa Monica Mountains and the Malibu canyons. This short day along a mostly flat coastline offers Southern California scenes from the bike seat.

Although there are numerous opportunities for a beach break, today also takes you into the metropolis of Los Angeles, so today's distance is designed to give you a half day in the big city if desired. Today's route stops at Santa Monica so you can plan your own experience of the nation's third-largest city by figuring what you want to see there and how many miles you want to go after your LA visit (see the Los Angeles city tour for suggestions).

From today's start at Sycamore Canyon, reach the next sandy spot in 5 miles at Leo Carrillo State Beach, which also has camping. Perhaps I should write "camping," because the parking areas along the road on these

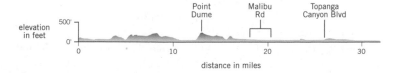

TACKLING LA

Cycling through Los Angeles can be challenging, with heavy traffic, intersecting freeways, and hills into some of the most desirable north-city communities. But a central spin through the city can be comfortably done on bike lanes and residential streets, venturing into congested areas only near the big tourist sites, like Hollywood Boulevard.

Keep this in mind: LA is huge. A route to downtown and back entails 40–50 miles, which at city speeds would be a long day, leaving little time for exploration stops. Best to tackle one section of the city at a time. Here are some ideas to focus your visit:

- **Soak up the beach culture.** Want to go surfing, people-watch with your toes in the sand, or just bask in the relaxed, sun-kissed vibe? Hang out on the Westside, in Santa Monica or Venice. Plenty of motels are within blocks of the beach, although they can be pricey.
- **See the stars.** If you're film-struck, head to Hollywood for the Walk of Fame, Paramount Studios, and the Hollywood Bowl. Look for a place to stay in central LA between Hollywood and downtown, a 10- to 15-mile flat ride from the beach.
- **Appreciate art.** The area's major museums are far-flung but worth the effort. The expansive LA County Museum of Art (LACMA) is centrally located and easy by bike; it takes extra effort to enjoy the downtown Museum of Contemporary Art, and you'll need transit to hit the elevated Getty Center. Stay in a beach community or anywhere midcity north of Interstate 10.
- **Take in a little of everything.** Ride this book's Los Angeles city tour, which edges Beverly Hills, hits Hollywood, samples old LA at its farmers market, bikes by LACMA, and loops back to the coast along a riverside bike path.

beach campgrounds are filled with RVs. Some are the homes of inveterate surfers, who ride the waves into their middle age. Others disgorge large older people who seem to think of "roughing it" as popping out the sides of their giant shipping containers with windows. Seeing hundreds of these lining the coastal route from the vantage point of a bicycle is incredible.

Leo Carrillo's beach adjoins the city of Malibu, although you wouldn't know it from the terrain. Malibu stretches out along many miles of oceanfront and into numerous canyons, so the city's 13,000 residents are spread thinly across the coastal landscape. Glimpses of ocean and beach appear sporadically between the fenced homes through Malibu, where you get used to dense green hedges and gates of all sorts.

Nicholas Canyon County Beach has a few picnic tables near the lifeguard station and food trucks in summer. El Pescador State Beach is a local favorite

SKIPPING LA?

If exploring LA is not on your list, consider traveling farther than Santa Monica before your motel night. Getting to the next campsite from Santa Monica entails a 75-mile day, not recommended because this section has a fair amount of slow urban cycling.

Since the route into Santa Monica is fairly short, you can add miles by riding part of the next day's route to shorten the next day. Marina del Rey buys you 5 more miles and has a nice bike path along its extensive pleasure-boat moorings and nearby hotels.

Or continue past Los Angeles International Airport (LAX)—and return to the coast at Manhattan Beach (13 miles from Santa Monica) or Redondo Beach (16 miles). Taking your motel night there would reduce the next day's route considerably, providing time to continue on to the next available hiker-biker campground, Doheny State Beach at Dana Point, which would be a comfortable 50-ish miles.

for surf fishing, and why not? The park's name is Spanish for "the fisherman." La Piedra State Beach offers a winding trail down from dramatic sandstone bluffs. All have restrooms and, of course, plenty of surfers.

Services consist mostly of small gas-station markets along this road. At 10 miles, find one of those at Trancas Canyon Road, but hold out a bit for a small shopping center with a coffee shop just uphill beyond Zuma Beach, where the route turns away from the water (Point Dume State Beach is out in the distance).

Continue east past Pepperdine University, sprawled on the hillside facing the sea, and into central Malibu. The sometimes-heavy traffic is manageable due to a decent shoulder lane, but the bike space disappears in the congested town center, so a right turn onto quieter Malibu Road is advised. Pass over the mouth of Malibu Creek and then by Malibu Pier before reentering a comfortable bike lane.

At Topanga Canyon Boulevard, with the grand, Spanish-inspired Getty Villa gleaming high above, the highway enters Santa Monica, a sign that today's route is near its end. Spend the last few miles on a sand-swept bike trail, accessed at Will Rogers State Beach at Temescal Canyon Road. The trail runs all along LA's beaches, lined with shops, cafés, and, of course, throngs of tourists, beach bums, and exercising locals. Pull over at the famous Santa Monica Pier.

A recommended stop is Santa Monica Bike Center, just two blocks from the beach at Colorado Avenue and Second Street. Bike Center offers repairs, friendly advice, and perhaps most importantly, secured overnight bike storage, making this a perfect staging spot for a visit to the City of Angels. There are no good camping options remotely near the coastal route here, so plan for a hostel or motel night (just up Second from Bike Center, adjacent to a shopping mall and Santa Monica's busy Third Street Promenade, is a hostel).

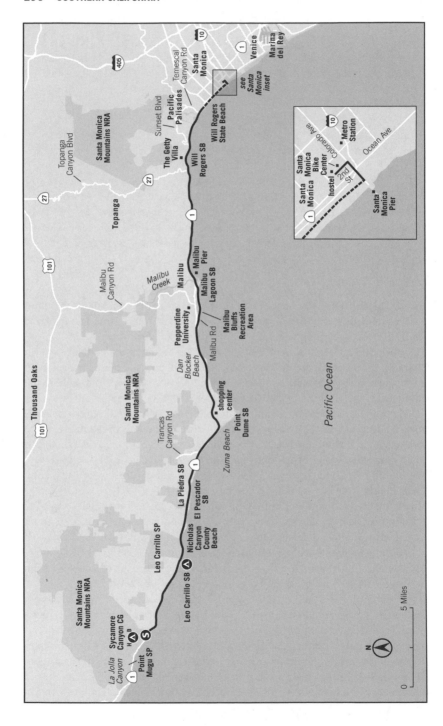

Attractions at the Santa Monica Pier sit beyond a sandy multiuse beach trail.

What interests you about Los Angeles? Answering that question will determine how far you travel today and where you stay tonight. If you want to explore Los Angeles (see the Tackling LA sidebar) or take the described city tour by bike, you'll need a second night. If you want to ride on past LA, see the Skipping LA? sidebar for ideas on where to stay tonight.

MILEAGE LOG

0.0   Depart Sycamore Canyon Campground, turning left onto SR 1.

5.1   Pass Leo Carrillo State Beach (restrooms, camping).

6.0   Pass Nicholas Canyon County Beach (restrooms).

7.5   Pass El Pescador State Beach (restrooms).

10.3 Pass Trancas Canyon Rd.

12.1 Pass Zuma Beach and Point Dume shortly afterward.

13.0 Pass shopping center with coffee shop.

16.9 Pass Corral Canyon Rd.

17.1 Pass Dan Blocker Beach (restrooms).

17.6 Right onto Malibu Rd.

18.0 Pass Pepperdine University.

19.1 Pass Malibu Bluffs Recreation Area.

20.2 Forward onto SR 1 as Malibu Rd. ends.

20.3 Pass Malibu Lagoon State Beach.

21.0 Pass Malibu Pier.

22.4 Pass Carbon Canyon Rd.

26.7 Pass Topanga Canyon Blvd.

27.9 Pass Will Rogers State Beach.

28.1 Pass Sunset Blvd.

29.3 Right at Temescal Canyon Rd., then immediate left onto bike trail at Will Rogers State Beach.

32.0 Arrive at Santa Monica Pier, at foot of Colorado Ave.

CITY TOUR: LOS ANGELES
Distance: 36.4 miles
Elevation gain: 890 feet

Choosing where to go in Los Angeles when you're just taking a day off the coast tour is a bit like choosing your favorite movie star. If you're thinking of drama, you'll go one way, but for lighthearted entertainment, another, and for a historical epic, a third. Stand in the sand at the Santa Monica Pier and try to decide what's most important.

Narrowing the choices down a bit is my preference for touring by bike in this city of cars. A second reality check comes when you consider the city's size: it sprawls high into the hills above canyons to the north and stretches into endless suburbs in all directions. A third consideration is available time. To see more, you'll have to pedal all day (see reality check two). To visit a grand destination, like Disneyland, you'd want the full day available for being a tourist.

Skirting the metropolis seems like a shame, because within the vastness of Los Angeles lies much diversity in population and attractions. I suggest a moderate distance that provides enough time to stop and savor the sights, on a route that tries for a little of everything: drama, entertainment, and history. Hopefully a day off in the city allows time to sample them.

Begin at the end of US Highway 66 (here called Santa Monica Boulevard). That's right, the famous Route 66 from Chicago comes right down to the sandy shore of Santa Monica. If you're staying at the nearby hostel, just a block from the full-service Santa Monica Bike Center (which even offers secured, indoor overnight bike storage), you'll be perfectly situated for the start of this city tour.

Head east away from the water through the beach community's bustling commercial center and onto Santa Monica Boulevard. A detour through quiet, shady side streets gets you to the bike-friendly section of the boulevard near Westwood. Bike lanes have proliferated throughout LA in recent years, and dedicated bike paths have sprouted and lengthened too; but on streets where there are no bike lanes, the determined, entitled big-city drivers will not suffer a foolish cyclist gladly. In other words, pick your route carefully.

First stop: Beverly Hills. Take a spin past the grand homes to the doorstep of the Beverly Hills Hotel. Known as the Pink Palace, the Sunset Boulevard hotel has been home to famous visitors for more than a century. Stars would

Will Rogers
Memorial Park

Hollywood
Blvd

Ballona
Creek Trail

elevation
in feet

500'

0'

0   10   20   30

distance in miles

hole up in its bungalows and hold court in its bar, and it's been the address of choice for visiting royalty. Ogle the hotel from a small park across the street that's dedicated to an honorary mayor of the town: Will Rogers. A bust of the much-loved humorist adorns the center of this lush triangular space. I never met a bust I didn't like.

Head south down the area's most famous street, Rodeo Drive. Shade trees loom overhead until you reach the shopping district, which gleams with marble, glass, and glitz. You might want to make sure to shine up your bike for this ride.

Next up is another shopping center with local history—and probably some things you can afford to buy. Due east is the Grove, which houses the city's historic farmers market, which dates to the 1930s. The farmers market's origins were in truck farms and grocers, not as much in evidence today, as the densely packed area, now surrounded by an open-air mall, attracts a different sort of shopper. The old market stalls retain their charm, and the crowded lunch counters and ice cream shops are today the destination for most shoppers.

In the northeastern corner of the property, where this tour exits, is the sobering LA Museum of the Holocaust. Just beyond looms CBS Television City, the studio complex where hundreds of TV shows have been filmed since the 1950s. If you're a fan of '70s humorist Carol Burnett, as I am, check out her show's spoof of the Italian classic film *The Bicycle Thief* (season 6, episode 6), filmed at this location.

Since you might have stars on your mind, next stop is Hollywood. Bike through quiet residential neighborhoods and then burst into tourist central. Join the hordes to gape at the Chinese Theatre, Wax Museum, and the Walk of Fame, a sidewalk full of bronze stars with famous names set into the concrete along with handprints of those being honored. Take in as much of the street as you can stand, but you'll likely be walking your bike while keeping a close eye on your possessions in the crowd. Be very concerned about the real-life bicycle thief.

From here the route reverses course and heads south to the La Brea Tar Pits, where the bones of Ice Age mammals have been found preserved in the ancient asphalt. A garden in the adjoining park showcases vegetation that would have covered the LA Basin eons ago. Next door is the next stop, the world-class Los Angeles County Museum of Art (LACMA). Walk your bike through the grounds between the museum's multiple buildings and past its grand outdoor sculptures. This is a great place for a culture break as well as coffee or lunch.

(If you are ambitious, you could head east from here and visit the urban center of Los Angeles. The high-rising financial district is 8 miles east, with highlights including Grand Park and its surrounding civic buildings, the Walt Disney Concert Hall, and storied Chinatown. A comfortable route can be

Will Rogers Park provides a lush stop on a Los Angeles City Tour, with the famous Beverly Hills Hotel behind.

found on the numbered streets Ninth to Eighth to Seventh. If you go that route, you could reach Union Station at Seventh and Main and might as well swing through the campus of the University of Southern California. USC is due west of downtown off Grand Avenue; on its edge are the city's natural history museum and science center.)

The route described here does not add that extra 15-mile loop, as the cycling day would be just too compressed for stopping and lingering along the way. Those sights would be an excellent destination for a second touring day, accessed via light rail. So instead, from LACMA head south into Culver City to ride a lengthy bike trail along Ballona Creek back to the beach communities.

Picking up the trail is tricky, as the creek exists in a concrete ditch below street level, tucked away between warehouses and a recent light-rail line. Look for the green playfields of Syd Kronenthal Park, along which a ramp leads to the trail's start. With a trickle of water and graffiti along the ramping concrete sides, the trail may seem more intimidating than inviting at first, but stay on the path, as it gets more interesting as you approach the ocean. The water level rises, waterfowl appear, and small parks pop up trailside for water and restroom breaks.

Near the ocean, the area south of the creek opens into an expansive nature preserve. The freshwater marsh comprises the last existing wetlands in the Los Angeles area, and environmentalists fought hard against developers to make it so. The site had been Howard Hughes's airport, and it was where he built the world's largest airplane, the *Spruce Goose*. Restoration of the site commenced after the state eventually purchased the land from Hughes's heirs and developers.

Pedal out to the end of Ballona Creek, then retrace a bit to the Marvin Braude Trail, which snakes through the boatyards of Marina del Rey into Venice. A quick ride through Venice to the multiuse trail along the waterfront takes you back to your beach beginning. There is plenty more to see in LA, but this 35-mile tour hits a few highlights.

MILEAGE LOG

0.0 From Santa Monica Pier, head straight across Ocean Ave. into bike lane on Colorado Ave.

0.2 Left onto 4th St.

0.4 Right onto Broadway.

2.3 Left onto Yale St.

2.5 Right onto Arizona Ave., which becomes Texas Ave.

3.4 Right onto Westgate Ave.

3.7 Left onto Ohio Ave.

4.7 Right onto Greenfield Ave.

5.0 Left into alley behind gas station.

5.1 Right onto Veteran Ave. In ½ block, left at stoplight onto Santa Monica Blvd. in bike lane.

6.8 Cross Avenue of the Stars.

7.0 Cross Century Park E.

7.5 Left onto N. Roxbury St.

8.4 Right onto Sunset Blvd.

8.7 Right onto N. Canon Dr. and into Will Rogers Memorial Park.

8.8 Right onto Lomitas Ave. at end of park.

8.9 Left onto Rodeo Dr.

10.0 Left onto Dayton Wy.

10.3 Cross N. Rexford Dr., then bear left on N. Alpine Dr. for 1 block.

10.4 Right onto Burton Wy.

11.1 Merge to left-turn lane onto Robertson Blvd.

11.2 Right onto W. 3rd St.

11.9 Left onto S. Orlando Ave.

12.0 Right onto W. 1st St.

12.6 Right onto S. Fairfax Ave.

12.8 Left into Farmers Market Pl. at pedestrian light to enter the Grove.

13.0 Left onto the Grove Dr. to depart farmers market.

13.1 Right onto Curson Ave.; in 1 block, left onto N. Curson Ave.

14.0 Right onto Willoughby Ave.

14.8 Left onto N. Orange Dr.

15.5 Jog right at Sunset Blvd. to stay on Orange.

15.7 Arrive at Hollywood Blvd. Reverse route.

16.1 Cross Sunset again on N. Orange Dr.

16.7 Right onto Willoughby Ave.

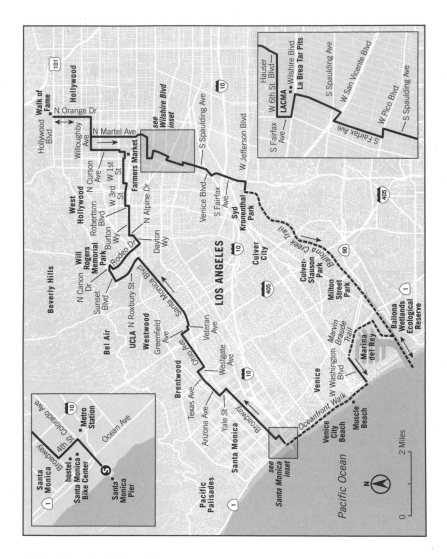

17.1   Left onto N. Martel Ave.

18.5   Cross W. 3rd St., then curve left as road becomes Hauser Blvd. Forward to stay on Hauser as it curves right.

18.9   Right onto W. 6th St.

19.1   Pass La Brea Tar Pits on left.

19.4   Left into pedestrian walkway at LA County Museum of Art (LACMA).

19.6   Left on sidewalk on Wilshire Blvd. in front of museum. (Detour left in 1 block onto W. 8th St. to downtown LA, Union Station.)

19.8   Right onto S. Spaulding Ave.

20.2 Jog right onto W. San Vicente Blvd. for 1 block. Caution: fast traffic.

20.3 Left onto S. Genesee Ave.

20.7 Jog left at W. Pico Blvd.; in 1 block, right onto S. Spaulding.

21.4 Right onto Venice Blvd.

21.7 Left onto S. Fairfax Ave. Caution: four traffic lanes to cross.

22.1 Cross under I-10.

22.5 Curve from S. Fairfax onto S. La Cienega Blvd.

22.7 Right onto W. Jefferson Blvd.

22.9 Right onto bike trail at National Blvd. intersection, then cross Ballona Creek.

23.0 Immediate right at Syd Kronenthal Park playfields down ramp to Ballona Creek Trail; right onto trail.

26.1 Cross under I-405.

26.3 Pass Culver-Slauson Park playground (restrooms, water).

27.2 Pass Milton Street Park.

27.6 Pass under Marina Freeway (SR 90).

28.2 Pass Ballona Wetlands Ecological Reserve.

29.7 Reach end of Ballona Creek Trail. Reverse route.

30.3 Left onto Marvin Braude Trail at end of jetty.

30.4 Right to stay on trail at end of Fiji Wy. at Marina del Rey.

31.7 Cross Admiralty Wy. after passing public library to continue on trail.

32.5 Left onto W. Washington Blvd.

33.3 Right onto Oceanfront Walk multiuse trail at Venice City Beach.

33.9 Pass Muscle Beach.

36.4 Arrive back at Santa Monica Pier.

SANTA MONICA TO NEWPORT BEACH
Distance: 54.2 miles
Elevation gain: 680 feet

Today, skitter south along the beach trail on the western edge of LA, dodging the fingers of sand drifting onto the trail and the toes of the drifters wandering along it.

Venice Beach announces itself with an open-air bazaar of colorful shops and temporary vendors that parallel the trail just a mile from Santa Monica. Pass the show-offs at Muscle Beach and the many street performers, artists,

and hawkers. The area reaches its densest mass on the weekends, when walking the bike might get you through more effectively.

Turn inland at Marina del Rey, as the beach trail ends on a spit where the marina and Ballona Creek join the ocean. Bike carefully up busy West Washington Boulevard in the bike lane to a right turn at 4 miles onto the Marvin Braude Trail, which snakes its way along the edges of the marina. Expensive hotels and restaurants line the popular pleasure-boat harbor.

At 6 miles, the trail turns and runs along the creek on a causeway, then crosses a bridge to continue south, a wide, paved path tracking down the center of the beach. Pass Los Angeles International Airport. You won't see LAX's ground activity due to towering embankments, but the heavy sky traffic right overhead is a good clue as to your location.

Ride along narrow Dockweiler State Beach past the airport, then pass Manhattan Beach at 13 miles. Its picturesque pier hosts a stately white building that is home to the Roundhouse Marine Studies Lab and Aquarium, open to the public, if you feel like a break, or turn inland off the trail here to the many shops and cafés in the surrounding blocks.

The trail continues past Hermosa Beach and into Redondo Beach, where it runs as a generous, protected two-way bike trail along North Harbor Drive. But the trail ends, and to avoid the hilly isthmus of Palos Verdes Estates, the route turns inland. You must traverse shopping and residential areas of Torrance and the industrial land of Carson before returning to a bike trail along the Los Angeles River that takes you into Long Beach.

In Torrance you'll need extra care navigating intermittent bike lanes and buses, and in Carson, pass shopping centers and Harbor-UCLA Medical Center, a major teaching hospital complex. Cross over Interstate 110 and skirt the edge of the massive port facilities that serve Long Beach, one of the nation's busiest shipping centers. The route parallels I-405 and then enters Long Beach by traveling over I-710. Loop through the adjacent neighborhood to access the Los Angeles River Trail, which takes you into the Long Beach waterfront, an area of linked parks and hotels serving the nearby convention center. Downtown is just a couple of blocks north of Shoreline Aquatic Park.

Across the bay sits one of the grande dames of ocean travel, the *Queen Mary*. The ocean liner, permanently docked in Long Beach, offers tours and hotel rooms. To visit it, turn left off the trail onto Golden Shore Road at the Aquarium of the Pacific. Travel two blocks on the well-signed side trail before making a U-turn to access the trail along Queens Way, a bridge that leads to the big ship.

On Long Beach's south shore, another marina at Naples Island requires you to jog inland a bit to skirt it before returning to the ocean at Seal Beach. The route continues on the shoulder of the Pacific Coast Highway (State Route 1), before returning to the oceanfront Huntington Beach Bike Trail. The trail carries you to Huntington Beach Pier and then along a small road

CONNECTIONS: LAX AND AMTRAK

If you're starting or ending your tour in Los Angeles, you can fly or take the train.

Los Angeles International Airport (LAX) is pretty easily accessible by bike, although it's a nerve-wracking last mile in heavy traffic. It's about 10 miles from the Santa Monica Pier; follow the main route's mileage log to the Marvin Braude Trail at Marina del Rey. When the path approaches Fiji Way, go left onto Fiji. This connects in one block with the Pacific Coast Highway (State Route 1), known here as Lincoln Boulevard. Turn right onto Lincoln until it intersects with Loyola Boulevard. Turn right on Loyola, then shortly turn left onto Westchester Parkway. Turn right on South Sepulveda Boulevard. Following signs for LAX, bear right onto Vicksburg Avenue. Stay to the right and approach the lower level of the airport terminal.

Amtrak is in LA's Union Station, the downtown transit center. Taking public transportation is easy: From the Santa Monica station at Fourth and Colorado, take the Metro light rail Expo Line ($1.75 at time of publication) to its downtown terminus on Seventh Street. Switch to the Red or Purple Line, which both end at Union Station, or bike the 2 miles to the station via Seventh and Main streets. When boarding Metro trains, look for a car with a bike symbol. Wheel your bike to the designated area and stand with it while traveling.

To bike from Santa Monica to Amtrak at Union Station, follow the Los Angeles city tour to Wilshire Boulevard, then detour east on West Eight Street as described in the city tour.

parallel to SR 1 that narrows to a trail and then to a wide sidewalk at Newport Beach, where a bike lane appears and becomes the better option.

Carefully navigate the big SR 55 interchange into central Newport Beach, where you will find plentiful cafés and overnight options. Lodging at this popular resort area is at a premium, so advance reservations are recommended. Eats and entertainment line the Pacific Coast Highway, with much more available on the Balboa Peninsula, at the end of SR 55. Here are a couple of options:

- If the urban setting doesn't appeal and you still have daylight and fuel in the tank, continue on to Crystal Cove State Park, an additional 7 miles. There are no hiker-biker sites at Crystal Cove's Moro Campground, so reserve in advance. Or really plan ahead to reserve a room in one of their historic cottages, which book up months in advance. If you do make it here, plan on some exploration. The park has a stunning, varied landscape. It goes from tide pools and a sandy beach to dusty trails through dry chaparral on the inland side of the park. A unique feature is a historic district by the beach that contains those cottages, preserved as they were in their vintage beach-culture heyday of the 1930s–'50s.

The mixed-use Huntington Beach bike trail offers regular stops for restrooms and refreshments.

- If you're really energetic, continue 20 miles south of Newport Beach to just beyond the town of Dana Point, to Doheny State Beach, which offers the first hiker-biker camping since Point Mugu. Reaching Dana Point would reduce tomorrow's ride into Encinitas to a moderate 43 miles.

No matter where you stay tonight, now that you've drifted south from LA, the end of the trek is nearly in sight. A sandy beach at the end of tomorrow's ride offers the last camping night on the Pacific Coast tour.

MILEAGE LOG

0.0   Depart Santa Monica Pier on the beach trail heading south.

1.5   Enter Venice Beach.

2.5   Pass Muscle Beach.

3.1   Left onto W. Washington Blvd.

3.9   Right onto Marvin Braude Trail at Mildred Ave.

4.6   Cross Admiralty Wy. and continue on bike path past Marina del Rey library.

5.2   Bike path curves right and parallels Fiji Wy.

6.0   Right onto bike path (follow signs) after passing Coast Guard facility (detour left on Fiji to LAX; see Connections sidebar).

6.1   Right onto Ballona Creek Trail.

6.7   Left onto bridge across creek as trail ends.

6.8   Right onto trail after bridge, into Dockweiler State Beach.

8.1   Pass Los Angeles International Airport.

13.1   Pass Manhattan Beach Pier.

13.6   Right at 35th St. and then immediate left onto the Strand, or continue forward in protected bike lane along Hermosa Ave.

14.8   Pass Hermosa Beach Pier.

15.5 Continue forward onto N. Harbor Dr. at Herondo St.; beachfront trail ends here.
16.0 Left onto Beryl St. in Redondo Beach. Note: Departure from ACA maps.
16.1 Right onto N. Catalina Ave.
16.7 Left onto W. Torrance Blvd. into Torrance.
16.9 Cross Pacific Coast Hwy. (SR 1).
19.2 Cross Madrona Ave.
19.6 Right onto Maple Ave.
19.7 Left onto El Dorado St.
20.4 Right onto Beech Ave.
20.5 Left onto Sonoma St.
20.8 Bear left onto Engracia Ave.
21.1 Right onto Cravens Ave.
21.4 Left onto W. Carson St. at intersection with Cabrillo Ave.
22.6 Pass Harbor-UCLA Medical Center.
23.0 Cross over I-110.
23.6 Right onto S. Main St.
24.1 Left onto E. 223rd St. in Carson.
27.0 Forward as 223rd becomes W. Wardlow Rd.
28.1 Cross over I-710 and then Los Angeles River.
28.5 Right onto Maine Ave. In ½ block, right on W. 33rd Wy., following bike trail signs.
28.7 Right onto Golden Ave. In ½ block, left on W. 34th St.
28.9 Straight at street end onto Los Angeles River Trail atop levee.
30.9 Trail goes under Pacific Coast Hwy. (SR 1).
32.6 Bike trail curves away from river at Golden Shore RV Park in Long Beach.
33.2 Trail crosses under Queens Wy. (detour right onto Queensway Dr. to *Queen Mary*).
33.3 Left at Shoreline Aquatic Park to continue around San Pedro Bay.
33.5 Pass Aquarium of the Pacific.
33.9 Right to stay on trail at Shoreline Village.
34.1 Left to stay on trail at waterfront.
34.5 Pass Alamitos Beach.
35.6 Pass Junipero Beach and Long Beach Museum of Art.
37.6 Left onto 54th Pl. as trail ends.
37.8 Right onto Bay Shore Ave.
38.1 Right onto E. 2nd St. onto Naples Island.
38.9 Cross Alamitos Bay into Seal Beach.
39.2 Right onto SR 1.
39.7 Cross San Gabriel River.
41.7 Cross Anaheim Bay.
42.4 Right on Anderson St. in Sunset Beach. In 1 block, left on S. Pacific Ave.
43.6 Forward onto sidewalk at street end. Continue into roundabout on Warner Ave.
43.7 Forward onto Huntington Beach Bike Trail halfway around roundabout.
45.1 Pass Bolsa Chica State Beach.

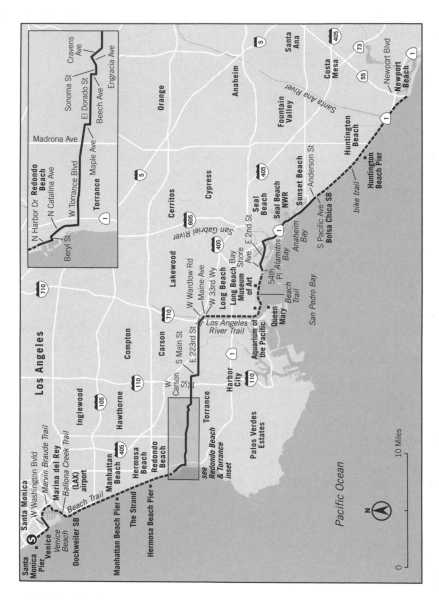

48.0 Pass Huntington Beach Pier.

52.2 Cross Santa Ana River.

53.4 Enter Newport Beach. Trail continues on wide sidewalk.

54.0 Trail continues under Newport Blvd.

54.2 Right onto Pacific Coast Hwy. as trail ends in downtown Newport Beach.

NEWPORT BEACH TO ENCINITAS
Distance: 61.9 miles
Elevation gain: 2710 feet

Depart Newport Beach through the busy town center, high-traffic blocks that require attentive riding. Cross the Newport Bay Bridge and pass Corona del Mar, and you're out of most of the dense resort development, back to the countryside. Today's ride is typified by a series of small rolling hills.

At 6.1 miles, pass the first entrance to Crystal Cove State Park. A side trail and a small road wind along the park, so you can easily detour through and check out the historic cottages and café, a half mile along, and return to the highway at Reef Point parking at 7.2 miles.

Continue into Laguna Beach, another crowded resort community that stretches for nearly 4 miles. You'll see the particular features of these towns again and again on the last two legs of the coast route: gated neighborhoods with large condo resorts, traffic-congested town centers lined with shops, and loss of the bike lane through the shopping district lined with parked cars. It is not a design encouraging the cycling tourist to linger. On the other hand, places to stop for coffee or ice cream are plentiful.

Whether or not you curse the town centers, they are often better in this stretch than the highway, so today's route detours away from the busy road through Dana Point, home to Doheny State Beach. Access to the park is circuitous. Return to the highway briefly when leaving Dana Point, then exit State Route 1 at signs for the Coast Highway and Doheny Park Road. With the highway curving off to your left, cross San Juan Creek and continue forward to a left-turn signal with a sign for Doheny Park. It loops around over the highway to access the oceanfront park and campground.

A bike trail parallels the highway south of the park to the turn to San Juan Capistrano as you enter San Clemente. The town of San Juan Capistrano, with its picturesque historic mission and yearly returning swallows, is about 4 miles inland but can be visited by a nice pedal up the San Juan Creek and Tarbuco Creek trails, accessed from Lantern Bay Park in Dana Point.

A snaky residential route gets you through San Clemente and past its state beach, which offers camping but no hiker-biker sites. At the south end of town you'll pass near but not within vision of Richard Nixon's "Western Whitehouse," a Spanish Colonial home and coveted retreat of the former US president.

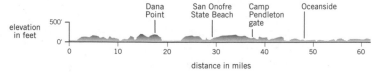

A bike path and park access road run along Interstate 5 to the long stretch of San Onofre State Beach, one of California's premier surfing spots. There are campgrounds at San Mateo and San Onofre bluffs but, alas, without hiker-biker sites.

Crossing onto Camp Pendleton is a serious experience. Just south of the San Onofre Nuclear Power Plant, the road ends and the military base, home to US Marines, begins with a self-service gate to a rough but serviceable paved bike trail. It winds through dry desert with the ocean a more distant view, then crosses under I-5 and briefly out of the camp. But you must reenter and continue south through the base, as bike traffic is prohibited on I-5 unless the camp roads are closed to cycling for military reasons.

A scenic lighthouse marks the marina and cafés of Oceanside.

Camp Pendleton allows bicycle travel only during the day (9:00 AM–3:00 PM weekdays; 7:00 AM–5:00 PM weekends), on a designated route. No stops or visits to the base towns or services are permitted. When the base access is closed, bicyclists are allowed to ride on the shoulder of I-5, but again only during daylight hours. To enter the camp at its guarded gate, you must have a valid photo ID or state driver's license.

You'll find little traffic on the quiet camp road. However, it is the only place on the coast route where you'll see signs for "tank crossing" or "troop crossing." You may see military training exercises in the distance or Marine aircraft overhead. Keep moving, soldier.

Exit the camp into Oceanside, once again avoiding the highway by making your way down to the oceanfront neighborhood. A marina with cafés greets you, followed by a lengthy residential stretch, which blends into the homes and beach resorts of Carlsbad and then, after a too-brief rural segment, into sprawling Encinitas. A campground exists at South Carlsbad State Park, but it does not offer hiker-biker sites, so keep rolling south.

San Elijo State Beach has two entrances, with the south one hosting the campground, which has a nice corral for cyclists at its south edge. It faces the beach and outlet for the San Elijo Lagoon, which can emit a rich organic odor. While Encinitas offers plentiful grocery stores and shops to provision for tonight's camp, there is also a well-appointed business strip just outside the campground, accessed at the stoplight at Chesterfield Drive in the grandly named community of Cardiff-by-the-Sea.

MILEAGE LOG

0.0 Depart Newport Beach heading south on Pacific Coast Hwy. (SR 1).

1.4 Cross over Newport Bay.

6.1 Pass Los Trancos, Crystal Cove State Park entrance (detour to trail through park).

7.2 Pass Crystal Cove's Reef Point parking (side trail rejoins highway).

9.0 Enter Laguna Beach.

9.4 Right onto Cliff Dr., following bike route signs. In 1 block, bear left to stay on Cliff Dr.

9.9 Pass Heisler Park.

10.3 Right onto SR 1, here quixotically called North Coast Hwy.

10.5 Cross Broadway St. at Laguna Beach town center.

13.5 Pass Aliso Beach County Park.

17.7 Right at Del Prado Ave. into Dana Point.

18.2 Cross Street of the Golden Lantern at Dana Point town center.

18.4 Forward onto SR 1 as Del Prado ends.

19.0 Right at off-ramp for Coast Hwy. (SR 1).

19.3 Pass exit to Doheny Park Rd. on left (detour to Doheny State Beach, hiker-biker camping).

20.2 Forward at Palisades Dr. onto bike path.

21.8 Forward as path turns into bike lane at Camino Capistrano.

22.7 Enter San Clemente.

22.8 Right on E. Avenida Pico. In 1 block, curve left to Boca de la Playa. In ½ block, at roundabout, curve right onto Calle de las Bolas.

23.0 Left to stay on Calle de las Bolas.

23.1 Bear right onto Avenida Florencia.

23.3 Left onto Avenida Pelayo.

23.5 Right onto Calle Puente.

23.9 Bear left at La Paloma to stay on Calle Puente.

24.0 Right onto W. Avenida Palizada.

24.1 Left onto N. Calle Seville, which becomes Avenida Santa Barbara.

24.5 Right onto S. Ola Vista.

25.9 Left onto Avenida Calafia; in 1 block, right onto Avenida del Presidente.

26.2 Pass turn to San Clemente State Beach.

27.0 Jog left onto Christianitos Rd. as del Presidente ends, then immediately right onto bike path next to I-5.

28.1 Forward through parking, then right onto Old Pacific Hwy. at San Onofre State Beach.

30.0 Pass San Onofre Nuclear Power Plant.

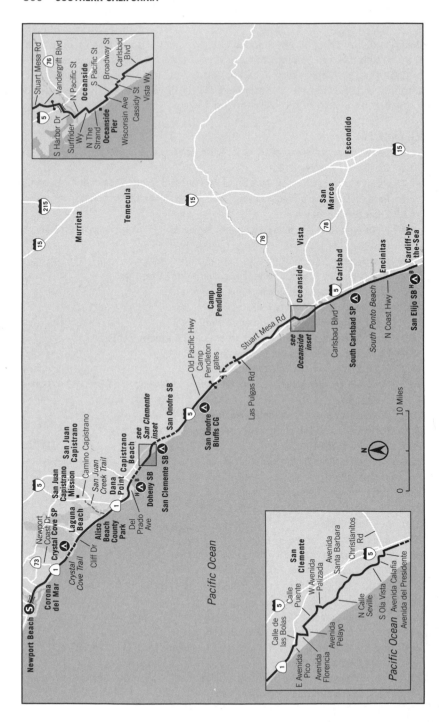

Stuart Mesa Rd
Vandergrift Blvd
N Pacific St
S Pacific St
Broadway St
Carlsbad Blvd
76
Oceanside
S Harbor Dr
Surfrider Wy
N The Strand
Oceanside Pier
Wisconsin Ave
Cassidy St
Vista Wy
5

Escondido
15

215
15
Murrieta
Temecula
15
76
San Marcos
Vista
78
Oceanside
Carlsbad
5
Carlsbad
Encinitas
Cardiff-by-the-Sea
San Elijo SB
see Oceanside inset
Stuart Mesa Rd
Camp Pendleton
Carlsbad Blvd
South Carlsbad SP
South Ponto Beach
N Coast Hwy

Old Pacific Hwy
Camp Pendleton gates
Las Pulgas Rd
San Onofre SB
5
San Onofre Bluffs CG
see San Clemente inset
Capistrano Beach
San Juan Capistrano
San Juan Capistrano Mission
Camino Capistrano
San Juan Creek Trail
Dana Point
Doheny SB
San Clemente SB
Del Prado Ave
1
5

Newport Coast Dr
Crystal Cove SP
Laguna Beach
Aliso Beach County Park
Cliff Dr
Crystal Cove Trail
73
1
Corona del Mar
Newport Beach S

Pacific Ocean

N

0   10 Miles

San Clemente
Calle de las Bolas
Calle Puente
W Avenida Palizada
Avenida Santa Barbara
Christianitos Rd
5
Avenida Calafia
Avenida del Presidente
N Calle Seville
S Ola Vista
E Avenida Pico
Avenida Florencia
Avenida Pelayo
1

Pacific Ocean

30.8 Pass San Onofre Bluffs Campground.

34.0 Forward through bike gate onto Camp Pendleton trail as road ends.

35.7 Curve left on trail under I-5.

37.3 Left onto Las Pulgas Rd. as trail ends. Proceed to Camp Pendleton's entrance gate.

37.6 Check in at camp gate with valid ID. Curve right to stay on Las Pulgas after gate.

38.0 Bear right onto Stuart Mesa Rd. at first intersection.

44.9 Right onto Vandergrift Blvd.

46.3 Exit Camp Pendleton; road becomes S. Harbor Dr.

46.6 Cross under I-5.

46.8 Left to stay on Harbor after railroad tracks.

46.9 Bear left at Y to stay on Harbor into Oceanside.

47.2 Left onto N. Pacific St.

47.9 Right on Surfrider Wy.; in 1 block, left onto N. The Strand.

48.0 Pass Oceanside Pier.

48.7 Left onto Wisconsin Ave. In ½ block, right onto S. Pacific St.

49.9 Left onto Cassidy St.

50.0 Right onto bike trail parallel to Broadway St.

50.3 Left onto Vista Wy.

50.4 Right onto Carlsbad Blvd.

50.7 Cross Buena Vista Lagoon.

50.9 Bear right at the roundabout to stay on Carlsbad, which becomes Coast Hwy. (SR S21).

51.5 Pass Carlsbad town center.

53.4 Pass first entrance to South Carlsbad State Park.

55.7 Pass entrance to South Carlsbad State Park campground.

56.9 Pass South Ponto Beach.

57.4 Enter Encinitas.

60.5 Pass San Elijo State Beach north beach (day use).

61.9 Arrive at San Elijo State Beach campground.

ENCINITAS TO MEXICO
Distance: 48.8 miles
Elevation gain: 1370 feet

You've arrived at the final day of the Pacific Coast route! An exhilarating feeling will carry you back out onto the highway. A statue of a surfer stands roadside next to San Elijo State Beach's south edge, facing the sea and ignoring the traffic roar. Follow his gaze and enjoy the thrill of surfers balancing on a wave's leading edge as you balance on your two wheels in the consistent bike lane.

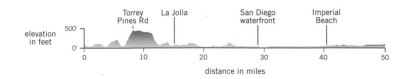

Seashore communities of Solana Beach and Del Mar lead you to a final hill climb (a steep, significant effort) into Torrey Pines, home of the University of California–San Diego. Pass the sprawling campus, with colleges named for Eleanor Roosevelt, Jonas Salk, Thurgood Marshall, and John Muir—a wide-ranging panoply of bold-faced names famous in fields as varied as politics, medicine, law, and the environment.

Wind your way down to La Jolla Shores and its dramatic coastline, past the Scripps Institution of Oceanography, which further solidifies this area as a world-class enclave of learning. At La Jolla Cove and Scripps Park, stop to marvel at the crashing waves and caves undercutting the shoreline. The contemporary art museum and luxurious homes overlooking the picturesque cove offer clues as to the wealth of the area.

The route enters Pacific Beach, a funkier neighborhood with colorful shops and smaller homes. Veer off the streets onto Oceanfront Walk, a trail that may be crowded and slow-going, but faces the beach and avoids congested commercial roads.

CONNECTIONS: SAN AND AMTRAK

San Diego offers absolutely the easiest connections for taking the rails or an airplane home after your trip. Leaving the city via mass transit is easy, with both the train station and airport centrally located. You can also bike to them.

San Diego International Airport (SAN): You bike right by the airport on your way into the city; simply turn off the North Harbor Drive trail at Harbor Island Drive, then merge left onto Airport Terminal Road in a quarter mile.

Amtrak: There are two San Diego stations—Santa Fe Depot downtown and the Old Town Station. Santa Fe Depot is two blocks inland from the Waterfront Trail; from Broadway Pier take West Broadway east two blocks, turn left onto Kettner Boulevard, and bike a half block north. Old Town Station is at the corner of Taylor and Congress streets, adjacent to the historic park (see the San Diego city tour).

If you're returning to Los Angeles, Amtrak runs multiple Pacific Surfliner regional trains daily from San Diego to LA, which allow cyclists to bring their bikes for a small additional fee and have them loaded onto the baggage car without boxing them.

Reaching Belmont Park, a retro-styled amusement park with a small roller coaster, exit the trail and continue on bike lanes past a series of parks that lead through the Mission Beach area, on a bridge over Mission Bay, and then onto the broad part of the peninsula that includes Point Loma and Cabrillo National Monument. The point, with its stunning overlook of San Diego Bay and the city (and views even to Mexico), highlights this chapter's second city tour. If you don't intend to take that tour, see it today by making a 9-mile detour along Catalina Boulevard. Pedal out to the point, then retrace your path down to the harbor to continue south.

A surfer statue near San Elijo State Beach

Soon you're bicycling along the San Diego waterfront, past the conveniently located, noisy, polluting airport and along the edge of downtown. A broad paved walkway makes off-street cycling easy. Pedal up to Broadway Pier, where the ferry to Coronado awaits. The rest of San Diego's city center and waterfront are also on the city tour, but again, if you're not planning to take that tour, spend a few more minutes and bike south a bit farther along the waterfront. You'll pass the USS *Midway* aircraft carrier, permanently berthed here and open for tours. It's a testimony to the very large presence of the US Navy in San Diego, a major military port.

Walk your bike onto the ferry and enjoy a quick 1.7-mile ride across the sparkling bay to the island of Coronado. The north part of Coronado is a large naval air base, but the ferry drops you at a park filled with restaurants and shops, and a bike trail leads south along the bay and a golf course. Pass the Hotel del Coronado, one of the nation's grand historic hotel destinations, and the Coronado Yacht Club. Pedal along the Silver Strand, a spit of land with beach on one side of a busy highway and you on the bike trail on the other. Look for the abundant birdlife in the wildlife preserve just offshore.

Leave the bike trail and ride south into Imperial Beach, the only community standing between you and the Mexican border. At the south end of this

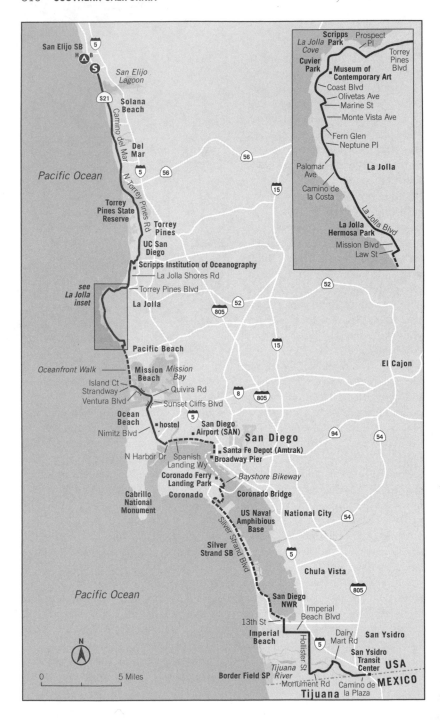

San Elijo SB

H B
S

San Elijo
Lagoon

S21

Solana
Beach

Del
Mar

Camino del Mar

Pacific Ocean

N Torrey Pines Rd

Torrey
Pines State
Reserve

Torrey
Pines

UC San
Diego

Scripps Institution of Oceanography

La Jolla Shores Rd

see
La Jolla
inset

Torrey Pines Blvd

La Jolla

Pacific Beach

Oceanfront Walk

Mission   Mission
Beach   Bay

Island Ct
Strandway   Quivira Rd
Ventura Blvd

Sunset Cliffs Blvd

Ocean
Beach   hostel

Nimitz Blvd   San Diego
                           Airport (SAN)

N Harbor Dr   Spanish   San Diego
              Landing Wy   Santa Fe Depot (Amtrak)
                           Broadway Pier

Coronado Ferry   Bayshore Bikeway
Landing Park

Cabrillo   Coronado
National
Monument   Coronado Bridge

                    US Naval   National City
                    Amphibious
                    Base

                Silver
                Strand SB

Silver Strand Blvd

Pacific Ocean

San Diego
NWR

                           Imperial
              13th St   Beach Blvd

              Imperial
              Beach

Hollister St

Tijuana
River   Monument Rd

Border Field SP

N

0   5 Miles

Dairy   San Ysidro
Mart Rd

San Ysidro
Transit
Center   USA

Camino de   MEXICO
la Plaza

Tijuana

Chula Vista

El Cajon

La Jolla inset:

Scripps   Prospect
La Jolla Park   Pl
Cove
                    Torrey
Cuvier   Pines
Park   Museum of Blvd
         Contemporary Art

         Coast Blvd
         Olivetas Ave
         Marine St
         Monte Vista Ave

         Fern Glen
         Neptune Pl

Palomar   La Jolla
Ave

Camino de
la Costa

                   La Jolla Blvd

         La Jolla
         Hermosa Park

         Mission Blvd
         Law St

community, pedal through flat farmland and horse country, turning east to meet the border crossing at Interstate 5.

The Adventure Cycling Association's maps end the bike tour at Border Field State Park, about 3 miles to the west. The low-lying road to that park can be flooded and muddy, so I recommend a visit to the bustling border crossing instead. Besides, after viewing the people streaming into Mexico and that country's huge red, white, and green flag flying proudly overhead, you can take the easy way back to San Diego: by rail. The San Ysidro Transit Center at the border includes a light rail line that whisks you the 7 miles back into the city ($2.50 at the time of publication). Or you can retrace your route and end your southbound journey along the Pacific Coast in a unique way: by pedaling north.

Two hostels are available in San Diego, one in the historic Gaslamp Quarter (on Market between Fifth and Sixth) and one in Point Loma (on Worden Street off Voltaire Street), along the main route into the city. Other overnight options abound.

MILEAGE LOG

0.0   Depart San Elijo State Beach campground, turning right onto SR S21.

0.2   Pass Chesterfield Dr.

0.4   Cross San Elijo Lagoon.

1.6   Enter Solana Beach.

2.2   Pass Plaza St. in Solana Beach town center.

3.4   Cross San Dieguito River.

4.4   Pass Del Mar town center.

6.3   Cross Los Penasquitos Creek.

7.3   Pass Torrey Pines State Reserve.

9.6   Right onto N. Torrey Pines Rd. as Genessee Ave. goes straight.

9.8   Pass University of California–San Diego campus.

10.8   Right onto La Jolla Shores Rd.

13.1   Bear right onto Torrey Pines Blvd. as La Jolla Shores Rd. ends.

13.8   Right onto Prospect Pl.

14.0   Right at Y onto Cave St.; follow sign down to Coast Blvd.

14.3   Pass La Jolla Cove and Scripps Park.

14.6   Right at Jenner St. as park ends to stay on Coast Blvd.

14.8   Pass Museum of Contemporary Art San Diego.

14.9   Right at Y as Coast Blvd. splits to stay along Coast Blvd.'s shore route.

15.0   Pass Cuvier Park.

15.3   Right at Olivetas Ave.; in 1 block, right at stop sign to stay on it.

15.5   Right onto Marine St.; in 1 block, left on Monte Vista Ave.

15.6   Jog right to stay on Monte Vista.

15.8   Right onto Fern Glen, which curves and becomes Neptune Pl.

16.4   Left onto Palomar Ave.; in ½ block, right on Camino de la Costa.

17.3   Pass La Jolla Hermosa Park.

17.4 Right at roundabout onto La Jolla Blvd.; enter town center.

18.5 Road curves left and becomes Loring St. for ½ block.

18.6 Right onto Mission Blvd.

18.8 Right onto Law St.; pass Palisades Park.

18.9 Left onto Oceanfront Walk mixed-use trail.

21.0 Left onto Island Ct. approaching carnival rides at Belmont Park; in ½ block, right onto Strandway.

21.1 Left onto Ventura Blvd., then forward onto W. Mission Bay Dr. at Mission Blvd.

21.7 Cross Mission Bay Channel.

22.1 Right onto Quivira Access Rd., then immediate left onto Quivira Rd.; follow bike route signs to downtown.

22.6 Left after Marina Village Conference Center onto bike path leading up to Sunset Cliffs Blvd.

22.7 Right onto Sunset Cliffs Blvd.

22.8 Cross San Diego River.

23.1 Merge left after bridge onto Nimitz Blvd. as Sunset Cliffs Blvd. curves right. Caution: heavy traffic.

23.4 Merge left across exit at W. Point Loma Blvd. to stay on Nimitz. Caution: heavy traffic.

23.7 Merge left across another exit signed for Cabrillo National Monument to stay on Nimitz. Caution: heavy traffic. (Detour right on Catalina Blvd. to Cabrillo NM. At 24.4, detour left on Poinsettia Dr., then Udall St. to the hostel at the corner of Worden St.)

24.9 Bear left to stay on Nimitz at Evergreen St.

25.4 Curve left onto bike lane on N. Harbor Dr. as Nimitz ends at a T.

26.0 Merge right onto harborside bike trail at Spanish Landing Wy. (or continue in bike lane).

26.9 Pass San Diego International Airport.

28.5 Pass Waterfront Park in downtown San Diego.

28.7 Pass Maritime Museum of San Diego.

29.0 Arrive at Broadway Pier. Buy ticket for pedestrian-bicycle ferry to Coronado Island.

29.0 Exit ferry onto Bayshore Bikeway (Silver Strand Bikeway). Continue south, hugging shore through Coronado Ferry Landing Park.

29.8 Pass Coronado Tidelands Park.

30.0 Forward as trail curves right and under Coronado Bridge.

30.4 Forward as trail curves left at Glorietta Blvd.

30.5 Cross Glorietta, then immediate left to continue on trail.

31.5 Cross Glorietta again; continue forward on trail.

31.8 Forward as trail curves left along Silver Strand Blvd. at Hotel del Coronado.

32.5 Pass Glorietta Bay Park.

32.6 Pass US Naval Amphibious Base.

35.8 Pass Silver Strand State Beach.

38.9   Trail curves left away from Silver Strand Blvd.

39.2   Enter Imperial Beach.

39.9   Right off trail onto 13th St.

40.2   Cross Palm Ave.

40.7   Left onto Imperial Beach Blvd.

42.0   Right onto Hollister St.

44.5   Left onto Monument Rd. as Hollister ends.

45.3   Forward onto Dairy Mart Rd.

45.8   Cross Tijuana River.

46.3   Right onto Camino de la Plaza.

48.5   Right onto pedestrian bridge to border crossing when approaching I-5.

48.8   Arrive at San Ysidro Transit Center and Mexico border crossing.

CITY TOUR: SAN DIEGO
Distance: 29.5 miles
Elevation gain: 1190 feet

There are plenty of superlatives about San Diego. The weather is nearly perfect year-round. Its natural deep harbor and many waterways make it ideal for shipping and boating. You'll find lush parks and areas with stunning vistas. And, with an impressive US Navy presence, it must be one of the most protected cities in America. Here's one more: it is nearly a perfect city for a day tour by bike.

San Diego, at nearly the south terminus of the Pacific Coast Bicycle Route, is a place to linger and enjoy your cycling achievement. Some will want to continue their tour into Mexico, but if you're ending your coast ride at the border, here's a strategy: ride down to the border on the main route as described, then put your bike on the light rail at the San Ysidro Transit Center and enjoy the train ride back into the city. Spend a day or two relaxing in this urban center, and use your bike to get out and enjoy the sights. The 30-mile city tour described here leads through many of San Diego's highlights, but visiting them fully would take much more time.

Begin this tour the way you came into town: along the waterfront. Keep San Diego Bay on your left and soon you'll have the San Diego airport on your right. Continue looping around the bay, climbing through the Point Loma neighborhood to Cabrillo National Monument. The monument honors

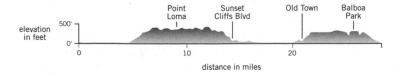

Balboa Park contains a variety of San Diego attractions, including its fine art museum.

Juan Rodriguez Cabrillo, the first European explorer to visit the area. He claimed the discovery for Spain in 1542.

Beyond the big statue of Cabrillo sits the Old Point Loma Lighthouse, one of two on the end of the peninsula. While the old one sits high above and distant from the bay, the newer one was placed on the very tip of the rocky point. A separate route, Cabrillo Road, accessed before you reach the monument, leads to the newer lighthouse and the stunning Point Loma Tide Pools, a rocky intertidal ecosystem teeming with sea life.

Pedal back past the regimentally straight rows of white headstones in the Fort Rosecrans military cemetery and tip your helmet in respect, then ride down to the Sunset Cliffs neighborhood, which offers more dramatic coastline. The park here is a popular surf spot. Next visit the Ocean Beach neighborhood, where a few blocks down colorful Newport Avenue will put you in mind of some refreshments, perhaps coffee, a fresh fruit smoothie, or the city's specialty: fish tacos.

Pick up the Ocean Beach Bike Path at Robb Field and pedal inland along the San Diego River. Pass under the big roads leading to Mission Bay, where a large park holds the SeaWorld attraction. Continue under Interstate 5 and enter Old Town, one of San Diego's earliest neighborhoods. Lock your bike and walk through the extensive Old Town San Diego State Historic Park, which has adobe buildings dating to the 1850s, a town plaza of the era, and many restorations. Surrounding the park are cafés, making this a great lunch spot.

Climb through Presidio Park and past the views at Fort Stockton, then edge through the Mission Hills neighborhood before dropping down into the massive local gem of San Diego's park system, Balboa Park. The home to famed San Diego Zoo, the park also houses a stretch of historic buildings with an array of museums, performing arts centers, gardens, and recreation areas. A half-mile ride down El Prado exposes you to many of the larger attractions, including the excellent art museum.

Finally, the route heads back to the city center, crossing the freeways to skirt the edge of the financial district and go through the Gaslamp Quarter, highlighted by Victorian-style architecture. Restaurants, clubs, and live theater animate this historic center at night, while by day it may be busy with festivals and thronged by visitors attending events at the nearby Convention Center. Pass by the waterfront Convention Center and its attendant hotel towers to return to the San Diego shoreline. End the tour by cycling past the massive USS *Midway*, an aircraft carrier permanently berthed and available for touring.

This tour does not expose you to all of the city's desirable spots, but it's a start. See the authentic, fun Little Italy and explore Coronado Island if you have a bit more time. Or simply enjoy the ever-present sunshine, light breezes, and glittering bay.

MILEAGE LOG

0.0   From Broadway Pier as you face San Diego Bay, turn right and bike north on sidewalk parallel to N. Harbor Dr.

2.0   Cross Harbor Island Dr.; pass entrance to San Diego International Airport.

2.3   Forward into parking lot from Waterfront Trail.

2.6   Forward back onto trail at end of parking lots.

3.2   Bear right as trail curves under N. Harbor Dr.

3.2   Bear left onto bridge on Halsey Rd. after going under N. Harbor Dr.

3.4   Bear left around USS *Recruit* displayed in Liberty Station Park, then right at its bow, and left onto street through shopping center.

3.6   Left onto Laning Rd.

3.7   Right onto N. Harbor Dr.

4.1   Pass Sun Harbor Marina.

4.2   Left onto Scott St.

4.6   Right onto Cañon St.

4.9   Jog right at Evergreen St. to continue on Cañon.

5.7   Pass Point Loma Community Park.

6.0   Bear left onto Catalina Blvd.

6.1   Forward onto quieter access road parallel to Catalina if desired.

6.6   Forward onto sidewalk as access road ends.

7.0   Forward onto street, then through gate at Naval Base Point Loma.

9.5   Reach Cabrillo National Monument entrance. Retrace route to exit.

12.0   Left onto Garden Ln. In 1 block, right onto Tarento Dr.

12.5   Curve left to stay on Tarento.

12.9   Bear left to stay on Tarento at intersection with Savoy St.

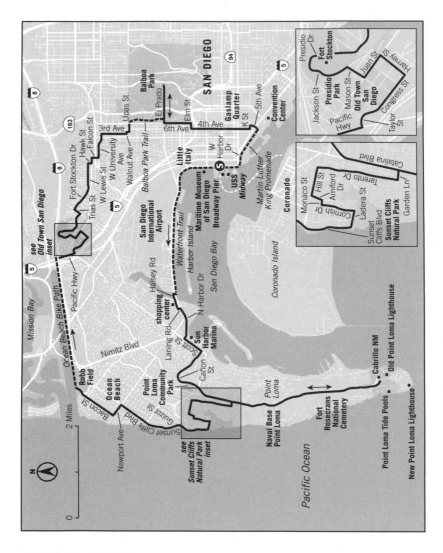

13.3   Left onto Hill St.

13.6   Left onto Amiford Dr.

13.7   Right onto Monaco St. In 1 block, left onto Cornish Dr.

14.0   Curve right onto Ladera St. Arrive at Sunset Cliffs Natural Park. Right onto Sunset Cliffs Blvd.

14.8   Left at stop sign at Guizot St. to stay on Sunset Cliffs Blvd.

16.1   Left onto Newport Ave.

16.4   Right onto Bacon St. (detour left 1 block to Ocean Beach pier and park).

17.1   Left onto Ocean Beach Bike Path.

17.4 Slight left to go under Sunset Cliffs Blvd.; stay on bike path.

17.6 Slight left to go under W. Mission Bay Dr.; stay on bike path.

19.5 Exit trail and veer right toward Pacific Hwy.; after overpasses, turn right onto Pacific Hwy.

19.9 Left onto Taylor St.

20.0 Right onto Congress St.; pass Old Town San Diego State Historic Park.

20.3 Left onto Harney St.

20.5 Left onto Juan St.

20.7 Right onto Mason St. In 1 block, left onto Jackson St.

20.9 Continue straight onto Presidio Dr.; pass Fort Stockton.

21.3 Slight left to stay on Presidio Dr.; follow scenic drive signs.

21.6 Bear right to stay on Presidio Dr. at intersection with Arista Dr.

21.7 Left on Trias St.

21.9 Right onto Fort Stockton Dr.

22.4 Left onto W. Lewis St.

22.8 Right onto Hawk St. In 1 block, left on Fort Stockton Dr.

23.0 Right onto Falcon St.

23.1 Left onto W. University Ave.

23.4 Curve right to stay on University.

23.6 Right onto 3rd Ave.

24.0 Left onto Walnut Ave. In 1 block, right onto 3rd, and in another block, left onto Upas St.

24.3 Cross Balboa Dr. and enter Balboa Park. Proceed onto trail through park paralleling Balboa Dr.

25.0 Left onto El Prado. Reverse route to return.

26.5 Left onto 6th Ave. to exit park.

27.0 Right onto Elm St.

27.1 Left onto 4th Ave.

27.7 Pass Westfield Horton Plaza park.

27.9 Enter Gaslamp Quarter.

28.2 Left onto K St. In 1 block, right onto 5th Ave.

28.3 Right onto Martin Luther King Promenade trail between second and third set of railroad tracks on approach to E. Harbor Dr. at Convention Center.

28.9 Cross onto W. Harbor Dr. at W. Market St.

29.1 Left at last light on Pacific Hwy.

29.2 Right onto waterfront trail.

29.4 Pass USS *Midway*.

29.5 Arrive back at Broadway Pier.

APPENDIX: PACKING LIST, BIKE MAINTENANCE, AND REPAIR

For a long trek, it's helpful to plan your packing and bike maintenance needs. Packing everything in advance and taking it on a trial run will make you more comfortable with your gear when you begin the tour.

PACKING LIST

Your packing list will be a bit different from anyone else's, but this overview will help you get started.

Bike clothing: padded shorts, bike jerseys, socks, shoes, fleece sweater, bike jacket, rain poncho, ear-warmer headband, underhelmet cycling cap

Casual clothing: shorts, long pants, T-shirts, short- and long-sleeved shirts, underwear, socks, sleepwear, camp shoes or sandals, light jacket, cap

Toiletries: towel, washcloth, shampoo, soap, toothbrush, toothpaste, deodorant, skin cream

First aid: sunscreen, bandages (assorted sizes), cotton gauze wrap, medical tape (small roll), insect repellent, painkillers

Food: coffee, tea, breakfast cereal, energy bars, freeze-dried breakfasts and dinners

Cycling gear: bike helmet, sunglasses, gloves, cycle computer, headlight, taillight(s), heavy bike lock, cable for wheel lock, light pannier cable lock, multitool, patch kit, extra tubes, pump (also see next section)

Camping gear: lightweight tent with a rain fly, ground cloth, sleeping bag, bag liner, inflatable pillow, camp light, tent light, headlamp, fire starter sticks, lighter or matches

Cooking: camp stove, fuel, solo cookset (pot, lid, cup), plate or bowl, multi-utensil cutlery, knife, bottle and can opener, sponge, biodegradable dish soap

Electronics: phone, camera, e-reader, chargers and cords for each piece of gear, portable rechargeable battery, extra disposable batteries

Miscellaneous: resealable plastic bags (various sizes), map(s), duct tape (small partial roll), 50 feet of nylon cord to hang camp food, notebook and pens, reading material, phone number list (travel services, reservations, emergency contacts), photocopies of important documents (ID card, driver's license, passport, credit cards)

BIKE MAINTENANCE AND REPAIR

Much appreciation for the technical advice provided here by friends at the Adventure Cycling Association, especially Joshua Tack, who wrote this section. Josh is membership manager at ACA and writes their Touring Gear and Tips column. See more of his work at www.adventurecycling.org.

Pretour Tune-Up Checklist

To prep the bike for a tour, a pretour tune-up is a good starting point. If you aren't familiar with working on your bike, see if your local bike shop will give you a crash course in bike maintenance and common repairs prior to the trip. The checklist below isn't meant to be a complete overhaul of the bike, but moving parts always wear the quickest, so give most of your attention to wheels, tires, chain, cassette (the cluster of sprockets attached to your rear hub), cables, and brakes. Running through this checklist takes 30 to 45 minutes and addresses current problems or imperfections that could create worse problems a few days into a trip.

1. **Frame:** Always start by giving the frame a good wipe-down with a clean rag, then check it over for any signs of cracks, which most commonly occur near welds.
2. **Tires:** Look for sharp debris, glass, or cuts in the tire. If the top tread is starting to become square (as opposed to rounded) or you can see the casing through the tread, it is time for a new tire.
3. **Wheels:** Spin the wheels to make sure they are round and true and there isn't any excessive friction in the hubs. Also squeeze pairs of spokes all around the wheel to check for consistent tension.
4. **Brakes:** Some brake pads have a wear indicator that shows when they need to be replaced. For others, make sure the rubber isn't wearing too close to the metal shoe that holds the pad. If they are in good condition, check the alignment to make sure the pads aren't rubbing on the tire or the rim. Lastly, check for good cable tension, so you don't have to pull on the brake levers too hard to get adequate stopping power.
5. **Chain and cassette:** Chain and cassette wear can wreak havoc on your shifting and increase the chance of a broken chain, especially when you're putting a lot of torque on the drive train with a loaded bike. If the cassette teeth come to a sharp point, the cassette should be replaced. Use a chain checker tool to make sure the chain isn't stretched. If you don't have one of these tools, you can look at how the chain lies over the front chain rings. If the chain doesn't seat itself on the chain rings properly, it is probably time to replace it.
6. **Shifting:** Run through the gears to make sure that the shifting is dialed in. Also look at the cables and housing for excessive friction or fraying.

7. **Rack:** Look for cracks in the rack, and make sure all the bolts securing it are snug. If the rack fails, you're likely hauling gear on your back until you can get a replacement, and that isn't a good thing.

8. **Bolts:** With a multitool, go over the bike from front to back, making sure all the bolts are snug.

9. **Take a spin:** The last step is to take the bike out and give it a quick spin around the block. Run through the gears while riding, try out the brakes, and listen for any creaks or unusual noises that might require further investigation.

Bike Gear for the Tour

The packing list for a Pacific Coast bike tour consists of specialized bike gear and a tool kit. The list needs to be tweaked for the climate and conditions of your tour. For instance, fenders can stay at home on a tour through Southern California, while they are advisable for touring the Pacific Northwest.

One component of my touring gear list that has consistently dwindled over the years has been my tool kit. I've learned that even when I feel as though I'm somewhere remote, I'm never far from either a bike shop or hardware store. Even a gas station can have a lot of useful items that can bail you out in a pinch, such as duct tape, hose clamps, adjustable wrenches, zip ties, a sewing kit, and even glue.

The list below is just a template. Your own tool kit depends on your skills, comfort level, and style of your tour. You should be able to assemble it all into a tidy little package. Here are some toolkit basics:

Multitool: Carry one compact device with many integrated tools. The Park Rescue Tool, for instance, is pretty much the only tool needed for disassembling and reassembling a bike for the airplane. It includes 1.5 mm–8 mm hex wrenches, 8 mm–10 mm box-end wrenches, a torque wrench, Phillips and flathead screwdrivers, a chain tool, tire levers, spoke wrenches, a knife, and a pedal wrench. Oh yeah, and a bottle opener!

Frame pump: A good tire pump strapped to the frame is essential, and the Topeak Road Morph is one of the best. It converts to a mini–floor pump and can hit high pressures with little effort.

Tubes and patch kit: Take one or two tubes and a half-dozen patches. I'm a huge fan of the Park Tool preglued patches.

Chain pins and chain link: You'll need a chain pin for the specific size of your drive train.

Spare spokes: A snapped spoke needs to be replaced right away. Since wheel sets have different spoke lengths, the FiberFix spoke is a good way to take care of any snapped spokes and at least get you to a shop where you can buy a steel spoke.

Chain lube and rag: Keeping the drive train lubed and clean of grit is a good way to extend the life of your chain and cassette.

Spare derailleur hanger: If you've never snapped a derailleur hanger, you're probably due. The Gimp multitool comes with one.

Cassette removal tool: A hypercracker is essential to break free the outer lock ring if you need to remove and replace the cassette.

Brake and shifter cable: Usually you can feel these reaching the end of their life well in advance, but spares don't take up much space and weigh next to nothing.

Band clamp: Carry two band clamps of different sizes, in case a rack or trailer part fails and needs to be cinched up until you can hit a shop.

Duct tape: Always carry some duct tape. A short end roll is enough.

THE TOURING CYCLIST'S TOOL KIT

Basics—items you would likely carry on a day ride:
- Multitool that includes 3 mm–8 mm Allen keys, a torque key, screwdrivers, and a knife
- Spoke wrench
- Mini or frame pump
- Spare tubes and patch kit
- Chain breaker
- Chain link

Extras for touring:
- Spare spokes or FiberFix spoke
- Chain lube and grease rag
- Small adjustable wrench
- Hypercracker (mini cassette lock ring tool)
- Emergency derailleur hanger
- Zip ties
- Band clamps
- Duct tape

RESOURCES

BOOKS

McQuaide, Mike. *75 Classic Rides: Washington: The Best Road Biking Routes*. Seattle: Mountaineers Books, 2012.

Moore, Jim. *75 Classic Rides: Oregon: The Best Road Biking Routes*. Seattle: Mountaineers Books, 2012.

Oetinger, Bill. *75 Classic Rides: Northern California: The Best Road Biking Routes*. Seattle: Mountaineers Books, 2014.

Thorness, Bill. *Biking Puget Sound: 60 Rides from Olympia to the San Juans*. 2nd ed. Seattle: Mountaineers Books, 2014.

Toyoshima, Tim. *Mountain Bike Emergency Repair*. Seattle: Mountaineers Books, 1995.

Weir, Willie. *Travels with Willie: Adventure Cyclist*. Seattle: Pineleaf Productions, 2009.

Wozniak, Owen. *Biking Portland: 55 Rides from the Willamette Valley to Vancouver*. Seattle: Mountaineers Books, 2012.

WEBSITES

Adventure Cycling Association: creator of the Pacific Coast Bicycle Route maps, www.adventurecycling.org.

BikingBis: calendar of West Coast rides, www.bikingbis.com.

MapMyRide, www.mapmyride.com.

Rails-to-Trails Conservancy, www.railstotrails.org.

Ride with GPS, https://ridewithgps.com.

Warm Showers: a community for touring cyclists and hosts, www.warm showers.org.

ROUTE-SPECIFIC

Canada

BC Cycling Coalition, www.bccc.bc.ca.

BC Ferries: ferries from mainland to Vancouver Island and Victoria, www.bcferries.com.

BC's Trans Canada Trail, www.tctrail.com.

Galloping Goose and Lochside Regional Trails Map: Victoria-area cycling trails, www.crd.bc.ca/parks.

Metro Vancouver Cycling Maps, www.translink.ca/en/Getting-Around /Cycling/Cycling-Maps.aspx.

TransLink: public transit to Vancouver International Airport, www.translink.ca.

Victoria and Gulf Islands Cycling and Walking Map, www.davenportmaps.com.

Washington

Bicycling the Olympic Peninsula Map, www.olympicpeninsula.org.

Bike Maps in Washington, www.wabikes.org/growing-bicycling/resources /bike-maps/.

Black Ball Ferry Line: ferry between Victoria, BC, and Port Angeles, Washington; www.cohoferry.com.

Cascade Bicycle Club: ·presenter of Seattle to Portland Bicycle Classic, www.cascade.org.

Metro Transit: public transit in the greater Seattle area, www.metro.king county.gov.

Olympic Discovery Trail Map, www.olympicdiscoverytrail.com.

San Juan and Gulf Islands Nautical and Recreational Planning Map, www.fineedge.com.

Seattle Bike Map, www.seattle.gov/transportation/bikemaps.htm.

Sound Transit: light rail to Seattle-Tacoma International Airport, www .soundtransit.org.

Victoria Clipper: ferry from Victoria, BC, to Seattle, Washington; www.clipper vacations.com.

Washington State Ferries: ferries to Sidney, BC, and San Juan Islands, Whid-bey Island, Olympic Peninsula, Kitsap Peninsula, and Seattle, Washing-ton; www.wsdot.wa.gov/ferries.

Oregon

Bike Portland, www.bikeportland.org.

Cycle Oregon: presenter of Cycle Oregon ride, www.cycleoregon.com.

MAX Light Rail: public transportation to Portland International Airport, www.trimet.org/max.

Oregon Coast Bike Route Map and State Bicycle Map, www.oregon.gov /odot/hwy/bikeped/pages/maps.aspx.

Oregon Coast public transportation: bus service between Oregon Coast cities, www.visittheoregoncoast.com/transportation.

Oregon Coast Visitors Association, www.visittheoregoncoast.com.

Oregon Scenic Bikeways, www.rideoregonride.com/bikeways.

Portland Bicycle Maps, www.portlandoregon.gov/transportation/39402.

California

Bay Area Rapid Transit: public transit in the San Francisco Area, including to San Francisco International Airport; www.bart.gov.

Bike East Bay, https://bikeeastbay.org.

Bus service, statewide: www.visitcalifornia.com/attraction/public-transportation.

California Bicycle Coalition, www.calbike.org.

Los Angeles Department of Transportation Bike Program, www.bike.lacity.org.

Los Angeles Metro: public transportation in the LA area, including to Los Angeles International Airport; www.metro.net.

Redwood Coast Heritage Trails, www.redwoods.info.

San Diego Bike Map, www.icommutesd.com/Bike/BikeMap.aspx.

San Diego County Bicycle Coalition, www.sdcbc.org.

San Diego Metropolitan Transit System: public transit in the San Diego area, including light rail from the Mexico border crossing at San Ysidro; www.511sd.com/sd511/transit/transithome.aspx.

San Francisco Bicycle Coalition, www.sfbike.org.

Sonoma County Bicycle Map, www.bikesonoma.org.

ACKNOWLEDGMENTS

Many cyclists, travel experts, colleagues, and friends contributed efforts over my two-year research phase to help bring this book to life, by suggesting routes, riding along, hosting me at their homes, and providing invaluable moral support. First and always foremost is my wife and traveling partner, Susie Thorness.

Thanks to Bill Alkofer, Doug and Ona Canfield, Brian Cantwell, Steve Cardin, Linda Conger, Elliott Crowder, Dempsey Dybdahl, Connie Fisher, Lawson Fisher, Ted Fry, Debbie Hinds, Tai Lee, Tim Olson, Alex Sawyer, Christine Sherry, Larry and Susan Snydal, Josh Tack, and Willie Weir.

Adventure Cycling Association has created an amazingly useful route map set, cramming a lot of detail into a compact package. The folks at Ride with GPS provided route-planning assistance with their excellent software. The staff at R&E Cycles in Seattle kept me on the road with stellar maintenance, and many bike shops along the route contributed route guidance along with service and supplies. Especially notable are Bike Newport in Oregon, American Cyclery in San Francisco, and Santa Monica Bike Center.

I greatly appreciate the professional effort of the team at Mountaineers Books, especially Kate Rogers, Laura Shauger, designer Jen Grable, cartographer Bart Wright, and my longtime editor and colleague Kris Fulsaas.

I also appreciate the efforts of other cycling guidebook authors who have guided and inspired me: Mike McQuaide, Jim Moore, Bill Oetinger, and Owen Wozniak. Jim and Owen contributed greatly to my Portland-area routes. I also would like to thank Vicky Spring and Tom Kirkendall, authors of *Bicycling the Pacific Coast*, the Mountaineers Books title that preceded this book. Their guide got me started exploring the coastal routes by bike.

Finally, many thanks to the cyclists that I've met in my travels. Some are quoted in this book, but many others provided companionship, good cheer, and inspiration. May this book help many more cyclists to join us in camaraderie out on the Pacific Coast.

INDEX

ABOUT THE AUTHOR

Bill Alkofer

Bill Thorness is a freelance writer and editor based in Seattle. He is the author of five books; in addition to this guidebook, he has written *Biking Puget Sound: 60 Rides from Olympia to the San Juans*, now in its second edition, as well as two books on edible gardening and a profile of an auto-industry executive. His articles have appeared in many regional publications, including *The Seattle Times*, *Cascade Courier*, *Edible Seattle*, and the *PCC Sound Consumer*, as well as numerous places online.

He has been a recreational cyclist since the mid-1980s, enjoying the mild three-season weather conditions of the Pacific Northwest. When he's not ditching his computer screen to research another bike route, he enjoys gardening, hiking, and skiing. Bill is a member of and ride leader for Cascade Bicycle Club, is a Route Ambassador for Ride with GPS, and is a supporter of the Adventure Cycling Association.

Professional affiliations include the Society of Professional Journalists and the Northwest Independent Editors Guild. See more of Bill's work at www.billthorness.com.

MOUNTAINEERS BOOKS

SKIPSTONE   BRAIDED RIVER

recreation · lifestyle · conservation

OTHER TITLES YOU MIGHT ENJOY FROM MOUNTAINEERS BOOKS

Biking Puget Sound
60 Rides from Olympia to the San Juans
2nd Edition
Bill Thorness

Biking Portland
55 Rides from the Willamette Valley to Vancouver
Owen Wozniak

Covers bike paths and city streets, with rides for cyclists of all abilities.

Urban Cycling
How to Get to Work, Save Money, and
Use Your Bike for City Living
Madi Carlson

All the information a novice
needs to ride their bike in the city.

75 Classic Rides Washington
The Best Road Biking Routes
Mike McQuaide

75 Classic Rides Oregon
The Best Road Biking Routes
Jim Moore

75 Classic Rides Northern California
The Best Road Biking Routes
Bill Oetinger

With turn-by-turn directions and downloadable cue sheets, these books will get you out on the road in no time.

Adventure Cycling Association Maps
Pacific Coast Bicycle Route #1–5